I0004402

A History of the Computer Industry

A History of the Computer Industry

From Relay Computers to the IBM PC

STEPHEN LINDFORS

Copyright © 2015 by Stephen Lindfors

All rights reserved, including the right of reproduction in whole or in part in any form.

ISBN-13: 9781514690802
ISBN-10: 1514690802

Table of Contents

One

Relay Computers

The first digital computers were built with relays, at Bell Labs, which was a part of AT & T at the time. Of course, AT & T used relays at that time for switching phone calls. George Stibitz, a mathematician at Bell Labs, built a very crude calculator in 1937, made out of relays, which added one-bit numbers to produce a two-bit result. He called it the Model K, because it was built in his kitchen, at home. His Model K attracted some interest, and Stibitz was asked to develop a more advanced digital calculator. He completed the new device in 1939 and called it the Bell Telephone Labs Model I Complex Calculator. It was constructed from 440 relays and could perform the basic arithmetic operations: add, subtract, multiply and divide. Numbers were entered with a keyboard. Managers at Bell Labs were discouraged by the cost of the Model I: $20,000. However, after World War II started, the U.S. government funded further development of relay devices at Bell Labs.

The Model II was the next in the series, and was used to test the accuracy of antiaircraft guns. Input and output for the Model II was in the form of paper tape. It was a general-purpose computer.

The Model III was completed in 1944 and contained 1400 relays. Model IV was completed the next year. Model V was completed in 1945 and contained

9,000 relays. It included floating-point arithmetic and could hold 30 numbers in memory. The last of the series, Model VI, was completed in 1949. It was a simplified version of the older Model V.

The Bell Labs relay computers soon became obsolete, mainly because they were too slow. The Eniac machine, also developed in the 1940s, was much faster than the Model V, because it used vacuum tubes.

Other relay computers were built in the 1940s. One of them was the Harvard Mark I, which was built by IBM. It was originally called the ASCC, or Automatic Sequence Controlled Calculator. It began as an idea from Howard Aiken, a graduate student at Harvard in the 1930s. The CEO of IBM approved the project in 1939, and it was built at an IBM lab in Endicott, NY. An IBM web site describes it well:

> It was 51 feet long, eight feet high and weighed nearly five tons. Consisting of 78 adding machines and calculators linked together, the ASCC had 765,000 parts, 3,300 relays, over 500 miles of wire and more than 175,000 connections. The Mark I was a parallel synchronous calculator that could perform table lookup and the four fundamental arithmetic operations, in any specified sequence, on numbers up to 23 decimal digits in length. It had 60 switch registers for constants, 72 storage counters for intermediate results, a central multiplying-dividing unit, functional counters for computing transcendental functions, and three interpolators for reading functions punched into perforated tape. Numerical input was in the form of punch cards, paper tape or manually set switches. The output was printed by electric typewriters or punched into cards. Sequencing of operations was accomplished by a perforated tape.[1]

IBM's CEO describes the inventors of the ASCC: "The original IBM automatic sequence controlled calculator, which was formally presented to Harvard University by IBM in August, 1944, was invented by engineers of IBM following the basic theory of Professor Howard H. Aikin [sic] of Harvard. Full credit for the invention should go to four engineers of IBM: Clair D. Lake, Frank E.

Hamilton, Benjamin M. Durfee and James W. Bryce. The machine was built
to their specifications after six years of laboratory work in the IBM plant at
Endicott, N.Y., with Mr. Lake in charge of the inventive work."[2]

The ASCC was a "technological dead-end."[3] That was because it was made
entirely of relays and was very slow. A multiply could take up to six seconds.

There was in addition a Mark II machine, also a relay computer, built by Aiken
and IBM, for the U.S. Navy. A Mark III machine, the ADEC (Aiken Dahlgren
Electronic Calculator) was also built for the Navy. It was built at Harvard and was
completed in 1949. It contained both relays and vacuum tubes, 3,000 relays and
4,500 vacuum tubes. The final machine in the series, the Mark IV, was also built
at Harvard and was completed in 1952. Unlike the other machines in the series,
the IV was all-electronic. It had a magnetic drum and magnetic core memory.

Until the first Univac computer was delivered, businesses and other organizations had to make do with electronic or electromechanical calculators, or electric
accounting machines. Of course, before the first Univac, a lot of development was
going on in laboratories, at IBM and elsewhere. Before the first Univac, the commonly-used products were Friden and Burroughs electromechanical calculators,
and the EAMs. The EAMs were typically used by businesses and other organizations
that had to process large amounts of data, such as for payrolls.

Jay Forrester at MIT developed an early digital computer called the
Whirlwind. It was originally conceived as an aircraft analyzer. An early name
for it was the Aircraft Stability and Control Analyzer project. At the time of
Forrester's proposed machine, analog computers were more commonly used for
aircraft analysis. But Forrester decided to use digital technology, at least partly
because it was successfully used in the Eniac machine. He made a proposal to the
navy in 1946 for his new machine.

The estimated cost, in 1946, of the entire project was $2.4 million, with
an estimated completion date of Dec., 1949. It was a major project; in 1947.
Whirlwind employed 50 people at MIT.

In 1946, Forrester initially considered electrostatic storage memory for his
Whirlwind machine. He also studied flip-flop circuits using vacuum tubes. Then
he looked into magnetic cores. By late 1952, he had decided to use ferrite cores
to replace the electrostatic storage then in use on the Whirlwind machine.[4] The

core memory was originally tested on the Memory Test Computer in 1952 with the assistance of Ken Olsen, who later founded Digital Equipment Corp. After a successful test on the MTC, the core memory was tested on the Whirlwind machine.[5] The Whirlwind's core memory consisted of 32 x 32 arrays of ferrite cores, which were 90 mils in diameter. The word size was 16 bits, with an additional bit used for parity checks in each word. Thus, there were 1024 words of 16 data bits each.[6] A small core memory was working successfully by May, 1952. The full-size core memory (1024 words) was working one year later. The full-size memory was moved from the MTC to the Whirlwind in August. The ERA firm decided to switch to cores for their 1103 machine soon after hearing about the adoption of cores in the Whirlwind machine.[7]

Forrester applied for a patent on his core memory. Other inventors filed similar patents. One was Jan Rajchman; another was An Wang and a fourth was Fred Viehe.[8] Rajchman was named the winner in Oct., 1960.[9] He won ten patent claims. The Board of Patent Interference decided on the winner. But many people had contributed to the development of magnetic core memories by that time.[10]

Two

M ore advanced than the relay machines was the Eniac, the first all-electronic digital computer, developed by John Mauchly and J. Presper Eckert, and the first general-purpose computer. It was completed in 1946, at the Moore School of Engineering at the University of Pennsylvania. Eckert was a graduate student when he started on the project, which began in 1943, the year he met Mauchly. It was an enormous machine, which weighed 30 tons and consumed 160 kilowatts of power. It was in use until Oct., 1955, when it was shut down for the last time. Parts of the Eniac reside in the Smithsonian Museum. Eckert and Mauchly formed their own company, the Eckert-Mauchly Computer Corp., which was purchased by Remington Rand in 1950. They later bought Electronic Research Associates of St. Paul, Minn. ERA developed the 1101, for the Navy, and the 1102, for the Air Force. The number 1101 was the binary equivalent of Task 13 in the Navy contract. William Norris was the CEO of ERA; he later was one of the founders of Control Data. Other ERA executives were Howard Engstrom, in charge of research and Ralph Meader, in charge of manufacturing (according to Norris). The two firms, ERA and Eckert-Mauchly, became the Univac Division of Remington Rand.

Another electronic digital computer built in that era was the EDSAC, built in England at the University of Cambridge. EDSAC stood for Electronic Delay

Storage Automatic Computer. It was built with 4000 vacuum tubes and had a mercury delay line memory.[1] That author expands on the EDSAC: "Although the EDSAC is often considered to be the first wholly electronic computer, we must recall that the first *computer* was the IBM SSEC—which, however, was neither wholly electronic nor a von Neumann machine."[2] But earlier on the same page, that author stated, "EDSAC ran its first program on May 6, 1949..." Thus, the Eniac machine was working much earlier than the EDSAC.

Delay line memory was an old technology developed for use in radar systems. Along with the Williams Tube, it was one of the earliest main memory systems used in electronic digital computers.[3] The Williams Tube memory came next. "What replaced delay lines as main memories were the Williams electrostatic tubes, which, as I have mentioned, were first used in the Manchester [England] machine." One disadvantage of the Williams Tube memories is that the data on the screen needs to be refreshed about 30 times per second.[4]

After completing the Eniac, Eckert and Mauchly started on a new machine, the Univac, in 1946. They worked on the new machine for several years and began to exceed their budget of $400,000, money they were receiving from the Census Bureau. Remington Rand bailed them out with the purchase of their firm in 1950, and the first Univac machine (later called the Univac I) was delivered to the Census Bureau, in 1951. That was before IBM had delivered a computer.

According to the Encyclopedia Britannica, a patent owned by Sperry Rand on the Eniac machine was voided in 1973. Consequently, the Atanasoff-Berry Computer was credited as the first electronic digital computer. But it wasn't actually completed. Mauchly had stayed at Atanasoff's home in 1941 and presumably obtained some of his ideas from that source.

IBM's first electronic computer was originally called the Defense Calculator, because it was meant for the military. It was later renamed the 701, the fist in a series of computers which went on sale in the 1950s. The first 701 machine was delivered in 1953. The 702 model was introduced soon after the 701, in September 1953.[5] This model was followed by the 704, the 705. the 709 and the 305 [6]

IBM built the 703 model computer, specifically for performing sorts, but they never sold it. One author described work on the 703. He said IBM "...later abandoned the project when, with the development of technology, it became possible to achieve adequate speeds without the need for special equipment."[7]

Solid-state computers became common in the 1950s. "The first computer to use transistors was the [French] SEAC, which was working in 1950, but in which soldered connections always gave trouble. It was used mainly for meteorology. Apart from transistors it had 750 vacuum tubes and about 10,000 diodes; all of its logic was in germanium diodes."[8] The second computer made mostly with transistors was the Transac S-1000, built by the Philco Corp. Philco produced other computer models in the 50s and early 60s, including the Transac 2000, the CXPQ and the Philco 212. Philco's computer division was eventually shut down by its new owner, Ford Motor Co.[9]

Another all-transistor computer was the Control Data 1604.[10] Other all-transistor machines included: the GE 210, IBM 1401, IBM 1620, IBM 7090, NCR 304 and the RCA 501. [11] Those machines were all introduced in June, 1959 or later.

A French company, called SEA (Societe d'Electronique et d'Automatisme) developed several early series of computers, including the CAB 500, the CAB 1500 and the CAB 2000. The name CAB stood for Calculatrices Arithmetiques Binaries.[12] The first of these used transistor technology and had a drum for main memory. It also used microprogramming. The 1500 series included virtual memory. The 2000 series was more advanced than the 500, with ferrite core memories. It had a word length of 22 bits and a main memory capacity of 128 words. It could do an add in .46 milliseconds and also used drum memory.[13] SEA produced their CAB 3000 series in 1958, which didn't sell well. It had a main memory also of up to 128 words.[14]

RCA Corp. developed a new mainframe computer, starting in 1952, called the BIZMAC. But progress was slow, and it wasn't delivered until 1958. That model had some impressive features, such as the capability to handle up to 200 magnetic tape drives (an enormous number). The fast memory was magnetic cores, with a drum as secondary memory. Memory was organized into words, unusual for a business machine. The BIZMAC had a six-bit character set (allowing 64 characters) and only 22 instructions, each with three addresses (very unusual). It had 4 K bytes of core memory, with an access time of 20 microseconds. It could read punched cards at a rate of 150 per minute. The BIZMAC had satellite computers, which were used to handle tape reads and writes. The satellite machines weren't very powerful.

RCA developed a database system for the BIZMAC, but it had some problems. "Before it could start to search for an item of data in the memory, the BIZMAC, like all von Neumann machines, had to spend a significant amount of time interpreting the instructions given to it; afterward it lost much time in moving the data to be processed from the secondary to the main memory and from there to the processor." RCA claimed that its BIZMAC was very powerful. "RCA, which had designed and built the BIZMAC, claimed that it was the most powerful computer in the world."[15] But despite its advanced features, the BIZMAC wasn't very popular.[16]

Three

ERA Company

The Engineering Research Associates company, where the Univac 1100 series began, was incorporated in January, 1946. The firm had its origins in the U.S. Navy's CSAW project, short for Communications Supplementary Activity—Washington. Their assignment was to break enemy codes and locate enemy ships during the war. The Navy wanted to retain the talented group that made up CSAW and offered some of them civil service positions. Two of the CSAW supervisors on the CSAW project, William Norris (later head of Control Data Corp.) and Howard Engstrom, decided that it would be better to start a business, hopefully getting some navy contracts.[1] But those two were unable to get adequate financing to form a new company, in late 1945. But later they got some help from a man named John Parker, who was an investment banker.

They were able to start the firm in 1946 with equity of only $20,000. They also obtained a $200,000 line of credit. Parker was named president of the new ERA firm. Norris, Engstrom and Ralph Meader, who had some experience with CSAW, were chosen to be vice presidents. They decided to name the company Engineering Research Associates, after trying some other names. ERA occupied a former glider factory in St. Paul, Minn.

Some of their early work involved digital calculators, which used thousands of vacuum tubes. In 1947 they started work on Task 13 for the U.S. Navy. The binary version of 13 is 1101, which was the name of their first computer. It was a "general purpose, stored-program computer."[2]

They used their expertise in digital calculators to write a book, High Speed Computing Devices. It became "the definitive study of the infant state of computing," according to a history of the ERA firm.[3]

Another project they worked on was magnetic recording. They developed a magnetic drum. It worked well enough that they used it in two new calculating devices, called Goldberg and Demon[4], which they delivered to the U.S. Navy in 1948. ERA's drums were "...the elite of the industry."[5] ERA obtained two important drum patents, which later became the property of IBM.[6]

They started building their 1101 computer for the Navy in March, 1948. It was code-named the Atlas. Of course, the 1101 was the first of many 1100 series computers built and sold by the Univac division of Remington Rand, later Sperry Rand. The ERA firm asked for permission to sell the 1101 to commercial customers. They Navy approved, after insisting on a few modifications.[7]

The 1101 computer had a 24-bit word and a drum memory. It had 38 hardware instructions. The Minneapolis Tribune described the 1101 "as the most reliable brain in the business."[8]

The ERA firm built other computer models after completing the 1101. The 1102 was built to process data from wind tunnel tests. The 1104 model was developed for controlling the BOMARC missile. And the Athena was built to work with the Titan ICBM.[9]

In Dec., 1951 the ERA firm was sold to the Remington Rand firm, according to John Parker, for about $1.7 million.[10]

Another large computer, the 1103, was announced by ERA in Feb., 1953. It was a commercial computer, based on a computer built for the Navy, with a 36-bit word and 16,384 words of memory. In 1954 they delivered the first computer with magnetic core storage, an improvement over the old Williams tube memory.[11]

Lacking sufficient capital, in 1955, the Remington Rand firm merged with Sperry Corp. to form the Sperry Rand Corp. ERA, Eckert-Mauchly and several other small companies were combined to form the Univac division of Sperry Rand.[12] After the merger with the Burroughs Corp., the company name of Unisys was adopted.

Typically, the chief developer of each system described here isn't known.

Univac I

The first commercial computer from the Univac division of Remington Rand (now Unisys) was the Univac I, invented by Eckert and Mauchly; Grace Hopper also worked on that model.

The Univac I was sold from 1951 to 1958; a total of 46 of them were sold. The first Univac I was delivered to the Census Bureau, in June, 1951. This was before IBM had delivered any computers; they delivered their first digital computer in 1953. The first commercial customer for the Univac I was the Prudential Insurance Company.

The Univac model also came with magnetic tape drives, the first computer to have them. Calculation speeds, of course, were slow, by today's standards, but were much faster than the calculators of the time. A typical instruction required about 500 microseconds. A multiply took 2.15 milliseconds, and a divide required 3.9 milliseconds.

The machine contained 5600 vacuum tubes and used mercury delay lines, one of the earliest memory technologies line for internal memory. The memory capacity was only 12,000 characters. Memory access was slow, requiring hundreds of milliseconds to retrieve an item of data.[13] The Univac I had a useful feature, allowing users to type data on a keyboard, which would be written directly onto magnetic tape. That system would also write the contents of punch cards onto magnetic tapes. That feature only worked with the common 80-column cards. Ironically, it would not work with the 90-column cards used by Remington Rand Corp.[14]

It was a huge machine, measuring 25 by 50 feet. It came with magnetic tapes and a typewriter, for input and output. (Some material from the Long Island Computer Museum.)

Univac II

The Univac II provided some advantages over the Univac I. It performed additions in 200 microseconds. A multiply required 1.9 milliseconds, and a divide took 3. milliseconds. Maximum memory was 120,000 characters or 10,000 words. Grace Hopper did some of the development work on the Univac II. It came with Uniservo II magnetic tape drives and a printer (600 lines per min.). That printer was fast for its time. A card reader was available for 80-column cards (120 cards/min.), as was a paper tape reader. The clock cycle time was 20 microseconds. The machine cost $970,000, not counting peripheral equipment. The first Univac II passed its first acceptance test in May, 1958, at Metropolitan Life.

Univac III

The Univac III, begun in 1958, was the division's first transistor computer. The first model III was delivered in 1962. It didn't have floating-point instructions, which their 1107 model did have. The 1107 was developed in St. Paul at about the same time.

Four

IBM's Calculators

IBM had experimented with electronic counters as early as 1941. Experimenters at Harvard Univ. were working on electronic counters as early as 1937.[1] Electronic counters were meant to replace the counter wheels, each representing one decimal digit, in the old calculators and accounting machines.

IBM developed many different electronic calculators, including the model 600 multiplying punch, the 601 multiplier, the 602 calculating punch, the 603 electronic multiplier, the 604 electronic calculating punch, the 607 electronic calculator, the 608 transistor calculator, the 650 Magnetic Drum Calculator, the ASCC, the NORC, the SSEC, and the Defense Calculator, which became the 701 computer. Some of those calculators were sold as products. Interested readers can find out more from <u>IBM's Early Computers</u>.[2]

The electronic multiplier was one of their earliest electronic calculators, with a demonstration model completed by the end of 1942. It would read two numbers from a card, multiply them and punch the result into another field in the card as the card was moved through the machine.[3] The machine wouldn't do divides.

IBM's next significant calculator project was the SSEC, which was based at least partly on the 604 electronic calculating punch. The Selective Sequence

Electronic Calculator was one of the more elaborate calculators developed by IBM. It was introduced to the public in Jan., 1948, when it was installed at IBM's headquarters in NYC. The IEC book describes it: "Designed, built and placed in operation in only two years, the SSEC contained 21,400 relays and 12,500 vacuum tubes. It could operate indefinitely under control of its modifiable program. On the average, it performed a 14-by-14 digit decimal multiplication in one-fiftieth of a second, division in one-thirtieth of a second and addition or subtraction of nineteen-digit numbers in one-thirty-five-hundredth of a second. With vast banks of tubes and flashing neon indicator lamps that were clearly visible from the street, the SSEC was an impressive sight."[4] The SSEC had only 160 digits of memory, tiny compared to IBM mainframes of a few years later.

IBM actually had a programming staff working on the SSEC. The machine was heavily used to solve numeric problems until July, 1952 (when it was shut down) and IBM didn't charge SSEC users who were solving pure science problems.[5]

In Aug., 1950, the U.S. Navy started discussions with IBM on a new machine that they wanted; IBM had earlier started planning on a similar machine, a successor to the SSEC. Byron Havens was the leader on that project. The plans called for a 16-digit word, hardware floating-point arithmetic, a million cycles-per-second clock, 2000 words of memory and tape drives. IBM estimated it would need about 6000 vacuum tubes and 15,000 diodes. The speed would be about 200 times faster than the Selective Sequence Electronic Calculator.[6] It would be called the Naval Ordinance Research Calculator (NORC).

The NORC cost about $2.5 million and was demonstrated in Dec., 1954. It was pretty fast for its time, with a one-microsecond clock. It had a 64-bit word and executed 15,000 operations per second. It had more memory than originally requested, 3,600 words and an 8-microsecond access time. It also came with eight tape drives, two printers and a card reader. The machine had 64 instructions, so it was effectively a mainframe computer.[7]

Another IBM calculator was the Magnetic Drum Calculator, which was developed starting in 1950.[8] It included a drum that was ten inches in diameter and revolved at 4280 RPM. It came with 1000 or 2000 words of storage and worked with various IBM products, including a tape unit and a 407 accounting machine. They were actually influenced on that project by a design from Engineering Research Associates, the small company later acquired by Remington Rand.[9] The 650 MDC was announced as a product in July, 1953.

The MDC was a type of stored-program computer, with the program stored on the magnetic drum.[10] Of course, the time to retrieve instructions from the drum was fairly long, compared to later computers, with their programs in core memories, for example. Reading a word from the drum could take up to 14 milliseconds, which was often much longer than the time needed to execute the two instructions in a word.[11]

The MDC was very successful. As one author stated, "The one runaway success, the one stunning surprise to its designers, was the IBM 650 [MDC]. A series of enhancements, beginning with the alphabetic and printer capabilities, sustained its initial popularity. In May, 1955, magnetic tape was offered to 650 users in the form of the 727 tape drive first used in the 702 system."[12] The 650 only had ten words of core memory, used for tape buffering. But later they increased memory to 60 words, providing a fast memory. The main memory on the 650 was a magnetic drum. The 650 could handle up to six tape drives.

The 608 model was solid-state, using over 2100 transistors, mounted on printed wiring cards. It could do an add in 0.22 millisecond, a multiply in 11 milliseconds and a divide in 13.5 milliseconds. The first 608 machines were delivered in Nov., 1957.[13]

Another important calculator from IBM was the 604 Electronic Calculating Punch. An important impetus for the 604 was Northrop Aircraft, which had connected some IBM hardware, a 601 electric multiplier and a 405 accounting machine to do some trajectory calculations. Later they substituted a 603 calculating punch for the 601. Other IBM customers, in 1948, requested similar combinations of hardware for their calculating needs.[14]

IBM's response was to develop the 604 machine. The normal configuration of the 604 was to connect it with a 521 card punch, a 402 accounting machine and, optionally, a 941 auxiliary storage unit, which held 16 numbers in its memory. The system of machines was called the Card Programmed Electronic Calculator. The 604 was commanded by the 402, which accepted commands and numbers read in on cards. Instructions were sent to the 604 by cable and results were sent to memory, the printer or a punch. The 604 performed calculations, including divides and square roots. But the pioneering Northrop Corporation didn't like that system, and they asked for more storage and more flexibility in their system. IBM consequently made some changes to the CPC, and the system became very popular. They sold almost 700 of the systems.[15] The CPC was used for scientific and business applications. Of course, these various combinations of machines were really crude computer systems, with their own input and output units, a central processor and memory.

IBM made some enhancements to the 604, such as adding a magnetic drum. That was in May, 1949.[16] At that time, the device was called the "drum-augmented 604." The magnetic drum wasn't an ideal storage device, at least partly because its access time was slow.[17] IBM executives later decided that the Defense Calculator was a higher-priority product, one reason being the Korean War, which began in June, 1950. The ERA firm was hired to produce a drum for the 604.[18] The 604 model was renamed as the "Magnetic Drum Calculator" or MDC early in 1950. It used vacuum tubes for its various circuits. The MDC would get its instructions and data from the drum; this was a big improvement from the paper tape input scheme originally planned for that device.[19] The instructions were to have a single address and the storage capacity was planned to be only 100 words.[20] But the project managers soon decided to offer larger memories, of 200 to 2000 words.

IBM was starting to feel the heat at that time from competitors in the calculator market. Some examples were Remington Rand's 409, Computer Research's 102-A and Underwood's Elecom 100.[21] One of the problems for engineers working on the MDC was that "[O]ur plans become obsolete more rapidly than the machines embodying them can be produced."[22] Originally, the group planned to build three prototypes of their MDC, but they had to settle for a single machine, which was ready for testing in Jan., 1952. The testing was completed by October.[23]

The MDC was announced as a new model, the 650 Magnetic Drum Calculator, in July, 1953; the project was 5-1/2 years old at that point. The MDC was offered with some peripheral equipment, including a 407 accounting machine (allowed printed output), a read-punch unit, and a magnetic tape unit. The magnetic drum capacity was up to 2000 words. The drum access time was given as 2.4 milliseconds, on average. They eventually added magnetic core storage, Type 653, as another option (from IBM archives, http://www-03.ibm. com/ibm/history).

The Defense Calculator

The Defense Calculator was the machine that became the 701, IBM's first commercial computer. Planning on that project began in Jan., 1951. It was meant to be used for scientific work and would use the binary number system, not decimal, for its internal operations; accounting machines had used decimal representation. Data values would be converted from decimal to binary, or the converse, as needed. An IBM executive, N. Rochester, commented on the binary approach: "Rochester favored a binary Defense Calculator not only for the sake of efficiency but also because binary had been chosen by most designers of machines for scientific applications."[24] The memory would be electrostatic, "Williams-type cathode ray tubes."[25] The word size would be 36 bits, due partly to the previously-chosen tape drives, which recorded six bits at a time. The tape drives recorded six tracks and a parity track. The memory would contain 2000 words of ten decimal digits. The instructions would occupy 18 bits each, with 5 bits for the op code and 12 bits for the address. An address would normally refer to a half-word of 18 bits. A one bit at the start of the op code would mean full-word addressing. Arithmetic could also be done with 18-bit operands, using the leftmost bit as the sign bit, as with the 36-bit words. The Defense Calculator planning group got some of their ideas from the Institute for Advanced Study computer, which was also in the design stage, in 1946.

Negative numbers in the Defense Calculator were represented as the magnitude and a sign bit. In the IAS machine, negative numbers were represented in complement format, with all bits toggled. The latter would become common in scientific machines using binary numbers.

The input and output devices they used were partly of the accounting-machine variety and partly new machines being developed at IBM. The calculator had a single input-output instruction, called COPY, which transferred data from the MQ register to or from a memory location. Of course, this turned out not to be very efficient, because the MQ (multiplier-quotient) register was also used for arithmetic operations. Programmers who used the COPY instruction had to know how data was recorded on the various media, including tape, drum and punch cards. [26]

IBM ran numerous tests on the Defense Calculator, using the Test Assembly, to find errors in the hardware and to determine processing speeds. The Test Assembly was a small test computer, based on the IBM 604 electronic calculator, which used CRT memory. They tested the conversion process, reading decimal data and converting it to the internal binary format. They also ran tests to solve differential equations. When they were checking for errors, "...[A] 44 minute run of over a million programming steps produced two known errors."[27]

In early 1951, IBM had received 27 letters of intent to buy Defense Calculators. But IBM management was becoming concerned about obsolescence, so they decided not to accept more orders about that time.[28]

The Defense Calculator had a debugging feature, wherein the next instruction was displayed on a console and could be executed by the operator. Numbers were displayed in binary format. Of course, IBM competitors later used numbers displayed in octal rather than binary.

Tape Processing Machine

The Tape Processing Machine (actually version II) eventually became the 702 model computer. One of the technologies used in the TPM was electrostatic memory, using cathode ray tubes (CRTs). A group at MIT was using this type of storage in their Whirlwind machine, being built for military use. It was called "Williams storage." With that type of memory, 500 pairs of spots on a CRT screen could store 500 bits of data.[29] This was in late 1948.

Around that time, IBM began to look at magnetic tape as a storage medium for computers. According to the IEC book[30], "Magnetic tape was by then [early 1949] generally regarded as the medium that would serve, in electronic computer systems, most of the file storage requirements to which the punch card had been applied in IBM's product line. By any reasonable estimate, tape could be expected to occupy less than 1 percent of the volume of punch cards for a given data storage capacity. And being erasable and reusable, it had potential for large savings in cost of the recording medium relative to cards." Also, tape read and write operations would be much faster than the corresponding card operations.

IBM also looked at another memory technology, called the mercury tank acoustic delay line. J.P. Eckert, of Eckert and Mauchly computer fame, invented that technology: "Eckert had invented the mercury delay line, prior to the Eniac project, for the storage of signals in radar applications. He recognized in the delay line a device capable of storing a large number of binary digits (bits) while requiring relatively few vacuum tubes."[31] Mercury delay lines used a quartz crystal transducer to produce waves in a tank of mercury, corresponding to zero and one values, which would be sensed by another quartz crystal and enhanced by electronic circuits, which would also reintroduce the signals at the other end of the tank.[32] Mercury delay lines were simpler and more economical than using flip-flop circuits, but they were slow, compared to the time to execute the typical instruction. IBM's engineers preferred CRT memory for their TPM machine, because it was fast enough and wasn't overly expensive.[33]

IBM decided to use the Williams tube, or CRT, memory also in its Test Assembly machine, a type of 604 calculator. "Its capacity was 250 words, each of five decimal digits plus sign, stored in six pairs of CRTs..."[34] The purpose of the Test Assembly was to test memory technologies and to test magnetic tape and tape drives. They also included a magnetic drum device. The traditional punch cards were also used, for input and output.

They purchased a magnetic tape recorder, which recorded on 13 channels, from the Cook Electric Company. Of course, it wasn't meant for digital computers. It recorded temperatures. The tape recorder was modified to work with the Test Assembly machine.

Their thinking about CRT memory was described in a few words: "...[I]n 1949, [Ralph] Palmer and Rochester regarded CRT storage as the most promising contender—indeed the most realistic choice—for fast electronic memory.

It was still unproved technically, but the economics looked right, and it could keep up with the fastest arithmetic units envisioned."[35] One of the employees who worked on CRT memories was Walter Mutter, who had just received his Ph.D. in physics from MIT.[36] He had earlier worked on electronic counters and other vacuum tube technologies.

IBM people found that their primitive Test Assembly machine worked pretty well for the purposes they intended. They learned about preparing and running stored programs in an electronic digital computer. "[N.] Rochester programmed it in March 1951 to solve second-order differential equations using ten-digit ("double-precision") arithmetic. More important, by year-end 1950, the Test Assembly had given Palmer's planner and engineers confidence that the basic technologies for a complete, large-scale [electronic digital] computer system were at hand."[37]

In March, 1950, IBM people (N. Rochester and W. Buchholz) wrote down their outline for the new TPM machine: 2000 characters of memory using CRTs, optional drum storage, magnetic tape units (number not given), and 40 instructions in the instruction set. They also planned on 200 characters of "accumulator storage." The TPM machine use vacuum tube circuitry. They expected fairly efficient use of tapes, since the machine could read from one tape and write another at the same time.[38] The actual building and testing of the TPM machine required two years, with some design changes, such as only allowing 100 characters in the accumulator storage; that meant a result of up to 98 digits. The planned concurrent reading and writing of tapes feature was discarded due to cost. Appendix B of the IEC book contains a detailed description of the TPM machine as it was actually built. The machine's instruction set is included there.

An instruction contained six characters, including one for the op code, four for the address portion and one character for a field mark. Instruction times were pretty slow: 1.28 milliseconds to add two small numbers and twice that to add two large numbers of 12 digits each. One reason for the slow ADD times was that the machine used a decimal adder, operating on a pair of digits at one time. "The adder operated serially on the low-order four bits of its two incoming characters. ... The accumulator was endowed with no arithmetic capability; it might have better been named 'general register' or 'arithmetic storage.'"[39] As can be seen from the previous sentence, the arithmetic/logic unit was fairly primitive.

A SUBTRACT was performed by adding the ten's complement to the operand value in the accumulator. Digits were represented in the TPM in the "excess-three" code, meaning that the internal value of a digit was larger by 3 than its actual value. This odd format was used because it simplified taking the ten's complement of a number. This was done by taking the nine's complement and adding 1. The nine's complement of a digit in excess-three format was obtained by toggling all of its bits.[40]

A MULTIPLY was performed by multiplying the value in the accumulator by the operand value in memory to yield a long result, of up to the sum of the two operand lengths. The result could be up to 47 digits. Of course, the result was an integer.

A DIVIDE was performed by dividing the value in the accumulator by the operand value in memory, with the quotient value in the accumulator. The remainder value's location was not given. Divides were done by repeated subtraction.

The instruction set also included READ and WRITE commands, which worked on one record at a time. The specific device was chosen with the SELECT INPUT-OUTPUT UNIT instruction. There was also an unconditional branch instruction, TRANSFER, and a conditional branch instruction, TRANSFER ON PLUS, which would test the sign of the value in the accumulator. To simplify input and output processing, there was also a TRANSFER EXCEPT AT END OF FILE operation. There were also instructions to simplify drum input/output. Six STORE instructions were included, most using field marks for the operand in memory. No LOAD instructions (opposite of STORE) are shown in the list of op codes for the TPM. But the RESET ADD instruction is the equivalent of a LOAD. The comment shows: "(Memory) replaces (accumulator)."[41]

The TPM machine was demonstrated to federal government people in early 1952, when it was still experimental. By the summer of 1952, the TPM was considered reliable. However, the machine became obsolete in 1953. "...[B]y 1953 the TPM was outdated in its circuit and device parameters and its overall design. A thorough-going redesign, for which planning had begun in late 1952, was promising a several-fold gain in speed." [42] One of the changes that they made in the TPM was to eliminate stops when errors occurred. They wanted the machine to keep going. As N. Rochester stated, "...[T]he true objective ought to be to keep a computer running, not to stop it."[43] They wanted the programmers to handle exceptional conditions in their own programs, rather than stopping the machine. Of course, hardware interrupts, such as for an illegal instruction, or a divide fault (on a divide by zero), were a way to prevent machine stops. If, for example, a programmer didn't handle a divide fault, the operating system could just terminate his program or job, with an error message. Hardware designers decided to include a "transfer (branch) on condition"[44] instruction in machines after the TPM to handle unexpected errors in programs.

Another unexpected problem for the TPM project was writing programs to replace accounting machine programs, wired into plugboards; the process took much longer than expected, which became typical for programming projects. Of course, sorts would have to be done by programs also, replacing the old sorting machines.

The TPM people soon found that their CRT memory was not very reliable. They got help in that area from the NORC (Naval Ordinance Research Calculator) people, but they still had some problems. As described in one source, "As it turned out, the memory was one of the most troublesome components of the TPM system, if not the most troublesome. Its erratic behavior was masked to a considerable degree, however, by a variety of problems throughout the system that stemmed from the experimental nature of many of its vital parts."[45] The "vital parts" meant the different types of electronic circuits, including the relatively new semiconductor diodes, made of germanium crystals.[46] AND and OR circuits were made of diodes, for example. [47] In an AND circuit, the output is "1" if both inputs are "1". In an OR circuit, the output is "1" if either input is a "1". The zero and one values are represented by different voltage values. These types of circuits are used to perform add and subtract operations in the hardware, among other uses.

The TPM II project soon followed the original TPM. It would be over five times faster than the original TPM, with a character cycle time of 23 microseconds compared to the original 128 microseconds. With Univac machines being installed at customer sites, there was pressure on IBM to announce the TPM II as a product. It was announced in September, 1953 as the 702 model. They described it as an Electronic Data Processing Machine.

There was some resistance from customers to the new magnetic tape medium that would be used with the 702. Of course, the data was invisible on tapes but easily viewed and verified on the familiar punch cards that many customers were using.

IBM built only 14 of the 702 machines. The CRT memories in the installed 702s were replaced by magnetic core memories. The 702 model soon became obsolete.

Gene Amdahl was put in charge of a group to develop an improved version of the 701 model machine. The new features would include floating-point arithmetic, index registers and faster arithmetic operations. They would also add 40 new instructions and much faster drum-to-memory input/output.

The improved 701 was announced in May, 1954 as the 704 model, with CRT memory. But by October, core memory was made available, a feature that greatly increased processing speeds. Originally, only 4096 words of core memory were offered, but several years later the size was increased to 32,768 words.

Five

Early IBM Mainframes

I BM's model 701 (an IBM trademark) was their first mainframe, which was installed in March, 1953, at their World Headquarters in New York city. It was originally announced by Thomas Watson, Sr. in April, 1952.[1] The letters IBM are also an IBM trademark. The Los Alamos laboratory was the second customer to have a 701 delivered. According to IBM, a large staff of people worked on the 701 project, more than 150 people. Presumably, this was because it was IBM's first electronic computer. The design process started on Feb. 1, 1951. Assembly of the first machine was completed in April, 1952. Some of the people involved were: Thomas Watson, Jr., M. Astrahan, J. Bartelt, P. Beeby, J. Birkenstock, and Werner Buchholz. The 701 model was originally called the Defense Calculator, because it was to be used by the military. Planning for the Defense Calculator began in Jan., 1951. It was composed of vacuum tubes. N. Rochester, C. Hurd and J. Haddad were responsible for much of the design.[2] The machine was manufactured at IBM's Poughkeepsie, N.Y. plant.[3]

IBM also announced some peripherals for the 701 in May, 1952, including a card reader, a card punch, a printer, a magnetic tape drive and a magnetic drum. Each of these was given a three-digit code, such at the 711, 716 and the 721. The name for the 701 came from the electronic analytical control unit, which was called the 701. An IBM web site[4] provided this and related information.

Some characteristics of the 701 model included: a word size of 36 bits or 18 bits, 33 operation codes, an integer add speed of 60 microseconds, a multiply and divide speed of 456 microseconds, a memory capacity of 2048 36-bit words (electrostatic storage), magnetic drums, magnetic tapes, a 150 LPM printer, a card reader (150 cards/min.), and a card punch (100 cards/min.).[5]

IBM's employees had gained experience with electronic calculation from other devices they had invented, including the Automatic Sequence Controlled Calculator, completed in Aug., 1944; the Selective Sequence Electronic Calculator, announced in early 1948[6]; the Electronic Multiplier, completed in 1942[7] and the Electronic Calculating Punch, the 604, delivered in fall, 1948.[8] There were other, similar devices, including: the 600, the 601, the 602, the 602A, the 607, and the 608.[9]

The next model in the series, the 702, was announced in September, 1953 and the first 702 was installed in July, 1955. The 702 was originally called the Tape Processing Machine, or TPM for short. By the time of that announcement, IBM also delivered a new printer, the 712 model, which had a speed of 1,000 lines per minute, which was six times faster than their earlier printers. IBM says it "…used the principle of wire printing." The so-called "wire printing" wasn't defined, but probably refers to the 5 X 7 matrix of wires used to print each character. Its memory was unusual, in that it used many cathode ray tubes. It required 23 microseconds to access a character from the CRT memory. The machine's speed was 10 million operations per hour (less than 3,000 operations per second), very slow by today's standards. Its speed for additions was 3,950 per second. It operated in decimal mode, which was also unusual. Most electronic digital computers operated in binary mode, then and now. Its tape drives had a speed of 15,000 characters per second. It could read punch cards at a rate of 250 per second. It also had a magnetic drum, which recorded data on a metal drum, rather than the metal platters that disk drives use. The CPU was leased for $8650 per month, not counting any peripherals.

Like the 701 model, it came with peripherals, including a card reader, a card punch, and a line printer. It also had an operator's console, which could display registers, and a typewriter for input and output. The 702 was designed mainly to solve business problems, but was also capable of handling engineering and scientific problems.

IBM's customers were concerned, at that time, about the integrity of their data stored on magnetic tape.[10] With punch cards, of course, they could actually see the data and verify it if needed. A vice president of the Met Life Insurance company described his concerns: "Perhaps the most radical idea which business is being asked to accept is the idea that a reel of tape can safely be used to carry information now being entrusted to visual card files... The adequacy of tape for this purpose has not been adequately demonstrated... We are not quite sure that the [tapes] are sufficiently safe from accidental erasure, loss of information through breakage, kinks, dimensional instability, flaking and other such occurrences. Nor have we been satisfied that the devices currently being employed to read and write on magnetic tape can be relied on to do so with accuracy."[11]

Some customers who purchased 702 machines still had a lot of punched-card equipment. Both types of equipment had their advantages.[12] The customers used magnetic tapes as a bigger computer memory. Later, they would use tape drives for sorting large data files. Some customers like the convenience of looking up customer data kept on punch cards. With the 702 model, customers noticed that their computers required a lot of time for training, writing programs and revising procedures—the price of a new technology.[13]

IBM found that, with the 702, too much time was consumed reading and writing tapes. IBM developed buffers, using magnetic cores, to speed up tape operations for some customers.[14] One of the problems with the 702 model was that it could only do one tape operation at a time, with multiple tape drives. Tape operations also could not be done at the same time as arithmetic operations in the CPU, making it a fairly slow machine.[15]

The 702 was made obsolescent soon after its announcement. One reason was that it lacked magnetic core memory. It used the older Williams-tube CRT technology. IBM eventually upgraded the 702s in the field, replacing CRT memories with magnetic core memories.[16] Only fourteen 702 models were delivered to customers.[17]

The next model in the series was the 704, which was announced in May, 1954.[18] Deliveries began in late 1955. The 704 was developed for engineering and scientific work.

According to IBM, it was the first machine to include full floating-point arithmetic, which simplified scientific and engineering programming.[19] A floating add, which required many hardware steps, took 84 microseconds. A floating divide took 240 microseconds. The word size was 36 bits. The 704 was the first in the series to use magnetic core memory, which became the industry standard for many years, until the early 1970s. As in later machines, it used tiny donut-shaped cores, strung on metal wires. As with other models, it came with a card reader, a card punch, printers, magnetic tape drives, and magnetic drum storage. A tape used on the 704 could hold up to 5 million characters. Processing could be monitored from the operator's console, which displayed register values and allowed changes in those values. The first Fortran compiler was developed for the 704 model, at IBM.

The 704 model was much more successful than the 702 model; 123 of them were produced. The system was greatly improved over the 702, with much larger memories (32,768 words vs. 10,000 characters on the 702), faster tapes and drums, and the previously-mentioned floating-point arithmetic. Another new feature was index registers, of which there were three[20]; they provide a way to speed up repeated program operations. The 704 also processed jobs up to 20 times faster than the 702 model.[21]

The next model was the 705, which was announced in Oct., 1954.[22] It was developed for business data processing and used vacuum tubes. It ran at 4,000 operations per second; it could do 400 multiplies per second. The word size was 35 bits. The 705 had a magnetic core memory of 20,000 characters. The 705 had the usual peripherals, such as card readers and magnetic tapes and used magnetic core memory. It also had an operator's console. It could do simultaneous reads and writes, correcting an old problem with the 702 model. The 705 had an instruction cycle time of 17 microseconds.

The 705 model came with an operator's console, which could be used to control the machine, display the contents of registers and the contents of memory. It also came with a typewriter, for printing out the contents of memory.

In 1955, IBM announced their Tape Record Coordinator, Type 777, which speeded up tape reads and writes. It included a tape controller and a tape buffer.

In Sep., 1955 IBM announced the 705 II model, which had twice the memory capacity of the older 705, or 40,000 characters.[23] The 705 III model was announced in Sep., 1957. It had twice the memory capacity (80,000 characters) of the 705 II and indirect addressing. Magnetic tape input and output was four times faster than with the 705 II's tape drives. The 705 III was IBM's last mainframe to use vacuum tubes.

IBM's next model was the 709, announced in Jan., 1957, which was designed for business and scientific data processing. It also had a 36-bit word and used vacuum tube technology.[24] It came with many different peripherals, including a card reader and card punch, magnetic tape drives, magnetic drums and magnetic core memory, which had a maximum size of 32,768 words. It could display results on CRTs, if needed. The 709 was much faster than earlier machines; it could execute integer adds and subtracts at a rate of 40,000 per second, for example. Floating adds and subtracts required 84 microseconds each.

An innovative feature of the 709 model was the Data Synchronizer, which overlapped input, output and computation. It included six input/output channels.

IBM announced their 305 RAMAC system in July, 1956. It was a small vacuum tube machine.[25] It came with a disk storage unit holding 5 million characters. The 305 systems had only one access arm for all of the stacked disk platters, making reads and writes slow. Later disk systems had one access arm per disk platter, to speed up access. IBM stopped producing the 305 systems in 1961.[26] RAMAC meant RAMAC disk system was used in the 704 model, the 680, the 1401 and the 7070. IBM sold over 1500 of the 305 disk systems.[27]

IBM announced another small computer, the 610 Auto-Point, in September, 1957. It came with a magnetic drum, an arithmetic unit, a paper tape reader, a paper tape punch, a plugboard, an operator's keyboard and an electric typewriter. There were three different levels of use for the 610: calculator mode, programmed mode, and an advanced programmed mode, where the machine was entirely under the control of a program. The "pluggable control panel" added flexibility to the machine in any of the three modes.[28]

One author called the 610 IBM's "first personal computer,"[29] but it wasn't very popular. It cost $55,000, and only about 180 were produced.[30]

Another early IBM calculator (called a computer by some employees) was the model 650 Magnetic Drum Calculator, announced in July, 1953. It came with a memory of 10,000 or 20,000 digits, a read-punch unit (up to three), magnetic tape units (one to six) and a 407 accounting machine (up to three), used for printing (from online IBM archives, http://www-03.ibm.com/ibm/history). A summary punch unit was also available. It wasn't a fast machine, performing 78,000 adds per minute and 5000 multiplications per minute.

The 650 rented for as little as $3250 per month.[31] It became very popular, with over 800 machines installed by 1958.

In 1955, IBM executives learned that the UCRL (Univ. of Calif. Radiation Lab) was interested in ordering a new, fast computer from IBM, which would be of a new design. Edward Teller, the famous physicist, was one of the principals at that site. IBM people discussed what to say to Teller, in an upcoming meeting: "…target delivery for no earlier than July, 1957, specify memory capacity of no more than 100,000 words, speak of a solid-state decimal machine with a 2 megacycle pulse rate, and mention 10 to 20 microseconds as the time for a floating-point multiplication."[32]

One result of that meeting was the creation of a team of a dozen men to work on the UCRL computer proposal. The goals were summarized as follows: "We are proposing a machine employing the latest and most advanced engineering techniques. The program will force the development of transistors, magnetic cores, new components, and system logic to the highest level of the art. The IBM LARC [Livermore Automatic Research Computer] proposal includes automation of construction and design as an integral part of the program.

The proposed technical computer has been specifically designed with the purpose of obtaining a good commercial machine as a modular by-product of the same program."[33] The initial designation for their new machine was the 707, which was later called the Stretch, meaning that the project stretched current technology.[34]

IBM's proposal to the UCRL contained this paragraph:

———◆———

"The University's [Univ. of Calif.] attention is particularly invited to the fact that, as a result of our study of this program and in the course of preparing the attached proposal, we have become convinced that far greater strides in the computer art than are specifically proposed herein will be possible within the next few years. Accordingly, it is our recommendation that between the time this proposal is accepted by the university and prior to January 1, 1956 the specifications be renegotiated in order that the University will be provided with a well-balanced machine operating in the eight to ten megacycle range similar in character to that proposed herein. Such a machine, which will be delivered in lieu of that specified herein, will be installed on the same time schedule as that for the machine proposed herein, but at a cost of $3.5 million. The University's favorable consideration of this alternative is strongly urged since the resulting computer will far surpass that outlined in this proposal."[35] The original machine for UCRL was expected to cost $2.5 million.[36]

An internal IBM document describes some of the machine's design: "...machine using ten megacycle transistor circuits with a high speed one-half microsecond memory and a large two microsecond memory. With the above will be the appropriate input-output, including high speed card reader, high speed punch, high speed printer, [and] very high speed tapes."[37] The document describes some other aspects of the machine: "...The contracted price is to be $3.5 million,...the AEC, Navy, Air Force and RAND [Corporation] constitute good prospects...the market survey indicated 37 machines [to be produced] during the first five years of production at a monthly rental in the neighborhood of $100,000."[38] The document was written by Cuthbert Hurd, an IBM executive. The quoted rental may be a record for a 1950s digital computer.

Sperry Rand won the contract for the LARC machine, due to their earlier delivery date.[39] IBM shifted their emphasis to the Stretch machine.

Of course, the Stretch machine was expected to perform calculations much faster than earlier IBM mainframes. An IBM executive, Stephen Dunwell, stated that the phrase, "100 to 200 times the 704,"[40] was often used to describe the speed of the upcoming Stretch machine. According to the IEC book, "In an IBM 704, a floating-point multiplication took 204 microseconds and a typical floating addition about half that time. Much of the time required for these 704 operations was owing to inexpensive, serial methods of shifting operands and propagating carries; he [Dunwell] expected to speed up these processes at the expense of more logical circuitry. If, as projected, floating-point multiplication could be done in less than 2 microseconds and if most supporting activities could be overlapped…then indeed the hypothetical Stretch could run 100 times faster than the 704."[41]

But the Stretch machine was found to have serious problems. Charles DeCarlo, an IBM executive, wrote about them in Feb., 1961: "Unhappily, after two weeks of trials with IBM and LASL [Los Alamos Scientific Laboratory] programs, it appeared that the system was slow by a factor of two; it was operating at 'approximately at four times [model] 7090 performance'."[42] IBM had expected that the Stretch machine would operate at about eight times 7090 perfor-mance.[43] Stretch was sometimes called the 7030, an advanced product version of that machine. Because of the speed problem, the 7030 version had its offering price reduced from $13.5 million to $7.78 million[44], a major embarrassment for IBM and a setback for the Stretch project. IBM soon decided to stop offering the product, beyond the current commitments, because each new 7030 was expected to lose money at the new price.[45]

The first Stretch machine was shipped in April, 1961 from IBM's Poughkeepsie factory. [46] It was shipped to LASL. After testing, it was accepted by the LASL people about a month later. Some characteristics of the system as delivered included core storage containing 98,000 words in six units, 2 million words of disk storage, 31 words of registers, including 15 special registers and 16 index registers, multiprogramming, interrupts, magnetic tape units, a card reader, a line printer, a card punch and an operator's console.

The history of the project shows that only nine Stretch machines were built, including one machine for LASL, seven 7030 models, and the Harvest machine[47], which was built for the National Security Agency.[48]

The Harvest machine was an enhanced version of the Stretch, with a 64-bit word, varied data formats, an enhanced instruction set, fast floating-point

arithmetic, decimal and binary arithmetic, table lookup instructions, reformatting and other new features. The machine was to be used in cryptanalysis.[49]

But the Stretch models led to newer and better machines, as described
by Thomas Watson, Jr., son of the founder, in an awards dinner speech:
"What I didn't stress and what I should have stressed was the fact that this
[the Stretch] was the lead machine at the time in the whole world...from
this machine derived most of the commercial features that enabled us to
prolong the 700 line into the 7000 line. ...I fear that the great contribution of STRETCH to our whole future in IBM got obscured and muddy.
And I think tonight at long last the situation is clarified. I think that the
Corporation, perhaps belatedly, has shown Red [Dunwell, an executive] and
his family what we really think of him, how much we prize his contributions,
and I just thought I would take the opportunity of publicly trying to correct
the record in saying that as an old-time salesman I repriced a product [the
7030] so that it would sell and in doing so perhaps besmirched some of the
great contributions of that product."[50]

Watson also said that the Stretch machine "maintained that position of [world]
leadership for a fairly substantial period of years. Also from this machine derived
... literally billions of dollars of revenue and growth for the IBM company."[51]

Another machine that followed soon after the Stretch was the 1401, which
was initially delivered in the fall of 1960.[52] The machine came with 1200 characters of magnetic core (later increased to 4000), punch card input, and later
tape units. IBM also offered an assembler for the 1401, called the Symbolic
Programming System (SPS) and later the Autocoder assembler. The machine
used transistor circuitry, with no vacuum tubes.

The basic parts of the 1401 were: the 1401 CPU, the 1402 card reader and
punch, and the 1403 printer. That model also came with optional tape units,
type 729. Up to six were allowed per system. The CPU had from 1400 to 4000
characters of magnetic core memory. The CPU wasn't fast, with a speed of 3200
integer adds per second and 417 integer multiplies per second.

The printer had a speed of 600 lines per minute and printed 132 columns. It
was a chain printer. The card reader and punch would read up to 800 cards per
minute and could punch 250 cards per minute. The tape units had various speeds,

from 15,000 characters per second to 62,5000 characters per second. IBM also offered a Fortran compiler for the 1401, despite the machine's small memory.

It provided a way to compile and test programs that were later run on larger machines. Unlike some other compilers, that Fortran read the source program only one time and then processed it in 64 phases. [53] According to the IEC book[54], "Compilation speed was startlingly high" for that Fortran, which is surprising considering the many phases. Those phases are described in the book, The Anatomy of a Compiler,[55] by John Lee. The phases are described in that book's Appendix A. The book only lists 63 of the phases.

In late 1962, IBM released two Cobol compilers for the 1401. They also provided the SPS assembler for the 1401 and the Autocoder assembler.

At some installations, the 1401 system was used mainly to handle input and output, meaning card decks and printed output, taking some of the load off of larger machines such as the 7090 model.[56] (IEC, p. 367) The early operating system SOS (Share Operating System) was replaced by newer systems, such as the FMS, the Fortran Monitoring System. More advanced operating systems (or monitors), IBSYS and IBJOB, were developed and released by IBM. IBSYS was released in Nov., 1961. It would run a new Fortran, a sort program and FAP (Fortran Assembly Program.). IBJOB was released in Feb., 1963 and ran Fortran IV, a Cobol compiler and a new assembler. It was more powerful than IBSYS. Both of those monitors could run concurrently on the same machine.[57] They would run on the 709 and 7090 models.

According to IBM, typical uses for the 1401 model were: payroll processing, accounts receivable and merchandising.

IBM announced their 1620 model (originally called the CADET) in 1959, just a few weeks after the 1401 was announced. It wasn't a powerful machine, because it didn't have an arithmetic unit. Adds and multiplies were done using stored tables. Each digit was used to look up the result from a table. The 1620 was a decimal, not binary, machine. Arithmetic operations were performed serially, rather than in parallel, as in most binary machines. The memory was magnetic core and held 20,000 digits. Each digit required six bits, with one bit used for parity and one used for an end-of-field marker.[58] The 1620 cost $74,500 to purchase and rented for $1600 per month. Despite its status as a low-power machine, it came with a Fortran compiler and an assembler. IBM also offered the Gotran interpreter, which processed a subset of the Fortran language.[59] IBM upgraded the 1620 later to provide a 60,000-character memory, and punch card devices were offered for input and output. The minimal instruction set was also enhanced. IBM delivered over 1000 of the 1620 models; they were described as "small scientific computers."[60]

IBM later decided to promote the 1620 model as a process-control computer. The machine was renamed the 1710 and was enclosed in special cabinets that protected it from hostile environments. The 1710 was connected to analog-to-digital converters. The new system was called the 1710 Control System and was announced in March, 1961.[61] By that time, IBM decided that their digital computers had become reliable enough to control industrial processes, which, if not run properly, could result in waste or possibly a disaster. Industrial processes were traditionally controlled by analog computers.

According to the IEC book,[62] "Industrial control systems that had been developed over the years, long before the advent of digital computers, employed devices that were actually analog computers. A process plant would typically use a variety of such devices, each tailored to a particular process parameter and supplied with inputs from appropriate sensing devices for temperature, pressure and so forth. ...The analog controller functions were all describable in mathematical terms and were therefore capable of being executed through the numerical methods developed for digital computers."

A newer model in the 1400 series, the 1410, was announced in Sep., 1960.[63] IBM soon announced an upgrade, a version with new disk drives. The 1410 model was originally called the 310. The renamed model also came with tape drives. Three different types of tape drives were available for the 1410, at various times. IBM also announced an input/output synchronizer, for use with the tape drives. The disk drives were an advanced version of the RAMAC drives (renamed as the 1405 drives), which came in 25-disk and 50-disk versions, holding 10 million to 20 million characters. (from IBM archives[64])

The 1410 also came with a card reader and punch, a printer and an operator's console. A paper tape reader and a magnetic character reader were also available.

The next machine in that line was the 1440 model, announced in Oct., 1962. It came with a magnetic core memory of 4000 to 16,000 characters.[65] It didn't allow magnetic tapes, but it did come with disk drives. It also came with a card reader and punch. In addition, it came with a printer, which had a maximum speed of 430 lpm. The 1440 was re-announced a year later as a tape machine. Despite that enhancement, the 1440 model never became very popular. As the IEC book [66] states, "...[T]he 1440 remained a mere shadow of the 1401 in terms of product acceptance." But it did come with a new type of transistor.

An important innovation for the 1400 series of machines was the software program RPG, the Report Program Generator, which simplified the transition away from punch cards for many users. As the IEC book states [67], RPG was "...a software method of easing the transition of wiring control panels [in accounting machines] to the preparation of programs for the 1401." It ran on 1401 systems that had only 4000 characters of memory. The RPG system included both a language and a generator, which produced the reports. It was a way to users to produce reports without writing programs in the 1401 assembly language. Writing programs with RPG was found to be much faster than writing them in assembly language. One result was that, "...RPG played an important part in the successful introduction of computers into small businesses."[68]

Another innovation for the 1400 series models was new, faster printers. One of he earliest of the so-called fast printers was a 150 line per minute printer developed for the 407 accounting machine. Various improved printers came after that one, including "wire" printers, a chain printer and a train printer. The wire printer formed characters from a 5 X 7 matrix. Chain printers were first announced by IBM in Oct., 1959. They were given the type 1403. Printing speeds for that model were up to 600 lines per minute.[69] IBM produced two wire printers, the 719 and 730, announced in 1955, which could print 1000 lines per minute.

The chain printer was an important development. In that type of device, a chain containing type moved horizontally across the page and hammers hit each character to be printed.[70]

IBM used five copies of each type font on a chain. The chain technology worked fairly well, but it had some problems, including chain breakage due to the high speed of 90 inches per second, the speed at which the chain moved, and the impact of the hammers. The breakage problem led to the train, which was somewhat similar to the chain, but the characters moved horizontally along a track. The train printers IBM developed were faster than the chain variety.

Another innovation was the 1443 bar printer, announced in 1962, which used horizontal bars from which type projected vertically. They were used with the 1440 model computer.

A new model in the 1400 series was the 1460, announced in 1963, which came with a faster memory than the 1401 and a fast chain printer.

Another new line of computers from IBM was the 7000 series. An early model in that line was the 7010, an enhanced 1410 machine, which was announced in Oct., 1962. The 7030 model, mentioned earlier, was a renamed and enhanced version of the Stretch machine.

Another model in the line was the 7040, which was announced in Dec., 1961. The 7044 model was a similar machine. Both of those models were derived from the 7090 model.

Many models in that series were solid-state machines, including the 7070, 7030, 7080, 7074 and the 7090.[71] The 7080 model was announced in Jan., 1960 and was a faster version of the 705 III model.

The 7094 model was a faster version of the 7090 and was announced in Jan., 1962. A faster version, the 7094 II, was announced in May, 1963.

IBM started planning their New Product Line, later called the 360 series (System/360), in Dec., 1961. This project was the result of a task force formed in the fall of that year, whose purpose was "to establish an over-all IBM plan for data processor products."[72] The group had members from the three main divisions (Data Systems, General Products and World Trade). The leader was John Haanstra. The group expected a 20 percent annual growth rate (number of machines) of the new systems in the U.S. An IBM document lists some of the goals of the NPL:

"It is recommended that the processor product line comprise five compatible CPU's. The internal performance ratio between successive entries should be between three and five, with the low end entries having smaller spacing ratios.

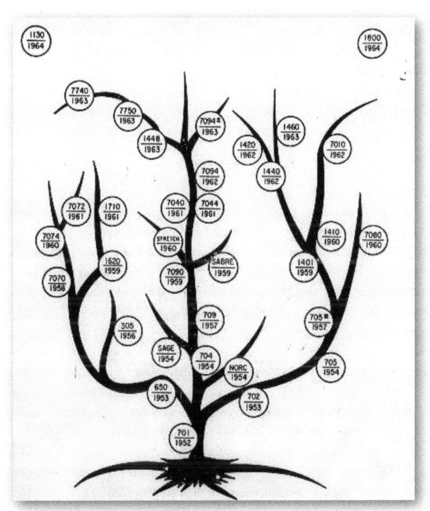

The above drawing shows IBM's mainframes before the System/360 series, over 12 years starting in 1952, with the 701 model. (Courtesy of IBM)

The line of CPU's must each be software supported and equipped with a selection of other devices which affect system performance: input-output channels of various data rates and various degrees of memory interference, memories of various sizes, and various complements of I/O devices.

Specialization in design for each customer must be achievable through the ability to couple any number and combination of CPU's into a single stored-program machine.

Each processor is to be capable of operating correctly all valid machine-language programs of all processors with the same or smaller I/O and memory configuration.

Each processor is to be economically competitive at the time it is introduced."[73]

———◆———

It was expected that the first two systems would be announced as early as the first quarter of 1964. The actual System/360 announcement was in April, 1964.[74] The five processors were expected to be from half the speed to 48 times the speed of the 709 processor, on scientific programs. The same ratios compared to the 7070 model would apply to business programs. [75] The 360 series machines would use the SLT (Solid Logic Technology) circuit technology.

This is the text of the System/360 announcement from April, 1964:

A new generation of electronic computing equipment was introduced today by International Business Machines Corporation.

IBM Board Chairman Thomas J. Watson Jr. called the event the most important product announcement in the company's history.

The new equipment is known as the IBM System/360.

It combines microelectronic technology, which makes possible operating speeds measured in billionths of a second, with significant advances in the concepts of computer organization.

At a press conference at the company's Poughkeepsie facilities, Mr. Watson said:

"System / 360 represents a sharp departure from concepts of the past in designing and building computers. It is the product of an international effort in IBM's laboratories and plants and is the first time IBM has rede-signed the basic internal architecture of its computers in a decade. The result will be more computer productivity at lower cost than ever before. This is the beginning of a new generation - - not only of computers - - but of their application in business, science and government."

More than 100,000 businessmen in 165 American cities today attended meetings at which System / 360 was announced.

Single system

System / 360 is a single system spanning the performance range of virtually all current IBM computers - - from the widely used 1401 to nearly twice that of the most powerful computer previously built by the company. It was developed to perform information handling jobs encompassing all types of applications.

System / 360 includes in its central processors 19 combinations of gradu-ated speed and memory capacity. Incorporated with these are more than 40 types of peripheral equipment which store information and enter it into and retrieve it from the computer. Built-in communications capability makes System / 360 available to remote terminals, regardless of distance.

The equipment is supported by programs which enable System / 360 to schedule its own activities for non-stop computing that makes most efficient use of system capabilities.

Internal processing power of the largest System / 360 configuration is approximately 50 times greater than that of the smallest.

The system's machine cycle time - - basic pulse beat of a computer - - ranges from one millionth-of-a-second to only 200 billionths-of-a-second.

System/360 core storage memory capacity ranges from 8,000 characters of information to more than 8,000,000. Information storage devices linked to the system can store additional billions of characters of data and make them available for processing at varying speeds, depending on need.

It is the balancing of these factors - - all available within a single system using one set of programming instructions - - that will make it possible for a user to select a configuration suited to his own requirements for both commercial and scientific computing. With the same type of input/output devices, a user can expand his System/360 to any point in its performance range, without reprogramming.

Computer advances

Some of the most significant advances represented by the new IBM System/360 include:

Solid Logic Technology. Microelectronic circuits -- product of IBM's Solid Logic Technology -- make up the system's basic componentry. System/360 is the first commercially available data processing system whose design is based on the use of microminiaturized computer circuits.

Called logic circuits because they carry and control the electrical impulses which represent information within a computer, these tiny devices operate at speeds ranging from 300 down to six billionths-of-a-second. Transistors and diodes mounted on the circuits are only 28 thousandths-of-an-inch square and are protected by a film of glass 60 millionths-of-an-inch thick.

Memory power. A hierarchy of memories within System/360 makes information in core storage available at varying speeds. Small local store memories operate in as little as 200 billionths-of-a-second. Control memories operate in as little as 250 billionths-of-a-second.

Powerful main memories - - containing up to 524,000 characters of information - - range from 2.5 millionths-of-a-second down to one millionth-of-a-second.

A key development provides 8,000,000 characters in bulk core storage - - each character available in eight millionths-of-a-second and each at the direct command of a computer programmer. This is over sixty times more directly addressable characters than were previously available in IBM computers. The computer's historic limitations on memory size are overcome by this development.

Application versatility. The traditional distinction between computers for commercial and scientific use is eliminated in System/360. Users will be able to process both business and scientific problems, or a combination of the two, with equal effectiveness. This versatility is reinforced by the variety of peripheral equipment which is part of the system.

Communications capability. Built into System/360 is the ability to respond to inquiries and messages from remote locations at any time. Hundreds of terminal devices can communicate simultaneously with a system while the computer continues to process the basic job on which it is working.

System/360 monthly rentals will range from $2,700 for a basic configuration to $115,000 for a typical large multisystem configuration. Comparable purchase prices range from $133,000 to $5,500,000.

Deliveries of the small configurations of System/360 are scheduled to begin in the third quarter of 1965. Deliveries of the largest configurations are scheduled to begin in the first quarter of 1966.

(Courtesy of IBM)

———◆———

After some name changes, the announced models were 30, 40, 65 and 75. One of the original models, number 60 (changed to 62 later) was dropped from the line due to speed improvements in the other models.[76] The model 30 machine would be relatively slow, operating on just one byte of data at a time, unlike the faster models.

In the software area, IBM decided to offer the languages Fortran, Cobol, RPG and PL/I with the 360 models.

IBM estimated that the cost of the 360 series hardware and software would be $675 million. They estimated the software cost at $35 million.[77] Later that cost ballooned to $60 million. The number of programmers needed grew from 200 minimum to an actual count of 2000. One of the software development managers, Fred Brooks, commented, "Adding manpower to a late software project only makes it later."[78] Brooks later wrote a book titled, The Mythical Man Month, published in 1975. That quotation is the main point of the book.

IBM decided to use magnetic cores for their entire 360 series. As one author stated, "Clever systems design techniques permitted IBM to use low-cost ferrite core technology in all its System/360 computers…"[79] Fortunately, the cost of magnetic cores dropped steadily. They achieved a "…dramatic 2000-fold increase in production capacity and 200-fold reduction in cost…" during the period 1955 to 1970.[80]

IBM had also looked at other types of memory for the 360 series. One of them was cryogenic logic, which used "persistent currents in cryogenic lines."[81] Another technology that they looked at was magnetic film, which was used by a competitor, Sperry Rand, in their 1107 mainframe. It was a fast memory, with a cycle time of 0.6 microseconds.

IBM also looked at Transformer Read-Only Store (TROS) memories, which used magnetic transformer loops. Another type was Card Capacitor Read-Only Store, or CCROS, a type of capacitance memory. An additional type, BCROS (Balanced Capacitor Read-Only Store), was used in some of the 360 models, the 50 and the 60, for the fast control store memory. The Hursley lab in England did much of the work on BCROS.[82]

The 360 series also included another type of memory, computer control stores, which held the microprograms needed to execute specific instructions. The floating-point instructions, for example, consisted of microprograms. The original idea for the microprograms came from M. V. Wilkes of the University of Cambridge. In his words, "it is necessary that the machine should contain a suitable permanent rapid-access storage device in which the microprogram can be held." [83] Another purpose of control stores was emulation, making one computer operate like another. In other words, it would be able to execute the other machine's instruction set. IBM's management learned the importance of control stores when they were used by Honeywell in their new H-200 model computer. Honeywell offered a program called "liberator" which translated IBM 1401 programs to run on the H-200.

However, technology was moving on, even though core memories were almost universal in 1960s mainframe computers. "In January 1968 IBM terminated its primary program to develop advanced ferrite core memories in order to concentrate its resources on the development of monolithic semiconductor memories…" [84] Ferrite core memories were fast and reliable. They had also been used with both vacuum tube and transistor technologies for 14 years. Semiconductor memories were still inferior to ferrite core memories in 1968.

However, IBM's research and development on semiconductor memories was successful, as shown by their model 370/145, with an all-semiconductor memory, which was announced in June, 1971. That model used 128-bit chips. [85] The use of semiconductor memory spread to other machines. As one author stated, "[T]he superiority of semiconductor memories was shown during the ensuing years as monolithic semiconductor memories became the dominant computer memory technology throughout the industry." [86] A later example of a semiconductor memory was that for IBM's 4331 model computer, which used semiconductor chips containing 65,536 bits each. That model was initially shipped in 1979.

Thomas Watson, Sr. and other IBM executives commented on the six management precepts that explain IBM's success: Well-defined goals and beliefs. Investment in the future. Commitment. Competition (external and internal). Free flow of information. Collective decision-making. [87]

Six

IBM AND THE EUROPEANS

A book by a European author, <u>And Tomorrow the World?...Inside IBM</u>, by Rex Malik discusses the European view of IBM. One important part of the book is IBM's typical backwardness in the technology area. Other books have pointed out that, even in the 1950s, they were two years behind, in that their first electronic digital computer was delivered two years after the first Univac computer.

Malik's book included a table[1] which shows how 12 IBM systems compete with competing machines. In only <u>one</u> case is the IBM product superior to the competing product (the 370/135). He goes on to say, "Two short periods excepted, IBM has generally been technologically backward."[2] On the next page, Malik states:

> Almost all the critical invention which has made the growth of IBM possible has originated elsewhere: components almost generally, discs and disc drives, tapes and tape drives, most of the communications technology, and as we have seen almost all critical invention within central processor and memory technology. What has made IBM strong has been its ability to improve on the work of others, the very process that it tries to deny anyone else the right to do.

———◆———

A nother important part of the book is the ethics of IBM's executives. For example, he lists some of the lawsuits against IBM (section titles from the book):

1) The USA versus IBM—1932-1936
2) The USA versus IBM—1946-1956
3) IBM's patent conspiracy
4) CDC versus IBM
5) Greyhound versus IBM
6) The Age of Aquarius: Telex versus IBM
7) IBM versus everybody

The big antitrust trial, USA versus IBM, was filed on Jan. 17, 1969, by the
Justice Department, in New York City.

The suit alleged than IBM violated the Sherman Act by attempting to
monopolize the digital computer market, in the business computer area.

The trial began in May, 1975 and was dropped in Jan., 1982, by the Reagan
Administration. Specifically, the Justice Department dropped it on Jan. 8, 1982.
William Baxter, a Justice Department official, stated that the charges were
"without merit."[3] It seems curious that the Justice Department spent so much
time and effort on something that had no merit.

Malik also lists other lawsuits against IBM: Catamore versus IBM; Equity
Funding shareholders versus IBM; Memorex versus IBM; Sanders versus IBM;
William Marrion, Inc. versus IBM; and Bunker Ramo versus IBM [4] That book
estimates the total of all the lawsuits against IBM at nearly $16 billion. And that
was just up to 1975, when the book was published.

The suit filed by CDC is interesting, for example. It was filed on Dec. 11,
1968 in a federal court. It is an example of David versus Goliath, and David
won in that case. Of course, most observers thought CDC would lose the case.

Control Data's view of IBM in that era was summed up by William Norris,
CDC's chairman, when he said, "IBM has been out to get us, and you can print
that."[5]

Malik describes the basis for the CDC lawsuit:

The case was defined by the Sherman Act, Section Two: IBM had monop-
olized and attempted to monopolize various markets and sub-markets
defined in the complaint. CDC sought to have IBM broken up and asked
for punitive triple damages (three times the damages adjudged suffered),
the standard plaintiff's remedies. However, the key complaints were those
for which it sought restraining injunctions. It listed thirty-six practices
of IBM, mostly out in the marketplace. They included such activities as
interfering in customer's negotiations with competitors and intimida-
tion of would-be customers' personnel—standard routines as far back as
Mr. Watson's NCR days. But more important, they also included another
group of practices. As a result of the CDC case a set of twentieth-century
industrial marketing phenomena enter the economic language: fighting
ships and phantom computers. It was these last that CDC was really after.

The lawsuit was settled on Jan. 12, 1973. CDC got IBM's Service Bureau
Corp. as part of the settlement, along with $29 million worth of contracts.
IBM also paid CDC's legal fees, and they paid SBC employee benefits for
ten years.[6] The two firms also signed a patent agreement, which gave IBM
knowledge in the terminals area, among other technologies. But CDC had to
destroy their document index as part of the settlement.[7]

———————◆———————

Malik goes on to discuss the Future System project, which occupied IBM's
time for several years before it was cancelled. Probably one reason for the
cancellation was the cumbersome software that they were working on, including
a new operating system called just Q.

Malik also discusses IBM's experiences with virtual memory, which IBM
didn't invent. He states, "…IBM for many years could not make advanced function [virtual storage] work with any worthwhile degree of efficiency…"[8] He

was referring to the 360/67 model computer. Malik also states that the virtual storage concept originated in Britain. [9] But British people often think the whole computer industry began in their country.

Malik relates another story about IBM's technology. He states that 14 airlines compared notes on their IBM mainframes. According to Malik, those firms were getting only 30% of the promised performance from their IBM systems. [10]

Possibly one reason IBM's technology is often lagging the competition's technology is that it was founded by a salesman, Thomas Watson, Sr., who was not an engineer or a technology expert. Sales and marketing seem to the areas where IBM excels. A competitor, the Hewlett-Packard company, was founded by two engineers. H-P seems to be pretty ethical, compared to IBM, and (speaking from this author's experience), their products are more reliable, maybe because engineers have more clout at H-P. H-P is now a larger firm than IBM, as measured by dollar volume of sales, and has been for several years. So the need to break up IBM, such as by divesting non-core divisions (e.g., Office Products), is not as great as it was when that book was written. Malik discusses how IBM might be broken up near the end of his book. [11]

Mr. Malik also discusses the European government view of the computer industry. Not surprisingly, their governments prefer to buy domestically-produced computers, such as Britain's ICL and France's CII. He also discusses R and D funding for domestic firms, provided by their governments. In fairness, the U.S government has provided some research and development that helped the U.S. computer industry, such as the Arpanet (from the Advanced Research Projects Agency, a DOD group); the Arpanet later became the Internet. The SAGE project also helped the U.S. computer industry. The Air Force also needed advanced circuitry for their Minuteman missiles, spurring the development of integrated circuits.

Of course, the European computer industry has not done well in general. This author has never used a European computer. The German firm SAP, however, has done well in the business software area. But that is one of just a few examples of European success.

Malik relates the view of some observers of IBM [12]. He calls it the "dumb funny company."

Of course, IBM is known for some important innovations, including the Fortran language and the first Fortran compiler, the PL/I language and relational databases, including the SQL language. And there is the IBM PC, but that came out five years after Apple Corp.'s first personal computer. IBM mostly used parts made by other companies when they produced that product, including the microprocessor (from Intel) and the operating system (from Microsoft). An industry, IBM-compatible PCs, developed after the success of the first IBM PC. IBM's OS/2 system for PCs is no longer in use. IBM is no longer in the PC business, having sold that division. Today, IBM is mainly in mainframe computers, software and services. So, the need to break up IBM is not as great as when Malik's book was published.

This author has used some IBM products. One was a Think Pad PC, which was very unreliable. It was a model A30, which constantly overheated, probably because the fan was only running two or three minutes per hour, even when it was always plugged in and charging. Just about everything in that machine had to be replaced, including several system boards, the disk drive and the DVD drive. IBM paid for the repairs, under warranty. In fairness, some other Think Pad models have a better design and don't overheat, according to users I have talked with.

IBM sold their PC division to a Chinese firm, Lenovo, some years ago.

Another product was an IBM operating system for mainframes, known as MVS/ESA and other names at different times. It was a very unusual system, with only one command, "Exec" (execute). The command was used to execute any program, including the customer's programs, IBM utilities and third-party programs. To delete a file, for example, one would call a utility program using the Exec command, which would read in the file name and then delete the file. Other operating systems that accept commands in text form, such as DOS and Unix, typically have several dozen commands.

When IBM was developing their famous 360 series, it did not go well. Thomas Watson, Jr. commented on that series in a speech to IBM's One Hundred Per Cent Club, for sales people: "Gentlemen, we made the decision to push back deliveries, and I know that you have had a tough time to convince those customers they will have to wait an extra year. When I leave here today, I have to go down and tell one of our largest customers he's going to have to wait a year, so I know exactly what you feel. But if we had to do it all over again, with the gamble and what it is, I would make the same decision." [13] Malik goes on to say, about the 360 series, "That the gamble was of the order of five billion dollars was due more to IBM management incompetence than anything else."[14] Earlier in that chapter, he stated, "…IBM executives still talk of the havoc that Series 360 caused. Production problems were horrendous: IBM's component plants were just not coming on stream according to IBM's required schedule. Domestic's Fishkill plant eventually had to be bailed out by IBM plants abroad…"[15]

IBM was initially very weak in time-sharing. At first, their famous 360 series didn't even have time-sharing. They tried to include it with the 360/67 model, for example, but the results were not very good. Rex Malik quotes an internal IBM document on the subject: "'It is our opinion that the Time Sharing systems being marketed today are *completely unserviceable in any manner that will result in customer satisfaction.*' [italics added by Malik]…. The system was clearly a loss leader; indeed, more loss than leader."[16]

He goes on to describe more of IBM's work on time-sharing: "Though IBM put on a brave face, releasing various versions of the software, the original 360/67 software development was never to succeed. Indeed, some of the versions that were to work were brought in by users without benefit of IBM; in one case, the customer, having done all the work, reputedly refused to let IBM have access to the software he had developed." [17] Imagine that, a customer that was better at developing software than IBM! Of course, IBM couldn't collect rental on systems that weren't actually working. They lost $78 million on the 360/67.[18] IBM did eventually produce a time-sharing product, which they called TSO, for Time Sharing Option. They offered TSO on their 370 series machines, starting in 1971.[19]

Another IBM product this author used was called CICS, which displayed data on terminals and accepted data entered by users, typically for updating databases. The databases I used were based on the IBM VSAM product, for direct-access disk files; VSAM allowed users to retrieve records, update them and delete them as needed. CICS was originally developed for electric utilities, but was later adopted by other industries, such as catalog sales and banking. [20] In catalog sales, it was used to process orders.

CICS is now over 40 years old. I found it cumbersome to use. It was difficult to install, and it was difficult to modify the screens used by other people, such as bank tellers. Microsoft Access has a simpler method called Forms to enter and view data, using their Windows systems. It is easier to use than CICS screens, and the forms are easier to modify. Relational databases are more flexible than databases using VSAM files; they are easier to modify. But the huge Oracle software firm was based on relational databases. Their annual sales are now over $38 billion. IBM has their DB2 product, which allows users to create and use relational databases. As with IBM PCs, other firms have often done better with a product or invention created by IBM.

Seven

Floating-Point Arithmetic

From the earliest days of digital computers, users (particularly scientists) wanted faster calculations. Of course, there were many techniques used to achieve this goal. Some of them were: faster circuitry, faster memories, parallelism, faster floating-point arithmetic, and faster peripherals, such as tape drives and disk drives.

Originally, floating-point arithmetic was done by software, which made it slow and, if the code was written by the users, prone to errors. The IBM 701 mainframe, for example, had software floating-point arithmetic, meaning the four arithmetic operations. The later 704 computer was the first to have hardware floating-point operations, according to IBM's archives.

Readers might think that floating-point operations for the hardware would be easy, but that is not the case. The instructions are easy to use, but the hardware has to do a lot of work to execute just one of those operations. A floating add instruction, for example, requires 26 steps.[1]

Many of the steps involve examining the exponents and determining the result's exponent. Also, the exponents must be made equal before the actual add can occur. It is in step 12 that the coefficients (mantissas) are actually added. Many of the steps involve checking for special cases, such as one operand's size being much greater than the other. In that case, the result is the same as the value of the larger operand. In other words, the value of the smaller mantissa is just shifted out of its register, at the lower end.

A floating subtract operation is almost the same as the floating add. Only three steps are altered to do the floating subtract. The subtract operation does an add of the complement of one operand.

The floating multiply only requires 21 steps.[2] Readers might wonder why there are fewer steps in the multiply than in the add, since a multiply is just a series of shifts and adds. The main difference is that the exponents don't need to be adjusted in a multiply. In the add, the mantissas (at least one) have to be shifted until the exponents are equal. (It is true that, if all the multiply steps are included, the floating multiply would have more steps than the floating add. The 21 steps for the floating multiply include just one step for the multiply of the mantissas.) The more important steps in the floating multiply are adding the exponents and multiplying the mantissas, as in an integer multiply. Typically, the two operands are normalized before the mantissa multiply is done, so that the binary point is just to the left of the mantissa. Normalization of the operands prevents loss of accuracy. After the mantissa multiply is done, the binary point is still just to the left of the mantissa.

The floating divide is similar to the floating multiply, with the exponents subtracted and the mantissas divided.

For any of the four operations, errors, such as overflow or underflow, are possible. An overflow means the result is too large, and an underflow means the result is too small in absolute value. A divide by zero, for example, results in an overflow. It may result in an interrupt. Some languages allow for trapping errors, such as dividing by zero. Visual Basic is such a language. The programmer can trap such an error, display or print out an error message, and continue or terminate execution.

You might ask why other operations, such as the square root, aren't done in the hardware. Probably the main reason is to cut costs. Functions to do the square root, sine, cosine, exponential, etc. are often supplied by the computer manufacturer or a software firm, as in the case of Visual Basic. Typically, they are included on a program library, in relocatable binary format, so that they can be pulled in at link-edit time, before the program is executed.

Other Techniques

Parallelism was another early technique for speeding up calculations. In the Control Data 6600, for example, there were ten functional units (see Supercomputers), which allowed overlap of calculations. In other words, a floating multiply, a floating add and a floating divide could all be executing simultaneously, with each one starting every 100 nanoseconds (one minor cycle). An operation would start immediately if the appropriate functional unit was available. In the 7600 model supercomputer, the minor cycle time was much shorter, about 27 nanoseconds, and calculations would execute much faster.

Both of those machines had an instruction stack, composed of fast registers, which would hold ten words on the 6600 model (for example). If the programmer could write a short loop, which would fit in the stack, it wouldn't be necessary to access the slower core memory until his loop was completed, which speeded up the execution.

Another technique to gain speed in the 6600 was the eight accumulators, which were 60 bits each. Performing calculations using data in those registers was much faster than retrieving data from the CPU's magnetic core memory.

Transferring values between registers required only 100 nanoseconds, compared to about one microsecond (ten times as long) to retrieve a value from core memory.

In the peripherals area, IBM steadily increased the speed and density of their magnetic tapes, starting in the 1950s. As one author stated, "The density of recording on half-inch tape had increased by a factor of 8, from 100 to 800 bpi; data rates had increased by a factor of 12, from 7500 to 90,000 cps [characters per second]; and the capacity of a reel of tape had increased by a factor of more than 11, from about 1.5 million to 17 million characters."[3] The quote describes the era from 1952 to the early 1960s.

Circuitry also became faster, partly because the circuits were becoming smaller, especially once integrated circuits came into use. Microprocessors allowed more shrinkage. Pathways became shorter. I.e., transistor circuits were smaller than vacuum tube circuits, integrated circuits were smaller than discrete transistor circuits, and circuits in microprocessors were even smaller. Electricity travels about one foot per nanosecond (maximum speed), so the length of connections is important in a digital computer.

IBM was able to speed up their core memories in the 1950s, so that the core memory for the SAGE project, for example, had a 2-microsecond access time per word.[4] Memory access times were later reduced to 0.7 microsecond in the Harvest machine.[5] Replacing the old Williams tube memory in the 704 model with magnetic core memory reduced the time for an add from 60 microseconds to 36 microseconds.[6]

Speeding up magnetic tape drives wouldn't speed up calculation, but it speeded up some types of processing, such as sorts, which sometimes used magnetic tapes. Disk drives were also speeded up in the 50s.

Starting in the 1950s, computer systems in general were also speeded up by multi-programming and by multiprocessing.

Multiprogramming was developed to make use of the wait time, such as when the central processor was waiting for data to be read from a tape drive or a card reader. If more than one program was waiting to be executed, the other program could be executing during the wait time. One author describes its origin: "One way of avoiding wasting time in this way [as described above] is to start a second program—that is, to resort to multiprogramming. The term seems to have been used for the first time by N. Rochester [1955] to describe a way in which the tape record coordinator [an electronic device] in the IBM 705 might be used to cause data to be read from a tape while the processor works on another task…"[7] Another way of looking at multiprogramming is that it increased throughput, the number of batch jobs processed per hour by a mainframe computer. It also increased the apparent speed of the computer for timesharing users.

Multiprocessing involved executing several programs, typically user programs, simultaneously. This meant that the computer had at least two central processors, or one central processor and a satellite processor, or input/output computer. The Univac LARC was apparently the first computer to use multiprocessing. An author describes the basics of multiprocessing: "…[I]n multiprocessing several units of the machine are working simultaneously on instructions belonging either to a single program or to several, all of which are able to access the memory or other common resources…"[8] As with multiprogramming, multiprocessing increased the rate of throughput for mainframe computers and the apparent speed of the computer for timesharing and online users (as with the SABRE airline system)..

Eight

It was well-known that keypunching was not a reliable method of recording data to be read by computers. IBM developed machines that would read printed documents, such as from a printing press, to eliminate or reduce the amount of keypunching required for data entry. One project in that area was VIDOR, or Visual Document Reader. VIDOR didn't become a product.

Another project in that area was MICR, or Magnetic Ink Character Recognition, announced in July, 1956 and used on bank checks. MICR was advocated by the American Bankers Association. Of course, MICR was successful. The process was developed by the Stanford Research Institute, which was responsible for the font and the recognition technique. [1] The checks were read horizontally by a magnetic read head. The font was designed to simplify the recognition process.

IBM announced their MICR-related machines in Jan., 1959. The machines included, "the 1210 sorter-reader; magnetic-ink inscribers by means of which the amount could be keyprinted on the face of the check; and control units to permit operation of the sorter reader with a computer, a magnetic tape unit, or an accounting machine."[2]

IBM developed other optical character recognition machines, the 1418 numeric reader and the 1428 alphanumeric reader. The former was announced in Sep., 1960, and the latter was announced in Aug., 1961. The 1418 was used with the 1401 computer and read only digits. The 1428 was used with the 1410 computer and read letters in a special font.[3]

Several years later, IBM developed a more-powerful machine that would read over 200 fonts, which had to be typed or printed. It was developed for the Social Security Administration.

Nine

MAGNETIC TAPE

M agnetic tape became an important technology in the 1950s. Before magnetic tape, there was wire recording, which is now over 100 years old. It was described in a September, 1900 issue of Scientific American. The article was about a new invention called the telegraphone, invented by Valdemar Poulsen. The device recorded sounds on steel piano wire, up to several hundred feet long, which was wrapped around a brass cylinder. According to the article, "… [T]he wire had to move at about 1.6 feet per second. For conversations lasting more than a few minutes, the drum and its single layer of wire could be replaced by a thin steel ribbon fed from one reel past the recording and reading station and wound layer after layer upon a second reel."[1] The article went to say that a recorded conversation could be played back several thousand times.

Edison's sound recording method became more popular, because of the weak signal produced by Poulsen's recording device.

Eckert and Mauchly wrote in 1945 that their EDVAC computer would use wire or magnetic tape to record data.[2]

The newer invention of recording using iron oxide on plastic tape was developed during the Second World War, by the Germans. That material was cheaper than wire and provided better quality sound recordings. Other advantages of tape were reusability and speed; it would be likely to keep up with the processing in digital computers. It was also a much denser recording medium than punch cards.

IBM started experimenting with magnetic tape recording in the late 1940s. Byron Phelps led a group to work on magnetic tape engineering at the Poughkeepsie facility. They looked at both metallic tape and oxide-coated plastic tape. The group decided that the latter medium was preferable, because the cost was lower, and the plastic tape weighed less.

Plastic recording tape was experiencing growing use in audio recording at that time. It could also be easily spliced, in case of breakage or for editing.[3]

John McPherson, an IBM manager, led a project starting in 1947 to get magnetic tapes working with the Selective Sequence Electronic Calculator, at the Endicott facility. But that project didn't achieve much. Magnetic tape development work was assigned to the Poughkeepsie facility in June, 1949.

In digital tape recording, some of the problems to be solved were: starting and stopping the tape, formats to use, and how to read and write the tape. IBM engineers looked at sound recording on tape, but the requirements there were different. Changes in sound were gradual and resulted in small changes in magnetization of the tape. With digital recording, however, the digital values were of the on/off variety, so that there was a large change in magnetization for a "1" value and the opposite magnetization for a "0" value. As the IEC book[4] comments, "Magnetic saturation of the tape was sought because it would help to make the system less sensitive to such unwanted signals [stray noise]; and the recorded transitions should be abrupt rather than gradual—more like square waves than sine waves—in order to produce the sharpest and most accurately timed signals in the reading process."

IBM people noticed that the BINAC machine, developed by the Eckert and Mauchly firm, running in Aug., 1949, used plastic magnetic tape in its system. The engineers noted that the recording device was similar to a reel-to-reel sound recorder.[5]

Some problems that IBM engineers worked on were: "starting and stopping it [the tape] rapidly, maintaining constant speed during recording or reading, controlling the supply and takeup reels…"[6]

IBM tried several methods for moving the plastic tape. One was the "electrostatic clutch," which they soon discarded. Another was the "pinch roller," which worked much better. In that mechanism, rotating and nonrotating capstans were used to move the tape either to the right or to the left. The tape was wrapped part way around an idler pulley on both sides of the read-write head. Once perfected, the pinch roller system was commonly used on IBM tape drives.[7]

They also developed a mechanism for starting and stopping the tape rapidly. Eckert and Mauchly favored spring-mounted pulleys. But at IBM, the vacuum column approach was found to work reliably. With that device, the tape was blown into two loops using air jets, one for the supply reel and one for the takeup reel. A slight vacuum was used to hold the tape in each column, which was made visible with a glass cover. Other devices were needed to work with the vacuum columns. The magnetic clutch, electrically-controlled, was used to stop the reel's motion. To sense the position of each tape loop, pressure-sensitive switches were used. These relied on the difference in pressure at the top and bottom of the columns. The pressure above the tape loop was atmospheric, and the pressure below the loop was slightly lower, so several switches were used in each column to sense the tape's location.[8]

Initially, IBM's engineers tried quarter-inch wide tape, but they soon switched to half-inch tape, to record data faster, meaning more characters or bits per second.

They also tried several different recording methods on magnetic tape. One was "discrete pulse" recording (DP), and another was "non-return to zero" recording (NRZ). In the former, short pulses of current sent through the read-write head would magnetize spots on the tape of the appropriate polarity. The area had to be first demagnetized with an erase head. With the NRZ method, current in the recording head was held constant in one direction to write a "1" and in the opposite direction to record a "0". This method required a separate timing track.[9] IBM's first commercial tape drives, for the 701 model, recorded at 75 inches per second.[10]

IBM produced many tape drive models in the 1950s, including the 727, used with the 702 computer, and the various 729 models (I, II and III), used with the 705 and 709 computers.

Ten

Magnetic Disks

Magnetic tapes were a step up from punch card storage once they became reliable, but they still had their problems. The biggest problem was that the access was only sequential. To find a specific record, the computer might have to search the entire tape, or even several tapes. That led to demands for some means of direct-access storage. An early invention in that area was magnetic drums, which were used, for example, in IBM's Magnetic Drum Calculator (model 650), which they developed in 1950. It used a drum that was ten inches in diameter. But the drum held only 1000 or 2000 words[1]. The machine also wasn't very fast, executing an add instruction in 769 microseconds.

But drums were found to have inadequate capacity and were too expensive to satisfy the needs of customers.[2] IBM employees, such as R. B. Johnson, began to talk about disk drives.

An early customer for direct-access storage was the U.S. Air Force, which was requesting a Material Information Flow Device, or MIFD, in late 1952. The purpose of the MIFD was to automate inventory accounting. The Air Force had ruled out punch cards and magnetic tape as storage media for that project. IBM proposed magnetic drums for the MIFD, but they were too expensive and didn't have the required capacity.[3] IBM didn't have a disk drive product at that point.

An inventor, Jacob Rabinow, wrote about disk drives in an engineering magazine. He stated: "A magnetic information-storage device now being developed at the National Bureau of Standards (NBS) combines advantages of large storage capacity and rapid access time. The new 'memory' stores data in the form of magnetic pulses on both sides of thin metal disks, which are mounted in a donut-shaped ring with the planes of the disks vertical. Each disk has a deep notch, and the notches are normally aligned so that a bank of recording-reading heads can be quickly rotated into position at any desired disk. Test results demonstrate that stored data can be reached in times of the order of 0.5 second... Two models are nearing completion."[4] Some readers may recognize the name Rabinow. His firm, Rabinow Engineering, was later acquired by Control Data Corporation.

Rabinow further commented that, because disks are three-dimensional, they make efficient use of space. He advocated a set of disks on a long metal shaft, with read-write heads mounted on a centrally-pivoted arm, which would move to a selected disk. A partial rotation of the disk was then all that was needed to access the required record on that disk.[5]

Disk drives are a form of semi-random access storage. Access to a word on disk is at least partly dependent on its location. Retrieval or writing of data is sequential, in general, for disk drives. The disk platters, of which there are one or more, typically revolve fast, meaning 3600 RPM or faster. The reads and writes are performed by read/write heads, of which there is at least one per platter (one circular disk). If there are several heads per platter, data transfer is done in parallel, meaning several words at a time.

For each platter, a head is moved to a specific track to do a read or write. Some wait time (latency) may be required for the disk platter to move to the desired location in the desired track. If the system wants to read, for example, the 10th word on the current track, the binary value 0110 is loaded into an address register. That value is compared with the word-mark track. When they match, the word has been located and the data transfer starts. Each platter also contains a timing track, which generates clock pulses needed for the read and write operations.

Another possibility is parallel data transfer, where each bit is located on a separate track. In that case, normally a group of words would be read or written at the same time, as the platter rotates.[6]

R. B. Johnson, a manager at IBM's San Jose facility, decided that they would develop a disk drive. As the IEC book comments, "During January [1953], Johnson chose the magnetic disk as the most promising medium for direct-access storage. [Arthur] Chritchlow [another manager], pushing ahead with a written proposal in early February, formulated challenging goals for a system with fifty disks, a capacity of 4 million characters (the equivalent, that is, of 50,000 IBM cards), and an access time of less than 1 second."[7]

One issue examined by IBM engineers was whether read and write heads would be allowed to touch the surface of disks. They decided that it would not be allowed; if a head could touch a disk, damage was likely. Some of the oxide might wear off. They planned to maintain spacing above the disk using "air-bearing techniques."[8]

One type of disk they examined was made of aluminum, 16 inches in diameter and .038 inches thick.[9] That seems very thin, since it is the thickness of an ordinary sheet of paper. Later IBM used thicker disks, one-tenth inch in diameter.[10] The test disk was coated with paint containing small particles of iron oxide. They got the disk working in June, 1953, writing a message on the disk and reading it back. They were able to prevent the head from touching the disk, but it came very close. Testing continued into the next year. One test involved reading a punched card with a card reader, writing it to a disk and then reading the data and sending it to a punch to punch it into a card.

Engineers at the San Jose facility had to examine, try, and discard various technologies before coming up with the best or adequate technology to use in a disk drive. The shaft for the disk was originally horizontal, but was later switched to vertical, for example. They tried seven experimental read-write heads, before finding the best one. One of the early working models was the Model II, which was demonstrated in May, 1955.

IBM described it as a set of 50 disks, 24 inches in diameter and one-tenth inch thick. The disks were 0.3 inches apart. The disks rotated at 1200 RPM. That model used air bearings to maintain spacing between the heads and disks.

Spacing was very small, about 0.001 inch. Each disk contained 100 concentric recoding tracks. The disks weren't perfectly flat, but this didn't matter. The disks were allowed to move up to .03 inch up or down. The recording method was called NRZI, for Non-Return-to-Zero-IBM, which was also used to record on tapes.[11]

IBM engineers noted that the equivalent magnetic drum (equivalent to the 50-disk system) would be 13 inches in diameter and 42 feet long.[12]

The San Jose facility experimented with different types of disks and access methods. They were able to develop a commercial disk drive, called the model 350., which was, "…the first movable-head disk unit in production."[13] The disks had 10,000 tracks, made up of 100 surfaces with 100 tracks on each surface. They would hold 500 characters per track, or 5 million characters in all. Johnson said a magnetic drum holding that much data would be 42 feet long and 13 inches in diameter, showing the relative use of space by each technology. The 350 was used in the 305 RAMAC machine, which was announced in July, 1956. It used vacuum tube technology.

IBM later improved the RAMAC disk system, increasing the capacity by ten times, or 50 million characters for the new system. They used a comb structure for the read and write heads in the new system. The engineers ran into many problems on that project. They had to improve their technology (working in San Jose) relating to magnetic heads, disk surfaces and magnetic recording techniques.[14]

Software technology was also improving at that time. Another IBM employee, Hans Luhn, came up with a "shrinking and randomizing" procedure which could be used to transform the original key of a disk file into an "…interval of storage addresses and effectively possessed the property of randomness."[15] The original key might be an inventory number, for example. Other names for this method were randomizing and chaining or hashing and chaining, which is also used in compilers and other language processors. The interval of storage addresses mentioned above is the chain that must be created initially or followed to f ind the specific record on a disk (or a symbol in a compiler). Ordinarily, the chain would not be very long. Of course, a long chain could slow down the retrieval of a record. Every record in the chain might have to be read and its key compared with the desired key to find the needed record.[16]That type of retrieval would be useful for generating invoices, with the appropriate data retrieved at random for creating or printing an invoice.

Luhn described his retrieval method in a memo: "The problem of automatic addressing for a random access storage unit is outlined and certain fundamental characteristics of this problem are given. Various methods for solving the problem and evaluations of this method are presented. A solution is presented which offers complete automatic addressing at a cost of about 20 percent of the random access memory storage capacity and an access time twice that of the basic random access memory. This appears to be the minimum cost now known for automatic addressing."[17]

A later disk project at IBM was the ADF, or Advanced Disk File, which began about November, 1957.[18]The resulting product was renamed the 1301 and was announced in June, 1961. It used the "slider" technology, which uses hydrodynamic air lubrication to separate the head from the disk surface. Work on that technology had started at IBM in 1954. A 1301 disk module could hold up to 28 million characters.

An improved disk product, the 1405, was announced in Oct., 1960 by IBM. It had four times the capacity of the old 350 disk product. It was used for a CIA project, called Walnut, which had as its goal storing and searching millions of documents.[19]

An enhanced technology, removable disk packs, were developed at IBM and announced in Oct., 1962. The product was called the 1316 Disk Pack. The pack held six disks and had a capacity of 2 million characters. The 1316 was used with the IBM 1311 Disk Storage Drive, which was available on the 1401 computer, the 1440 computer, and other models. Of course, removable disk packs provided some advantages. They could be moved to another drive, they could be secured in a locked cabinet, and they could be shipped to another facility. The removable disk pack helped to achieve the end of the punch card era.

Magnetic drums were another early semi-random access storage device. Data on drums was recorded and read in the same way as for disks. With drums, the read and write heads were fixed in location. So, the access time could be long. The drum rotation speed was high, up to 24,000 rpm. But it could still take up to 250 milliseconds to access data. Consequently, data was usually transferred to or from the drum in large blocks. As with core memories, drums would have a data register (DR) and an address register (AR) The CPU would send commands that included READ, WRITE and RESUME. The latter command means that the CPU is ready to receive another word from the drum when reading.[20] The RESUME command, when writing, is used to notify the drum circuitry that another word is available in the DR from the CPU.

Besides slow access, another disadvantage with drums was the low density. The interior of the drum was not used at all for recording data, making the recording density quite a bit less than with disks.

IBM nevertheless used drums in several of its early products, including the 650 Magnetic Drum Calculator and the 610 Auto Point Computer.

Eleven

Magnetic core memories were a replacement for the old Williams-tube memories. That memory technology used cathode ray tubes to record and retrieve data. Ferrite core memory was invented by Dr. An Wang, who later founded Wang Laboratories. Wang described the new technology in his own words: "Magnetic cores with a rectangular hysteresis loop are used in a storage system which requires no mechanical motion and is permanent. The binary digit 1 is stored as a positive residual flux and the binary digit 0 as a residual flux in the opposite direction."[1] The state of a core was detected by sending current through the wire wound around the core, which switched it to the 0 state. Another wire wound around the core detected the induced voltage, meaning the 1 state. This output signal was used to switch a nearby core to the 1 state, thus preserving the data value. Wang used a ferromagnetic nickel-iron alloy in his ferrite cores.

IBM eventually bought the rights to use Wang's ferrite core patent for several hundred thousand dollars.[2]

IBM improved on Wang's approach by, for example, developing non-destructive readout of data and coincident-current core memory. In the latter, half-currents are used together to switch a magnetic core when they work together at a specific location. I.e., the vertical and horizontal wires together supply enough current to switch the specific core.[3]

Mike Haynes at IBM did a lot of work on coincident-current memories that allowed non-destructive readout. In a letter to another IBM manager, he stated, "I have found a way of sensing, or reading out, the information content (binary) of the core without the necessity of changing its state and subsequently regenerating. Using this, I have worked out a proposal for a static magnetic core storage system." [4] The technique was described as follows: "using small pulses of short duration he [Haynes] was able to detect the state of the core without destroying the information." [5] The state of a core was altered by the two (X and Y) wires, threaded through the core, which together had large enough current pulses to change the magnetization, effectively changing it from 0 to 1 or 1 to 0, as needed.

IBM did extensive work on ferrite core memories in the early 1950s. An example was the 960-bit memory developed to hold the image of a punch card (12 rows X 80 columns). The cards were read by a model 405 accounting machine and used to punch cards with the Type 517 card punch. The memory acted as a buffer. That project was proposed by Edward Rabenda, who wanted to convert the punch card data to BCD codes. [6] Rabenda used cores that were 240 mil outside diameter (.240 inches), 150 mil inside diameter and 45 mil high. The cores required 2.5 amps each to store data. The project wasn't a commercial success, however, because the cores weren't reliable enough. [7] Other IBM people, such as Werner Buchholz, looked into using ferrite core buffers with card readers, card punches, and printers, but the cores that they were buying, from General Ceramics, weren't reliable enough.

IBM soon began using ferrite cores with printers [8] used with the 702 and 705 model computers. In Feb., 1953 IBM got a 960-bit ferrite core memory working with a printer and card reader used with a TPM machine. [9] The TPM machine later became their model 702 mainframe computer (actually the TPM II).

An early use of ferrite cores was in Project SAGE (Semi-Automatic Ground Environment), an air defense computer project. The SAGE computers were named AN/FSQ-7. The computers used 33 memory planes of 64 X 64 cores each, or 135,168 bits. The read-write cycle time, as described above, was 7.5 microseconds for the SAGE memory. They later reduced the time to six microseconds.

IBM decided in July, 1954, to use ferrite core memories in commercial computers. The RAND Corporation requested a core memory of over 1 million bits, in mid-1955. IBM was able to ship them its Type 738 memory, containing 32,768 words of 36 bits each, with over 1.1 million bits. The cost to RAND was $1,040,000. The 738 memory was a big improvement over the Type 737 memory, used in the 704 model computer.[10]

IBM started work on a faster memory system in Jan., 1956, called Project Silo, which was partly financed by the NSA. The goal was to develop a 2-microsecond memory of one million bits and a smaller half-microsecond memory, both using ferrite cores. These faster memories were later used in the Stretch computer.[11] The Stretch's main memory had a 2-microsecond access time. The memory was cooled with a liquid, transformer oil, which IBM adopted after trying Freon, grease and other liquids and solids.[12] The half-microsecond memory had a lot of problems, so it was dropped as a requirement for the Stretch project in July, 1959. [13] But the faster memory was still required for NSA's Harvest computer. IBM was able to provide a 0.7 microsecond memory for the Harvest machine, compared to the preferred 0.5 microsecond memory. The Harvest machine had 1024 words of memory, with 72 bits per word, or 73,728 bits total. Each bit of memory used two ferrite cores between 30 and 50 mils in diameter and 11 mils high. Two cores were used to improve noise rejection.[14] The memory was made available in Dec., 1960. But the Harvest machine wasn't delivered until Feb., 1962.[15]

One type of ferrite core used by IBM in that era was CuMg, or copper magnesium. Of course, ferrite also contains iron and oxygen. The CuMg variety was obtained from Philips, the big electronics firm.[16]

Ferrite cores were originally wired by hand, with an X-Y plane of 4096 cores for Project SAGE taking 40 hours to wire, for all four wires going through each core. Due to the high labor content, IBM management searched for a way to automate the wiring process. They used a technique from MIT which positioned the cores in depressed areas on a plastic plate. The cores were than wired with a needle-like device, which pulled a wire through a set of cores and was then attached at the edge of the core array. The needle was then pulled back through the cores and re-threaded[17] By late 1963, IBM was producing over 1 billion ferrite cores per year.[18] Earlier, they had made cash licensing payments to An Wang, Philips Corp. and others. The final licensing payment IBM made as related to ferrite core memories was $13 million paid to MIT for Jay Forrester's patent for coincident-current core memories. MIT originally had asked for a payment of 2 cents per bit.[19]

A typical magnetic core memory worked as follows: For a write, the word (or byte) address is first placed in the address register, AR. The value to be written (0101) is placed in another register, DR. The cores at the address AR are cleared to zero before the write. The AR value is used to select the word driver for the specified word in memory. A full-read current is sent to the word line for the specified word. The 1 values are set in the word by the word driver and the bit drivers using half-currents. I.e, the appropriate bits in the chosen word are set to 1, the other bits having been cleared.[20] The memory circuitry issues a CYCLE COMPLETE signal when the data value has been placed in the DR register. This prevents the CPU from getting ahead of memory processing and possibly using an old value in the DR.

To do a read, the address is placed in the AR register. The word driver sends a full read current to the word line for that address. Wherever the word bits are 1, voltages are sent to the corresponding bit lines because of the bit magnetizations.

The sense amplifiers detect these voltages and send them to the DR. The DR value is sent to the processing section, which requested the read and is expecting the new value. If the read operation is destructive, the value in the DR is used to select bit drivers which rewrite the data into the selected word.[21] For the read operation, a DATA READY signal is issued when the word is available in the DR register. A CYCLE COMPLETE signal is sent after the word is re-written to the specified location.

Twelve

Programming on the early IBM computers was originally done with plug-boards, a cumbersome technique. According to <u>IBM's Early Computers</u>, "Most of us in those days were plugboard men. There were a few stored program people, but not many. We decided what we wanted was the best of both worlds...We decided that one could transfer data best with stored programs—that was always a nuisance with all those wires to string—but one could make decisions a lot easier on plugboards."[1] In a later chapter, the IEC author states, "But the fundamental change in the application development process would be in the final step, where programming would replace panel wiring."[2]

Certainly, stored programs were an improvement, where the program could alter itself (such as by computing and modifying addresses) and new programs could be placed in memory, in seconds or minutes at most. Use of subroutine or function libraries would be another improvement, where a program could call in standardized code, such as for computing a square root (SQRT in Fortran), which could be used many times in each program. With a function like the square root, the argument value is placed in a specific register or other required location, the result is returned in some other register and the function returns to a specified location in the calling program. Typically, that was (and is) done with a "return jump" instruction which stores the current address + 1 at the start of the function (stored in an instruction's address field), which then returns to that address when the calculation is complete. In today's program libraries, such functions are kept in relocatable binary format, where addresses in the function are modified by adding the initial location of the function to get the correct absolute addresses.

The next step in programming was to use machine language, which is just numbers. The numbers, typically printed or displayed in hexadecimal (base 16) or octal (base 8), consisted of instruction codes and addresses (or small integers), which the hardware executes. Of course, this was an error-prone process at first. The programming process was simplified by assembler programs, such as the SOAP assembler (Symbolic Optimal Assembly Program), originally written for the 650 machine. It was written by Stanley Poley and Grace Mitchell. A listing in the IEC book[3] shows that it is like modern assemblers, in that it accepts mnemonics for the instruction codes and symbolic locations in the program, rather than absolute addresses. Data is also referenced by symbolic locations. Of course, these locations need to be relocated before the program is executed by the hardware.

Another early assembler form IBM was Autocoder, written for the 702 model[4] and later modified for newer models, such as the 705. Another early innovation was a simulator, which interpreted programs written on the 702 model which were to be used on the new 705 model, which was not yet available. Other early assemblers written at IBM were SOAP (Symbolic Optimal Assembly Program) and SPS (Symbolic Programming System).

One of the most important programming innovations in the 1950s was higher-level languages, such as Fortran. John Backus at IBM was placed in charge of a group, in 1954, to define a higher-level language, called Fortran. They completed the language definition in 1954. Backus was then authorized to develop a compiler for the language. A few compilers had already been written by that time, such as Grace Hopper's A-0 compiler[5]. Backus's group worked on the compiler in 1955 and 1956.

The first Fortran compiler was shipped in April, 1957.[6] It ran on the 704 model. One of the first papers ever written on Fortran, by Backus et al., was "The Fortran Automatic Coding System."[7] The compiler ran in three phases initially. The first phase would process the source code, written in a user-friendly language (unlike assembler code), and the third would produce relocatable binary code, which was then processed by a link-editor or a loader before being executed by the machine's hardware. Other phases were later added to optimize the generated code, to make it run faster.[8]

The Fortran compiler and language were well-received by customers. Early on, 26 installations were using the compiler.[9] Fortran was found to be very efficient. The IEC book stated that, "Productivity studies at the General Motors Research Laboratories installation showed that compared to assembly language, Fortran reduced programming and coding effort by a factor of between five and ten. Taking into account machine and programmer costs for programming, compiling and debugging, development cost was reduced by a factor of 2.5." [10]

After they had been using Fortran, customers noticed that there was a lot of "down" time on their computers, when no programs were being run. As the IEC book states, "Some innovative work had already been done to reduce the 'between jobs' periods during which one programmer was removing card decks and tapes and the next-scheduled programmer was mounting his. The proportion of time devoted to setdown and setup could be high in installations where numerous jobs were being debugged and run."[11] These concerns led to operating systems, which reduced the unproductive time.

One response by IBM was the Share Operating System (SOS) for the 709 model.[12] An initial version of the system was shipped by IBM in Aug., 1958. As the IEC book states, "In August, the chairman of the SHARE SOS committee reported that 'SOS was distributed on Aug. 7. Although there are still many bugs in the system, it operates correctly in all important respects, and many packages of additional corrections are in the late stages of completion or distribution.'"[13] Share was one of IBM's user organizations.

Another response, by IBM users, was the 709 Fortran Monitor, developed at Rocketdyne and released in late 1959. It became very popular with users and was known as the Fortran Monitor System, which was also adapted for use on other IBM models.[14]

Another important software product from IBM was CICS (Customer Information Control System), which simplifies terminal input and output, such as for bank teller terminals. It is an old product, but it is still in use on many IBM mainframes. CICS is often used with some Cobol compilers, which include enhanced verbs for using CICS. CICS is an old product, which was first released in 1969. Terminal users can bring up predefined screens with the appropriate user-defined four-character commands, such as IQML, for displaying loan data at a bank. The user would type in a loan number, and CICS would display some of the customer data for one loan. Function keys would allow displaying additional data. Other commands, such as ANML, would allow for defining a new loan. By today's standards, CICS is an old and cumbersome product to use; defining a new screen for a terminal is tedious. An IBM web site comments, "[U] pwards of 300 billion transactions flow through CICS systems each day. CICS has been at the forefront of innovation throughout its life."[15]

An important feature used by CICS programs and Cobol programs was IBM's VSAM file structure, which was used for direct access files. Users could retrieve and update records using a key with the VSAM structure. VSAM files were useful in database systems, but relational databases are more useful and more flexible than VSAM files. For example, to expand a record defined in a VSAM file, every program using that record would have to be recompiled. But a new relational database table (like a VSAM record) can be defined or expanded on the fly, without bringing down the database system.

Working with American Airlines, IBM developed the Sabre system, a real-time system for airline reservations. It was officially called Sabre starting in 1957. The project was in the study phase for four years at IBM. It was transferred to SEPD (Special Engineering Projects Division) group in 1958, under J. A. Haddad. Sabre used the IBM 1301 disk system, or Advanced Disk File, to store its data. Project people had earlier looked at many other data storage options, including punched cards. The system also used IBM Selectric typewriters as the terminals. They weren't really fast (15 cps), but they worked. Sabre used developments from the earlier SAGE system. The airline allowed only a three-second response time (maximum) at its terminals.[16] The airline people could display a lot of useful information using Sabre, such as the number of seats available on a specific flight and information on a specific passenger, including special meals.

Sabre initially used a pair of 7090 mainframes and included more than 1000 terminals. It used 16 of the 1301 disk systems, which held up to 800 million characters of data. The system began operations in 1962.[17] It was working in many cities by 1964. Other airlines later developed their own reservations systems. The Sabre system was also a model of how distributed computing could work in other industries.

Thirteen

O ne of the most important concepts in modern digital computers is the stored program. This means that the program could modify itself[1]; this can still be done with assembly language or machine language programs. The earliest programs of this type were written in machine language, composed of instructions (processed by the CPU) and references to data, normally in registers or RAM memory. Compiled programs today typically don't modify themselves, except for the return jump instruction, which stores a return address in the instruction to which it is transferring, allowing it to return to the calling program. It is possible to generate or write code which never modifies itself, which is sometimes called reentrant code. At least in theory, a reentrant program can be executed by several users simultaneously, with base registers used to access the data for each user.

Machine Language

The earliest computer language was machine language, which consisted of hexadecimal (base 16) or octal (base 8) numbers; hexadecimal uses the letters A through F to represent the digits from 10 to 15. The numbers displayed were a sequence of op codes and operands. An op code corresponded directly with a hardware instruction, such as ADD, meaning add two integers. The operand for each op code was either an address in memory or a small integer. A machine language program, if displayed or printed out, would be in hexadecimal or octal. (Utilities, such as CMPSDMP on the CDC 6600, existed to make a machine language program look like assembly language, which could then be printed.) Howard Aiken proposed, in the 1930s, creating a translator to read higher-level language programs and produce machine language executable by the computer. Aiken was a mathematician. John Backus' Fortran compiler was one of the first translators of this type.

Writing in machine language was and is very tedious and error-prone. It survives today mainly in the form of "patches," which are typically a few instructions written to replace bad code in a compiled or assembled program. Today's PC users probably wouldn't understand a lot of this.

Assembly Languages

To simplify writing machine language, assemblers were developed. An assembler is a translator that converts symbolic assembly language to machine language, which may be absolute (not later altered) or relocatable. The latter is converted by a link-editor or loader to absolute machine language, by adding the program's initial address to all relative locations. An example follows:

```
LDA     Const1
ADD     Var1
STA     Var2
```

This short program fetches the Const1 value from memory, adds Var1 to it and stores it in Var2. Each of the op codes above is converted to a different binary value, which would later be translated by the machine's central processor to obey the program's commands. Typically, some explanation in English would follow each instruction in a well-written program. An operand in assembly language was typically an address in memory, or a small integer constant. The format is as follows: Opcode, Index, Address.

In the above example, the Opcode is six bits, the Index is three bits, and the Address is 15 bits. This is the old Control Data 1604 instruction format. Each instruction occupied 24 bits, or one half-word. In most cases, the value in one of six index registers was added to the 15-bit address. Index registers are useful for looping.

Commercial assemblers typically included other features, such as ways to define large integers, floating-point constants, character strings and to reserve blocks of memory. Other features sometimes included commands to reference external functions or procedures and macros. A macro is a facility to define a set of instructions that can be referenced by a single name. When the name is referenced, the op codes are generated, along with variables that may be included when calling the macro. An example follows.

Addseq	Macro	Name1,	Name2
	LDA	Const1	
	ADD	Name1	
	STA	Name2	
	Endmac		

The macro is named Addseq, with two arguments, Name1 and Name2. When Addseq is called, the two names from the Addseq call line are substituted before the three instructions are generated. With some assemblers, default values can be provided so that only the macro name is needed in the call. The code produced by the macro is the same as the three-instruction sequence shown just above the macro definition.

To reference an external procedure, such as a square root function, a command such as EXT might be provided. Typical syntax would be: "EXT SQRT", which would appear at the beginning of the program. EXT is used instead of EXTERNAL because programmers aren't known to be verbose; they prefer abbreviations. The result of such a command is that the reference becomes part of the assembler's output, which is then used by a link-editor (see Glossary) to search a system library file for the SQRT function. The function is then read into memory, with the user's program, and the address of SQRT's entry point is substituted in the user's program as the executable code is being generated. Assemblers sometimes contain extra features, such as the ability to generate code for several target machines, such as the Unisys Meta-Assembler. Another feature in some assemblers is the absolute option, which generates absolute code; absolute code isn't relocated. An extensive discussion of assembly language is included in the multi-volume series by Knuth, The Art of Computer Programming. Knuth uses a hypothetical assembly language, Mixal, but the first volume describes how to write a Mix language simulator. The first volume also discusses computer science techniques, which are often more important than knowledge of specific languages.

On the first supercomputer, the Control Data 6600, two assemblers were available, ASCENT and COMPASS. The latter was technically a meta-assembler, because it produced code for two machines, the central processor and the peripheral processors. The central processor had a 60-bit word and did the difficult work. The peripheral processors, of which there were ten, were 12-bit machines and did the simpler tasks, such as input, output and memory management. Of course, they had separate assembly languages. Most people used only the CPU's (central processor's) language. The Compass assembler had all the features mentioned above. Compass was used to write library routines and compilers, such as the MNF Fortran compiler for the 6600. MNF was Minnesota Fortran, written by University of Minnesota staff members, who didn't like Control Data's Fortran compilers, called Run and Fun. A University of Minnesota honors graduate, John Norstad (BA Math, 1971), stated in his autobiography, "MNF was the standard compiler for teaching programming at universities all over the world in those days."

Another university, Waterloo in Canada, developed its own Fortran. They called it WATFOR, which ran on a 360/75 mainframe. One author describes the WATFOR compiler project: "WATFOR was written by four third-year math students in the summer of 1965. It was a fast in-core [in RAM memory] compiler with good error diagnostics, which proved especially useful to students for debugging their programs, as well as speeding up execution."[2] (It is unlikely that math students would know much about compilers, unless they had studied the subject extensively in their spare time.) They later revised the WATFOR compiler and called it WATFIV. It should be noted that there are at least two types of compilers.

One is typically fast at compiling and generates adequate code. The other is slower and generates "optimized" code, which is designed to run fast. Optimizing code is a difficult task for a compiler. The optimization strategy may be different for each computer model. It would depend on the instruction set. Thus, the WATFOR compiler likely didn't generate optimized code.

As with virtual memory, code optimization isn't as important as it used to be. Computers are much faster and cheaper than they used to be, and they contain much more fast RAM memory.

One of the earliest compilers ever written was developed for the Whirlwind computer at MIT in the early 1950s. It was sometimes called an "Algebraic System." The program would read in commands from a user and generate machine code. It wasn't clear if the program was a compiler or an interpreter. It was developed by Laning and Zierler.[3]

Fortran Language

Despite their extra features, assemblers were still difficult to use for many people. It wasn't practical for scientists, engineers and accountants to learn a computer's instruction set, for example (of course, some learned it anyway). Consequently, higher-level languages, such as Fortran and Cobol were developed. Fortran was developed at IBM by John Backus and others, who worked at IBM's Watson Scientific Laboratory. Backus had earlier developed a language at IBM called Speedcoding. (Backus had graduated from Columbia with a masters degree in math in 1949 and was hired by IBM in 1950.) The Fortran group developed their first version of the language in Nov., 1954, called Fortran I. It was pretty primitive, with only two-character variable names. They soon released an improved version of the language, Fortran II. It allowed six-character variable names and formatted input and output. Fortran I did not allow formatted output. There was also a Fortran III, developed by a Backus colleague, Ziller. The better-known Fortran IV appeared in 1962. Early Fortrans didn't have strong variable typing. Initially, integers were defined by used of I through N as the first character of the variable name.[4] Other prefixes designated type Real, meaning floating-point, variables. Type statements, such as "Type Real A" and "Type

Integer B", were adopted later. Some early Fortrans allowed short character strings, which were typed as integer. An example is

$$NAME = 5HSTEVE$$

The above statement stores a five-character string in the integer variable NAME, which could then be printed out, possibly in a report title. The letter H (short for Hollerith) indicates that a string constant follows. Fortran systems often allowed the reading in and writing out of character strings using the A (for alphabetic) specification in FORMAT statements.

Recent Fortran compilers often have type statements for complex, double precision and for character variables and strings. User-defined record structures may also be allowed. Most Fortran compilers allow a Type Logical, to define logical variables and arrays. Type Logical variables and arrays can then be used in logical expressions, along with the constants True and False. The logical operators include at least AND, OR and NOT. Logical variables and expressions can also be used in IF statements.

The Fortran compiler developed by the Backus group was announced in 1957 and ran initially on the IBM 704. It is described in the article, "The Fortran Automatic Coding System," written by Backus, et al.[5] Backus later helped to develop an early version of the Algol language, called Algol 58; Backus is also known for developing the Backus-Naur form, for defining the syntax of programming languages. An excellent survey of early computer languages, before 1967, is contained in Programming Systems and Languages, (McGraw-Hill, 1967) by Saul Rosen.

The advantages of Fortran (short for FORmula TRANslation) were that the programmer didn't need to know the machine's instruction set or even how it worked internally. A scientist, for example, could write a program or procedure to multiply two matrices (a mathematical operation) without knowing how the calculations were done internally—usually in floating-point. Other advantages were the built-in formatted input and output. This feature provided automatic conversion of integer, floating-point and character values from an input file to internal binary for use by the program. On output, conversion from binary was provided, so that results were available in user-readable formats. In recent years, new features were added to Fortran, including the new data types Complex, Double Precision, Character, and record structures. Some Fortrans include an interactive debugger. (An interactive debugger is a tool, built into the compiler, which allows the user to execute his program one statement at a time. The user can also set breakpoints, which allow the program to stop at specific statements. He can then display or change variables and arrays at that point or just resume execution.) There is even a Visual Fortran, for creating Windows programs. Some Fortran compilers are available free for downloading, from the Internet.

IBM later released compilers for Fortran II and Fortran IV, more advanced versions of their original language.[6]

Cobol Language

The Cobol language began with a meeting at the University of Pennsylvania in April, 1959. Attending were manufacturers, university people and some computer users. They agreed that there was a need for a business-oriented language that would be independent of computer models. The Defense Department at that time was developing its own language, AIMACO. But that department expressed some interest in discussing a new language.[7]

There was a second meeting about Cobol in May, 1959, a meeting of 26 organizations [8], mainly from the private sector, at the Pentagon. The group decided that a new, business-oriented computer language was needed. A subcommittee began working on the new language the next month, starting with the old language Flow-Matic, developed by Grace Hopper; Hopper was eventually promoted to rear admiral in the Navy. (Hopper was born Grace Murray and married Vincent Hopper, an English professor; she obtained a Ph.D. in math in 1934 and had earlier started teaching at Vassar.) The subcommittee also looked at two other languages, AIMACO and Comtran, from IBM.[9] But the syntax of Cobol is very similar to the Flowmatic syntax. As one author wrote, "The main features of the new language [Cobol], and especially the use of natural-language words, were taken from the FLOWMATIC language used widely on Univac machines. Objects could be given code names of up to 12 characters, so that either their usual name could be used or, at worst, a close abbreviation."[10]

Specifications for the new language were completed by December, 1959. The language was called Cobol60. The federal government released a report on the language in April, 1960. A language manual was made available to the public in 1961. The name Cobol is short for COmmon Business-Oriented Language. Many organizations participated in its development. The initial language is described in the paper, "Basic Elements of Cobol 61,"[11] by Jean Sammet. Cobol was designed more for business use than for scientific use. The syntax was (and is) much more English-like than Fortran's syntax, for example. The Defense Department decided that computer manufacturers offering the Cobol language would be given preference as vendors. They either had to offer Cobol, or a language that would be better.

Remington Rand and RCA were the first two companies to get a Cobol compiler running on their computers. Remington Rand got its Cobol running on the Univac II, and RCA got a Cobol running on their 501 model, by late 1960 or early 1961.[12]

A typical executable statement in Cobol is: Multiply A by B giving C Go To Alpha. Cobol was later expanded to allow sorting and report generation. In the late 1960s, the Codasyl committee (Conference on Data Systems Languages) introduced a database feature that worked with Cobol, which was later extended to other languages, such as Fortran. The Codasyl database would consist of fixed-length records, which would be read in using a key, possibly updated and then written out if desired. Today Codasyl databases are not very popular, since relational databases (often using the SQL language) are easier to use and modify.

A Cobol program consists of four divisions: the Environment Division, the Data Division, the Identification Division and the Procedure Division. The first three parts of the program contain declarations. The last part, the Procedure Division, contains only executable statements, called verbs.

The Cobol source statements must be in specific columns, as with the Fortran language; this requirement was left over from the punch card era.

The Environment Division and the Identification Division were typically pretty short and not very significant parts of Cobol programs. The former might only contain statements about the source computer and the object computer, which were usually the same. The latter might only contain the author's name and the installation where the program was to be written or used. Consequently, the Data Division and the Procedure Division are typically more important.

The Data Division is used to describe structures of files to be used in the program, formats of records and working storage, which can be used to define the format of print output.

Important parts of the procedure division include the arithmetic statements ADD, SUBTRACT, MULTIPLY, DIVIDE and COMPUTE, plus IF, MOVE and GO TO. The first five of these are called the Arithmetic verbs. The first four verbs perform the indicated arithmetic operation and store the result in a variable. COMPUTE is used to compute the value of an expression and store it in a variable. The IF clause is the start of a conditional statement that performs one sentence if the value is true and another if the value is false; an ELSE clause is allowed in the IF, to execute the specified sentence when the value is false. MOVE starts a sentence that moves data in memory. The result is that data is copied from one location to another, with possible reformatting as part of the move. The GO TO verb transfers control to another part of the program.

Statements for input and output include: OPEN, CLOSE, READ, WRITE, DISPLAY, and ACCEPT. OPEN causes a specific file to be accessed and opened for processing, meaning reading or writing. CLOSE places a specific file in an inactive state. READ reads a record from an input file. WRITE writes a record to an output file. DISPLAY writes a message to a specific device. ACCEPT reads a short message from a specific device. Formatted output was allowed, using the versatile Picture clause in data definitions. It specifies the format for printing or displaying data. Other verbs include PERFORM (like a Fortran call) and EXAMINE. The latter allows a programmer to count specific characters in a character string or to replace characters, such as a string of zero characters, with some other character. The ALTER verb allows changing the destination of a GO TO statement. The STOP verb stops the program, with an optional message. The ENTER verb allows calling a program written in a language other than Cobol. The EXIT verb returns to the caller from the current procedure.

Algol Language

Algol (ALGOrithmic Language) was another early higher-level language, introduced in Europe in 1958. It is described in "The Algol Programming Language," an article by Saul Rosen.[13] The language was more popular in Europe than in the U.S. Its syntax structure is similar to some newer languages, including C, C++, Pascal, Ada and Visual Basic. The above paper includes some examples. The language is free-format, unlike Fortran and Cobol, which require statements and labels to be in specific columns. Their formats were influenced by the old 80-column punch cards, a restriction that doesn't apply to Algol.

The history of Algol began in early 1958, with a meeting in Zurich, which was led by F. L. Bauer and A. J. Perlis. John Backus also attended.[14] The result was a paper defining a language called the International Algebraic Language. They later renamed the language and called it Algol. That language shared some features with Fortran, IT (Internal Translator) and MATHMATIC.[15] MATHMATIC was developed at Univac by Grace Hopper for the Univac I.[16]

The IT language was developed by Al Perlis at Carnegie-Mellon University for the IBM 650, a primitive computer. The compiler generated assembly language which was later translated to machine language. It used the assembly language SOAP.[17]

The first version was Algol 58. IBM started writing a compiler for Algol in 1959. Among IBM users, Fortran was more popular than Algol; most people in their SHARE users group preferred Fortran. IBM had sent out a good version of their Fortran compiler in early 1957. One problem with Algol was that it was weak on input and output, unlike Fortran.[18] They could have used Fortran-like input and output in Algol, but there is no sign that they ever did that. Cobol also had better input and output than Algol. As one author stated, "But the most serious drawback was the almost complete lack of concern [in Algol compilers] with input and output."[19] Another problem for Algol was, "Algol's limited commercial success was, as we have seen, that many computer users had just adopted Fortran and saw no reason why they should change."[20]

A new version of the Algol language was published in early 1960, called Algol 60. At this time the meta-language BNF (Backus Normal Form) was developed, for defining languages. One useful feature of Algol is recursive functions, wherein a function can call itself. Algol also has block structures. A block starts with BEGIN and ends with END. One reason for block structures is that variables can be defined to exist only within a block, which saves on RAM memory.

Another Algol version, Algol 68, was published, by Winjgaarden. The Pascal language was developed as a variant of Algol 58, by Wirth and Hoare. Pascal became popular at colleges and universities.[21]

There was a system based on Algol, called MAD, for Michigan Algorithmic Decoder. An author describes it: "MAD offered fast compilation, essential for a teaching environment, and it had good diagnostics to help students find and correct errors. These qualities made the system not only successful for teaching, but also for physicists, behavioral scientists, and other researchers on the Michigan campus.... Unfortunately, few industrial and commercial installations realized, as MAD's creators did, the importance of good error diagnosis."[22] Yes, good diagnostics save time. I remember one compiler that only had one error message: "Syntax error in above program." Of course, that was a useless message.

Another language derived from Algol was Jovial (Jule's Own Version of IAL), developed by Jules Schwartz. Schwartz wrote a compiler for Jovial on the IBM 709, which was completed in 1960.[23]

PL/I was introduced by IBM in 1964 and was an attempt to combine the best features of Cobol, Fortran and Algol; it was meant to be a universal language. PL/I was developed in England and was originally called NPL.[24] The language tried to do everything for everyone, and consequently was not very successful. There are many languages derived from PL/I, including PL/8, EPL, PL/M and others.

Pascal Language

Another language that was popular is called Pascal, after the French scientist who wrote three classical books, including <u>Scientific Treatises</u>. The language was invented by Niklaus Wirth and was popular in the 1970s and 1980s. It was based on the oldest version of Algol, known as Algol 60. Pascal was popular in academia and was typically used to teach programming. It includes the data types Integer, Real, Character and Boolean, as well as record structures. Users can define records as types, which are then used to define variables or arrays.

Structured programming is encouraged in Pascal with procedures, functions, if/then/else structures, for loops and other loop structures. The language has built-in input/output features, but they aren't as user-friendly as those in Fortran. Newer languages, such as Visual C++, which is also related to Algol, have eclipsed Pascal in popularity.

The C language was developed by Bell Labs, which was a division of AT & T. It is a fairly primitive language compared to C++ and the other improved versions of C. For example, to compare two strings, you need to call a function rather than just use the "=" or other operator between two strings.

APL Language

APL is another language from IBM. It was first defined in a book by Ken Iverson, A Programming Language, published in 1962. APL was initially a type of notation. One author describes how APL began: "Originally APL, due to Kenneth Iverson, was designed as a tool for the description and formal analysis of a computer. It was used in 1962 to describe the IBM 7090, among other applications and in 1964 the IBM 360....At the end of the 1950s Iverson extended the work he had done for his doctoral thesis by developing subroutines with which he could test the relative merits of different methods for solving systems of differential equations. Experience with this work led him to the decision that an APL program should consist of a 'central body' that could call any number of independent subroutines and that like Fortran it should not have a block structure."[25]

Iverson commented on how an APL interpreter might work: "Iverson convinced himself also that data items should be handled very dynamically during the running of a program and therefore should not be frozen by initial declarations; in APL, therefore, names are not declared at the start of a program."[26]

After Iverson created the definition of APL, someone wrote an interpreter for it (about 1964), making it a computer language. It is a powerful language, but it includes many cryptic operators and an alternate keyboard in its original definition, making it hard to use. The old APLs typically use a system like DOS or Unix, where one can type in a statement, have it executed immediately and type in another statement. Some APLs use a different set of operators and the standard Windows keyboard, such as an APL written by this author, making it much simpler to use.

Classic APL uses both cryptic operators and standard operators, such as + and − for add and subtract. Some of the cryptic operators include a leftward-pointing arrow, which means Specification or "is defined as." A rightward-pointing arrow means "go to" a label. The Greek rho letter means "reshape" or "size of." The Greek letter iota means "index generator" or "index of." APL programs can be concise and powerful, such as

($DOM 4 4 $R 2 1 5 1 1 1 -3 -4 3 6 -2 1 2 2 2 -3) $IP 4 1 $R 5 -1 8 2

which solves a 4 X 4 set of simultaneous equations in one line, using an alternate set of APL operators. One of the reasons for the power of APL is that variables and arrays are declared and initialized in just one line of source code. For example, an array of 100 integers can be defined as

A $S 10 10 $R $I 100

The above statement creates an array of 100 integers, from 1 to 100 and stores them in the array A, which is defined with two dimensions, 10 by 10. In classic APL, the $S operator would be written as the leftward-pointing arrow, the $R would be written as the Greek letter rho and the $I would be written as the Greek letter iota.

ADA Language

The Ada language was developed to meet the needs of the U.S. Department of Defense. The development process began in 1975, with the High-Order Language Working Group (HOLWG). [27] Software was and is a major expense for the DoD. In 1973, for example, they spent $3 billion on digital computer software—mostly for maintenance (fixing errors and adding needed features).

56% of that money was spent on embedded systems, such as for Minuteman missiles. They used a staggering 450 general-purpose computer languages in the DoD.[28] At that time, in the 1970s, much of their software was written in assembly language. Of course, that means that errors in the programs were more likely and maintenance was difficult. Today, higher-level languages such as Visual Basic, C++ and Java are used to make programming easier and to make the programs more reliable. The HOLWG group decided that no existing language met all their requirements. Consequently, they decided to develop a new language, which became Ada, named for Ada Lovelace, the first programmer.[29]

The DoD in the 1970s had a list of preferred programming languages, which included: ANSI Fortran, ANSI Cobol, Jovial (two versions), Tacpol, SPL/I and CMS-2. Only the first two were widely known and used at that time. Jovial was based on Algol. HOLWG looked at the existing languages and made some conclusions: "that no language was suitable in its current state, that one language would be a desirable and achievable goal, and that development should be started from a suitable base, such as Pascal, PL/I or Algol 68."[30]

HOLWG's new language was created in stages, from April 1975 to June 1978. The stages were: Strawman, Woodenman, Tinman, Ironman, Revised Ironman and Steelman. The DoD people decided on eight criteria that the new language would need to satisfy: Generality, Reliability, Maintainability, Efficiency, Simplicity, Implementability, Machine independence, and Complete definition (must be completely defined).[31]

DoD people asked contractors to produce a definition for the new language, starting in April 1977. Seventeen firms submitted definitions. Most of them were based on the then-popular Pascal language. Four contractors were chosen as the winners: Cii-Honeywell Bull, Intermetrics, Softech and SRI International.[32] About two years later, the Cii-Honeywell Bull team was chosen as the winner. The language was officially named Ada about that time also. In June 1979, the Preliminary Ada Reference Manual was sent to over 10,000 people.

Classes to teach Ada were also established. Jean Ichbiah, of Cii Honeywell Bull, was the first person to teach those classes. The Ada language was modified and improved until December, 1980, when it became a military standard,

MIL-STD-1815.[33] Ada became an ANSI standard in February 1983.[34] The U.S. government established an Ada Joint Program Office, to coordinate Ada activities. Ada became the required language for mission-critical systems in the DoD. Many U.S. allies also adopted Ada for their new military systems.

An APSE, Ada Programming Support Environment, was created to use the language and compilers. There was also a Kernel APSE and a Minimal APSE, including an Ada compiler. These environments were created to provide an interface between the user and Ada. The DoD set up the Ada Compiler Validation Capability (ACVC), which included about 3000 tests. They consisted of correct and faulty Ada programs, to test compilers. An Ada Implementer's Guide was also written and published, to help compiler writers.[35]

As implied above, Ada is based on the Pascal language.[36] The Pascal language was developed by Nicklaus Wirth. He developed an early version of the language in 1968, and he completed a Pascal compiler in 1970. It became popular at colleges and universities. Pascal was based on the Algol 60 language. As one author stated, "Pascal has become very popular because of its clarity and simplicity and has been extended from its initial definition to add features necessary for the actual production of large programs by teams of programmers."[37] But Pascal had an important weakness: it was weak on input and output. Cobol and Fortran had more elaborate features for those processes.

The Ada language has added features to improve error checking at run time and to detect errors at compile time, such as trying to read from an output-only procedure argument. Strong type checking also prevents storing the wrong data type in a variable or array. Exceptions are included in Ada to handle error conditions, such as a stack becoming full.[38] In computer science, a stack of objects is like a stack of dishes, with an object added to the top or removed from the top.

Ada allows block structures, using "Begin...End", which also allow defining of local variables, which become undefined at the end of the block. Ada also allows procedures, pointers, functions and arrays. The main risk with pointers is than one of them could be null, which could cause a serious error. Other languages, such as C and C++, include pointers. Pointers can be used to construct linked lists[39], but they can also be created using just offsets. I.e., a stack can be created as a linked list, using offsets.

The Ada language doesn't limit the number of dimensions in an array. As stated by one author, "Arrays are not limited to one dimension. In fact, there are no language-defined limitations on the number of dimensions allowed in an array."[40] However, an Ada compiler may impose a limit on the number of dimensions.

Like Pascal, Ada has strong typing, which includes user-defined records and subtypes using integers, such as "subtype stack_index is integer range 0..400". Of course, the type included must be a previously-defined type, including user-defined types.

Operators allowed by Ada include the normal arithmetic operators, plus exponentiation using the "**" operator, like Fortran. It has its own set of rules for that operator, such as not allowing a negative exponent with an integer base. Ada also allows conditional expressions, such as

$$\text{If } A < B \text{ and } C > 100 \text{ then } \ldots \text{ end if;}$$

Ada also has control structures like Pascal, including loop types. Examples of looping structures include: "While…loop…end loop", "For…loop…end loop" and "Loop,,, end loop". The latter example might be an infinite loop, so an explicit exit from the loop is required. The For loop above can include an "in" clause, as in "For I in 1 .. max loop…end loop". Ada provides a Goto statement, which can be used to exit a loop. Of course, transferring inside another loop is not good practice. Ada also allows the structures "if…then…end if" and "if…then…else…end if". Another allowed control structure is "case…is when…end case". Any number of "when" clauses are allowed in the case statement.

Another feature Ada allows is sets, which the user can create. The user can also test for membership in a set.

Ada has an error-handling feature called Exceptions, which are defined as "Events that cause suspension of normal program executions."[41] Ada also has the "raise" statement, to draw attention to the event. Ada also handles exceptions, meaning that the program can take action related to the exception.

Another important Ada feature is the package, which restricts access to names and data. As one author states, "It is the main structuring unit of Ada and typically encapsulates data and processes that provide access to that data....The package specification can contain type definitions, data declarations and specification parts of subprograms or tasks."[42]

Ada also allows tasks, which allow concurrent execution of procedures. This is an example of multiprogramming or multiprocessing, depending on whether multiple processors (CPUs) are available. Ada has features, such as semaphores, to allow synchronization of tasks. [43] Of course, two tasks can't be allowed to alter the same data record at the same time, which would produce erroneous results. Another feature for tasks is sending a message to another task. There is a related feature, the Accept statement, for reading a message from another task.[44]

Ada systems also have the APSE, meaning the Ada Programming Support Environment. One author defines it as, "It is the set of software tools that will be used to design, develop and maintain Ada programs—the programmer's workbench."[45] The Department of Defense wrote a document about the APSE, "Department of Defense Requirements for Ada Programming Support Environments." It was published by the DOD in Feb., 1980.[46]

PL/L (NPL) Language

PL/I, originally known as NPL, began in Oct., 1963. It was a result of the Advanced Language Development Committee of the Share Fortran project. Share was an IBM user's group. They decided on three goals for the language:[47]

1) To serve the needs of an unusually large group of programmers. This included scientific, commercial, real-time and systems programmers. The language was intended for novice and expert programmers.

2) To take a simple approach which would permit a natural description of programs so that few errors would be introduced during the transcription from the problem formulation into NPL.

3) To provide a programming language for contemporary (and perhaps future) computers, monitors [operating systems] and applications. As

a frequent benchmark, the committee chose not the familiar "Can we write NPL in NPL?" but "Can we write, in NPL, a real-time operating system to support NPL programs?" (i.e., an NPL language machine).

The first version of the NPL language was presented to the parent group SHARE in March, 1964. They approved that version. After many suggestions were received, a second and then a third version was published, which is described here.

PL/I was originally named NPL. However, an organization in England called the National Physical Laboratory asked IBM to change the name. They decided to call it PL/I. IBM also trademarked the names PL/2, PL/3, ... up to PL/100. The first compiler for PL/I was developed at IBM's Hursley Laboratory in England.

PL/I seemed to have as its goal to do everything for everybody, which is why some subsets of PL/I such as PL/M were developed.

The ALDC decided on six design criteria for NPL: (1) Anything goes, if it has a useful meaning. (2) Full access to machine and operating system facilities. (3) Modularity. (4) Relative machine independence. (5) Cater to the novice. (6) NPL is a programming, not an algorithmic, language.[48] They were influenced, in developing the language, by Fortran and Algol. NPL includes Begin and End blocks, for example, and Do loops.

PL/I has functions and procedures, like Fortran. It also has four kinds of storage allocation: External, Internal, Static and Controlled. External means the variable is defined outside the current block. Internal means a variable is only known to the current block. Static means the variable is declared once for the entire program, a type of global storage. And Controlled means a block of storage is explicitly allocated and freed by the program, with an Allocate or Free statement. Procedures can be reentrant or recursive. A procedure is declared to be reentrant, which means two or more users can execute it at the same time.

PL/I has many data types, including binary, decimal, floating-point and character. It even has Picture clauses like Cobol. An example is

DECLARE X Picture (ZZ.999)

which declares a six-character decimal value with three digits after the decimal point.

PL/I also allows structures, which are like records. One author defines structures as follows: "A structure is an ordered collection of scalar variables, arrays and structures, not all necessarily of the same type or characteristics."[49]

Attributes for files the program is using can be declared with a DECLARE statement. Attributes allowed include Input, Output, Tape, Plot (for data to be plotted), Even or Odd (parity of data), and Tape. PL/I also allows Open and Close statements for using files.

PL/I allows data-directed input and output, as in

$$READ\ DATA\ (X, Y, Z)$$

which reads data from the standard input. The input stream might contain "X = 57, Z = 1.45E10". In that case, X and Z get the specified values but Y is not changed.

Another useful statement is "On condition action". An example would be "On overflow X = Xmax". If the condition occurs, an asynchronous interrupt of the current task occurs. PL/I can also trigger an interrupt if an array subscript is out of range. PL/I can also detect an end-of-file condition, floating-point overflow and other conditions, which can trigger a user task. PL/I detects errors such as the above if the user doesn't specify an action on detecting a problem.

PL/I allows conditional statements, using the sequence "if...then...else...;" It also allows the PLOT statement, which requests plotting of a data file. Transfer of control is done in PL/I using the GO TO statement.

PL/I programs can create new tasks, which are then executed. A WAIT statement causes the program to wait until the specified task completes. A DELAY statement is used to wait until a specified task has completed.

PL/I allows compile-time facilities. These are: "Hints to the compiler. Commands to the Compiler. Macro variables and procedures."[50] Hints might include procedure attributes such as reentrant or recursive.

Commands to the compiler are preceded with the % character. The commands are used to modify the source input which is then compiled like a normal source program. Variables can be declared and initialized at compile time and then used to modify source statements. Even compile-time if statements are allowed in PL/I.

Macro variables allow compile-time declarations of variables and procedures. These are processed to produce new source statements which are then processed later as normal programs.

Machine Arithmetic

Two kinds of arithmetic are included in most computers: fixed point and floating point. For most users, fixed point means integer calculations. It is possible to have fractional values, such as 10.35, with fixed point arithmetic, but then the user must keep track of the decimal point. Floating point is more convenient, since the machine keeps track of the decimal (or binary) point.

Integer arithmetic produces exact results, unless overflow or underflow occurs. These errors can also occur with floating point. (Another problem with floating point is rounding errors.) The following Fortran program causes overflow on most machines:

```
            REAL V, X
            V = 1.E200
            X = V * V
            PRINT 10, X
10          FORMAT (' Big number = ', E20.10)
            END
```

The program computes the square of 10 to the 200th power. The result of the above program is likely to be "Big number = Infinity". To produce underflow, you need only change one line, the "V = " line, to V = 1.E-200. The result in that case will likely be "Big number = 0".

Another type of arithmetic is double precision, which is also floating point, but with twice the accuracy of the normal floating point calculations. Double precision instructions are included in the hardware of some computers. They are used like the normal floating point instructions. If double precision instructions are included in the hardware, floating point is often referred to as single precision. Either type of arithmetic is subject to truncation or rounding problems, but they are less likely to occur with double precision. Many computers have a 32-bit word length, so floating point calculations don't have much accuracy in that environment. Double precision would thus be a better choice. If additional precision is needed, specialized software could be used. Loss of accuracy in machine arithmetic is covered in numerical analysis books.

Another type of arithmetic, complex, usually isn't included in the hardware. It is more likely to be done with software. Some Fortran compilers include both complex and double precision arithmetic. Each one has to be declared as a type. Thus, a variable or an array can be declared as type complex or type double precision. In either case, the calculations are done in that type of arithmetic, and library functions, such as SQRT (square root) and COS (cosine) may be available to assist the programmer using any of those three types. In other words, there would be three square root functions, for example, one for each type (SQRT, DSQRT and CSQRT). A good Fortran compiler would generate a call to the appropriate version of the square root function, depending on the type of its argument. E.g., SQRT becomes CSQRT if the argument is type complex.

Basic Language

Dartmouth college invented timesharing in the early 1960s, according to the Lundstrom book. They also developed the BASIC language, which was used by students. They also wrote a user manual (published in 1964) for that language, which wasn't as powerful as Fortran, for example. The number of FOR loops (like a Fortran DO loop) was very limited, along with the amount of data that could be read in by a BASIC program. Variable names were limited to a single letter, plus an optional digit. Their versions of BASIC also included some built-in math functions, such as EXP and SIN, for the exponential and sine functions.

Their user manual also included a discussion of the Dartmouth Time-Sharing system some commands for using it, such as HELLO to log on and RUN to compile and execute a newly-typed program. Since their BASIC only had 15 statements, they are listed here: LET, READ, DATA, PRINT, GOTO, IF-THEN, FOR, NEXT, END, STOP, DEF, GOSUB, DIM, RETURN, REM.

Dartmouth used a GE 235 computer to run BASIC. Timesharing was meant for undergrads at Dartmouth, and BASIC was the only language they had there. One author comments on BASIC: "…[T]he programming language they developed, BASIC, became one of the most widely used computer programming languages in the world, with an influence that extended well beyond the timesharing system for which it was written."[51] Timesharing was later offered on other machines, including the PDP-11/45 and the HP-2000.

Dartmouth college also had a more advanced version of BASIC, which they called CARD BASIC. This version had fewer restrictions than the other BASIC and included a matrix processing option. The keyword MAT had to precede each matrix-processing statement, as in

$$\text{MAT X} = \text{ZER}(10,10)$$

which created a square matrix, X, with the dimensions shown containing all zeros, and

$$\text{MAT C} = \text{INV}(A)$$

which computed the inverse of A, a square matrix. The MAT keyword also worked with vectors (one-dimension arrays). Unisys also had their own version of BASIC, which included matrix processing.

At DEC, a group of developers wrote the RSTS-11 operating system in BASIC. They used enhancements to BASIC, to make calls on the operating system and to read and write specific memory locations, using the PEEK and POKE commands in BASIC. Of course, altering any instructions in the operating system with a POKE command could cause serious errors.[52]

Despite the popularity of BASIC, many universities in the sixties continued to use Fortran and Cobol, in batch mode, with programs typed in on punch cards. Fortran was adapted to run in time-sharing mode, by Univac, using their CFOR (Conversational Fortran) language. CFOR was an interpreter. Of course, today Fortran compilers can be downloaded from some web sites at no cost. Pascal took over from BASIC at some universities in the 70s, because it was more powerful. It also offered new features, such as record structures.[53]

By the late 1980s, keypunches weren't used much anymore. (The last time this author saw a keypunch was at a bank in St. Paul, Minn. in 1990.) Programs could be typed in with a, text editor, similar to today's Notepad program, used on Windows systems. Some development systems, such as Visual Studio, include formatting text editors, which indent the code as needed and check for missing end of loop statements, etc.

None of the early languages worked with icons or a mouse, so the input and output was typically numbers and/or text. Graphic output was sometimes available using a plotter, by special request. Some systems allowed punch card output, in character or binary format. The icon-and-mouse environment was invented by the Xerox Palo Alto Research Center. But they found their first widespread use in products from Apple Computer (now Apple Corp.), such as the Macintosh machine. Later, Microsoft started to use them in their Windows system, which was meant to replace DOS.

In the 1950s and early 1960s, computer manufacturers typically used their own character set, with each character occupying six to eight bytes; examples include IBM's EBCDIC and Control Data's Display Code. Starting in the early 1960s, the new ASCII character set became the standard, which was published in 1963 by the American Standards Association; ASCII stands for American Standard Code for Information Interchange. At that time, it consisted of 128 characters (requiring 7 bits), but it occupied eight bits per character on most machines. The new character set included the upper and lower case letters, the ten digits, punctuation characters and non-printable control characters, such as end-of-text (ETX). A newer character set, Unicode, is in use today, which allows the large Asian character sets. It allows 8-, 16- and 32-bit formats. Another newer standard is UCS, an ISO standard character set.

SQL Language

The SQL language is the most common database language used today. It was invented by E. F. Codd, who described it in a June, 1970 article, "A Relational Mode of Data for Large Data Banks," in the Communications of the ACM. It is used for relational databases and is, like Cobol, an English-like language, except for long, complex queries. An example is

SELECT * FROM EMP-REC
WHERE SALARY > 50000.

The "*" symbol means display all the columns in the table EMP-REC. (If the user is using a system like Unix, the output from the query can be saved in a file, for later use.) If the WHERE clause is omitted, all rows in that table are displayed. Data in relational databases is arranged in tables, which contain one or more columns and a key. The language contains many other commands, including INSERT, UPDATE, DELETE, CREATE, DROP and security commands such as GRANT and REVOKE.

IBM developed the first database system using the SQL language, at their San Jose Research Lab, in the 1970s. Oracle developed their own relational database system in the late 1970s, using the SQL language. The first version was released in late 1979. Other firms, such as Sybase and Microsoft, introduced their own database products using the SQL language.

One of the advantages of the SQL language is that the database is easily changed, using SQL commands. E.g., one can create a new table using the CREATE command, or insert new rows in a table with INSERT, or even add or delete columns from a table. It is also possible to alter the format of a column. UPDATE is used to change the contents of records in a table, and DELETE can be used to delete some or all the records in a table. Of course, some of these commands are not easily reversible, so organizations usually perform database backups often. SQL became an ANSI (U.S.) standard language in 1986. The database administrator has his own set of commands available, using SQL, such as CREATE DATABASE and CHECKDB, which verifies the integrity of the current database. SQL commands are divided into the DDL and DML categories, meaning the Data Description Language and Data Management Language. DDL commands are for the DBA to use. Examples of those commands are CREATE TABLE and ALTER TABLE. Examples of DML commands are INSERT and UPDATE.

Other variations of the SQL language exist now, including PL-SQL, which adds programming features, and T-SQL, for transaction processing, and MYSQL, another database product using the SQL language. According to IBM, MYSQL was invented by Michael Widenius and is available as a downloadable product. It is an open source product, according to Mr. Widenius. He has his own blog, at http://monty-says. blogspot.com/2008/11/oops-we-did-it-again-mysql-51-released.html.

See also: http://www.computerhistory.org/timeline/

Details of Languages

The Algol language was developed in Europe, starting with a meeting in 1958. After several other meetings, a description of the language was produced, called the Algol 60 report, [54] The report was written by John Backus, et al. and edited by Peter Naur. Input was solicited from the United States in defining the original Algol language. The report document was adopted at a meeting in Paris in Jan., 1960.

The original language included only a few types, integer, real, string and Boolean. String constants were allowed, and they could be used as actual arguments of procedures; "Strings are used as actual parameters of procedures," according to the Algol 60 Report. Procedures, functions, arrays and constants were included, such as integer, real, and Boolean constants (true and false) and string constants. If statements were included, with optional Else clauses, along with For loops, including While and Until clauses. The original report had the foresight to include upper and lower case letters, but input and output statements or procedures were not discussed. Labels and Go to statements were allowed. A small set of math functions was allowed, including: Abs, Sign, Sqrt, Sin, Cos, Arctan, Ln and Exp. So, the original Algol had fewer capabilities than the original Fortran, due to its lack of input and output statements or procedures.

Fortran Language

The statements included in most Fortrans are described below. Each keyword is followed by a colon and a description.

DO: This keyword starts a loop. It must be followed by a statement number and loop limits, as in Do 20 I = 1, 100.

IF: This is a conditional statement that tests a numeric expression and goes to one of three statements, as in If (A-B) 30,40,50, depending of whether the expression is negative, zero or positive.

IF (alt. format): In the alternate format, only one statement number is referenced, as in If (X .GT. 10) Go to 50 . If the expression is false, control falls through to the statement after the IF.

FORMAT: This is a statement that specifies the format of values to be read in, printed out or written out. An example of a complete statement is 100 FORMAT (1x, 5I10). Some Fortran systems allow format statements to be defined in arrays.

READ: This statement tells the compiler that you will be reading in data from some kind of file, probably on disk or tape. An example is: READ 200, array . 200 in that case is a Format statement specifying the format of the input data.. Another example is: READ (10,300) Array.
The second example reads from unit 10 with the format specified in statement 300.

PRINT: This statement tells the compiler that you are writing output on the standard print file, in the specified format, as in: PRINT 10, array2. This statement says to print the contents of array2 in the format specified by statement 10.

WRITE: This statement is a more generalized version of the PRINT statement. It allows you to write on any unit, in character format (as in the PRINT statement), or in binary format. For character format, you could write WRITE (10,200)

LIST: For binary format, you could write WRITE (20) LIST. The latter example doesn't use a format statement number.

PUNCH: This is similar to the PRINT statement, but may not be allowed in your Fortran. It used to refer to a card punch connected to the computer, but now it may default to another unit, probably a disk or alternate print file.

CONTINUE: This is a do-nothing statement that is often used to terminate a DO loop. A statement number is allowed before the CONTINUE keyword.

DIMENSION: This statement defines one or more arrays. In Fortran, an array can have from one to three dimensions. An example is: Dimension List(10,20,30).

TYPE: This statement allows the programmer to assign a specific type to one or more variables or arrays. The normal types are: Integer, Real, Complex, Double, and Logical. Some Fortrans may not have types Complex or Double.

GO TO: This statement transfers control to a specific statement number. You can't go outside of your program, subroutine or function with this statement. Computed GO TOs are also allowed, as in GO TO (10, 20, 30), VAL1. If Val1 has the value 1, control goes to statement 10, etc.

PROGRAM: This statement is normally required at the start of a program and may include parameters for the compiler.

FUNCTION: This statement starts a function, which typically has one or more arguments. The calling program retrieves the value from the function's name. An example is: FUNCTION

CUBERT(ARG). The calling program would get its result, for example, by using the statement

$$X = \text{Cubert}(10.5).$$

SUBROUTINE: This statement begins a subroutine, which may or may not have arguments. It is terminated with and END statement.

assignment statement: This is a statement that stores a new value in a variable. It consists of an "=" character, with a variable name at the left and an expression (formula) or another variable name at the right of the "=". An example is $Z = \text{EXP}(2.0) * 3.0$. Any variables in an assignment statement can be subscripted.

CALL: The call statement is used to call a subroutine, which returns to the calling program. Actual argument values may be included in the call statement, if the subroutine was defined with arguments.

RETURN: This statement is used to return from a function or subroutine. Normally, a return statement isn't needed, since the END statement does a return.

STOP: A stop statement ends execution of the current program, regardless of where the statement is located; it can be used in a function, subroutine or main program.

END: Ends the current program, function or subroutine. It performs a return to go back to the calling program.

DATA: A non-executable statement which initializes variables or arrays at compile time. Examples follow: DATA X /3.14159/ and DATA LIST /5,4,3,2, 1/

COMMON: This is a declarative statement which places variables and arrays in a special area of memory which is also used by subroutine and functions called by the current program. It can be used in place of arguments to functions or subroutines.

EQUIVALENCE: This is a declarative statement which allows variables and arrays to share memory with other variables and arrays. This could cause problems if, for example, double precision variables share memory with type real or integer variables. Example: EQUIVALENCE (A, B, C), (ARRAY1, LIST1). In this case, A, B and C all share the same location, as do ARRAY1 and LIST1. ARRAY1 and LIST1 are at different locations from A, B, and C.

Type statements: TYPE REAL, TYPE INTEGER, TYPE DOUBLE, TYPE COMPLEX, TYPE CHARACTER and TYPE LOGICAL. These are used to assign specific types to variables or arrays; usually the TYPE keyword can be omitted. Some Fortrans do not have the DOUBLE or COPMPLEX types. If you use variables that do not appear in any TYPE statements, they receive implicit typing, as follows: variables that start with the letters I through N are type INTEGER, and variables that start with other letters are type REAL. Type LOGICAL variables can appear in logical expressions and in IF statements, using a GO TO.

OPEN: Opens a file for a specific use and assigns a unit number to the file.

CLOSE: Used after an OPEN statement to free the file.

BACKSPACE: Used with a sequential file to position the file before the preceding record.

ENDFILE: Writes an end-of-file mark on a file.

REWIND: Positions a sequential file at the first record.

The Fortran 77 standard included type character, structures and records. An HP-3000 manual describes how to use these newer features. Type character has a slightly different syntax from the others, as follows: CHARACTER * 20 FNAME. This means the string FNAME can hold up to 20 characters. A structure is like a type, which is used in a later declaration to define a record, typically used for input and output. This is an example:

```
STRUCTURE /student/
STRUCTURE /name/
    CHARACTER*20 last, first, middle
    END STRUCTURE
    CHARACTER*1 sex
LOGICAL*1 school_yr
END STRUCTURE
```

To use the structure named student, a record declaration is needed:

```
RECORD /student/ class(30).
```

(Above examples from the Hewlett-Packard Corp.)

A Fortran standard definition is available at: http://www.fortran.com/F77_std/rjcnf.html. New standards occasionally are being developed.

It is possible to write an ambiguous Fortran program, as in the following example:

```
            Program Test
            Dimension Format(10), Common(20)
            Do 20 i5 = 1,10
20          Format (i5) = i5
            print 20, format
            Do30J = 3.14159
30          Common(j) = 0
            end
```

Note that arrays called Format and Common are being defined and that the second statement in the first DO loop is partly ambiguous. The Print statement is not likely to work, since statement 20 isn't really a FORMAT statement, but it appears to be one until the "=" is encountered. The assignment statement referencing the variable Do30J appears to be the start of a loop, but the loop upper limit is missing. Some Fortrans allow type REAL loop indexes, but they are usually integer variables, as in DO 30 J = 1, 10. Programs like the above are best avoided unless you are testing a Fortran compiler or interpreter.

Pascal Language

Some important statements in the Pascal language include: program, procedure, function, begin and end, type, const, var, array, if, else, while, repeat, for, case, record, goto.

PROGRAM: Starts a new program.

PROCEDURE: Begins a new procedure; terminated with END.
FUNCTION: Begins a function; terminated with END.

BEGIN: Starts a group of statements, which can then be referenced as one statement.

END: Ends a group of statements; must be preceded by a BEGIN statement.

TYPE: Allows the user to create a new type, such as INTEGER, REAL or a record definition.

CONST: Begins a constant defintion.

VAR: Begins a definition of one or more variables. Examples are VAR X: int, Y: real

ARRAY: Begins the definition of an array.

IF: Starts a conditional IF statement.

ELSE: Begins an IF statement clause (optional).

END IF: Ends an IF statement, or an ELSE clause.

WHILE: Starts a conditional loop; tests a variable or function value. Syntax is
WHILE <expression> DO <statement>.

REPEAT: Starts a conditional loop. Syntax is
REPEAT <statement> UNTIL <expression>.

CASE: Starts a CASE statement. The syntax is

CASE <expression> of
<case-clause1>
END.

Multiple case clauses are allowed. Control transfers to the appropriate labeled statement (<case-clause>, depending on the value of <expression>.

RECORD: Starts a record definition. The syntax is RECORD <field1> END. Multiple fields are allowed, if separated by commas.

Input and Output statements include:

READ, READLN (read one line), WRITE, WRITELN (write one line), OPEN (open a file) and CLOSE (close a file). These are technically library procedures. The four read and write procedures read or write variables, not binary values.

Pascal also allows assignment statements, as in Fortran, where a variable to the left of the := (assignment operator) is replaced by the expression value to the right of the := operator. Input and output statements are also included, such as READ, WRITE and WRITELN. Pointers are also allowed, with the syntax "^" followed by a type identifier, such as Integer. Of course, pointers add some complexity and risk to a program, in that a pointer may point to an incorrect address, and using pointers makes the source code more difficult to understand. The language also allows character strings, delimited by double quotes, as in "string". Expressions in Pascal include arithmetic, conditional and logical expressions, using the AND and OR operators. The above discussion doesn't include all Pascal features, and shouldn't be used to write Pascal programs, except for a trivial example. The program below shows how to write a trivial example which writes a line of output to your PC.

```
program HelloWorld;
begin
writeln('Hello World');
end.
```

As you might have noticed, input and output in Pascal is weaker than in Fortran, which has the rich formatting language, included in FORMAT statements, providing automatic conversion for variables and arrays being read or written. Fortran also includes binary input and output. In some Fortrans, such as the old MNF, an array of character strings can be used as a FORMAT statement.

Basic Language
What follows is a short description of the original Dartmouth Basic language.

The LET keyword means an expression follows; the variable after the LET is being set to the value of the expression after the "=".

The READ keyword is a command to read in data following the program's executable statements.

DATA indicates that numeric or text data follows, which will be read in by the program.

PRINT with an expression or list displays the output.

GOTO transfers control to a specific line number in the program.

IF-THEN goes to a specific line number if the condition is satisfied.

FOR starts a loop, using a specified variable.

NEXT ends the loop, for the specified variable.

END ends the current program.

STOP stops the program.

DEF starts a function definition.

GOSUB calls a subroutine.

DIM defines an array.

RETURN returns control from a subroutine.

REM is the start of a comment line.

Quick Basic, an interpreted form of BASIC from Microsoft, is similar to the early versions of that language. That version of Basic was included on some older versions of Windows, as Qbasic.exe; it was designed to run on DOS systems.

Fourteen

O ne author describes the earliest days of computer science: "At the beginning of the 1950s business people were regarded as lower-class citizens as far as computer science is concerned, unable to appreciate such elegances as floating-point arithmetic or to comprehend a computational procedure. But this attitude changed drastically by 1963; as the dominant users, they were given much more consideration."[1] He continues, "...[B]y 1963, the range of applications of computers had become so wide that computer science was no longer the private territory of the mathematicians, but had become a new science in its own right, with its own fields of research, its own applications and an industry that both led and followed it."[2]

One of the first computer science books published in the U.S. was Computer Programming: A Mixed Language Approach,[3] by Stein and Munro. It isn't nearly as sophisticated as Knuth's multi-volume series on computer programming, but it does discuss some important topics, including digital computer structure, early programming languages and machine arithmetic. Knuth's books discuss computer science techniques, such as stacks, queues and linked lists, in much greater detail; many of these techniques are used in today's PC software products.

This author met Dr. Stein (now deceased), one of the authors, who stated that the book was written on his kitchen table, with each writer producing alternate chapters, which the other would then critique.

The machine used in that book was in the scientific computer category, the Control Data 1604. Their book goes into great detail about the computer's organization and the instruction set, which had 62 instructions; an appendix in their book explains each instruction. The values 00 and 77 octal were not used. The CDC machine had a rich instruction set, with a full set of floating-point and fixed-point arithmetic instructions. It also had search instructions and looping instructions, such as Index Jump. There were other conditional jump instructions, based on the value in the A register or the Q register. The latter two were the principal arithmetic registers and were used for multiply and divide instructions. The 1604 also had input and output (I/O) instructions.

The languages used in that book were Fortran, the most commonly-used scientific language of that era, and the 1604 assembly language. They even show assembly language instructions mixed with the Fortran source code, which isn't likely used now. The risk in that case is that the compiler might be using some register values, such as loop index registers, that the assembly language program could alter, making the results worthless. Of course, mixing user-written assembly-language functions with a Fortran program, or vice-versa, would work much better. (Some readers might not be aware that Fortran has been evolving, with some compilers now allowing Type Complex, Type Double (double precision), character string arrays, and records. Of course, it helps to have library functions and subroutines that handle the new types, such as for the trig. and hyperbolic functions; examples would be CSIN, complex sine and DSQRT, double precision square root. There is also a Visual Fortran.)

The book discussed some techniques which aren't used today, such as altering addresses used in the program by, for example, with the 1604's substitute index upper (SIU) instruction. Today the program wouldn't be altered, but addresses would be altered by changing index registers, for example. In computer science, this is called reentrant programming, which allows two or more users to execute the same program at the same time; each has his own set of registers so the data is accessed separately for each user. With today's multi-gigabyte RAM memories, this technique isn't as important as it was formerly.

An important topic of the Stein and Munro book is fixed-point arithmetic, which requires the user to keep track of the exponent, with the operands scaled so that the decimal or binary points are aligned. The latter step is done automatically with floating-point arithmetic. Scientists and engineers use floating-point so they don't have to be concerned with scaling. It also allows them to do calculations using very large and very small numbers.

Another important topic is how input and output was done in assembly language. The 1604 had three instructions for input and output, INT (input transfer), OUT (output transfer) and EXF (external function). This topic isn't often studied today because driver programs handle it.

In the Fortran language, input and output was (and still is) done with Fortran statements, such as READ, WRITE and PRINT. FORMAT statements were and are used to read data in the right format and to write or print it in a readable format. Reads and writes could also be done in binary, without using FORMAT statements.

In those early days, the computer communicated with the operator using an electric typewriter, which would be used for input and output. The contents of the operational registers (not RAM memory) were also displayed on the console, when the machine was halted (not executing any programs). Of course, that was primitive and slow. In their next scientific machine, the 6600, CDC used cathode ray tube displays to communicate with the operator. The 1604's operating system was also primitive. It would only execute one user program at a time, and that program could alter RAM memory used by the operating system. That problem could be corrected by re-booting the system from a tape drive. A copy of the autoload program, for booting the 1604, follows: The 74 op code means External Function (EXF).

CDC 1604 Autoload Program

Address	Instruction	Comment
000000	74 0 32005	Rewind the tape
	74 7 32000	Wait for ready
000001	74 3 00002	Activate (FWA = 000002)
	74 7 32000	Wait for ready
000002	XX X XXXXX	Will be the first word
	XX X XXXXX	read from tape
000003	74 3 00002	Second word read from tape
	74 7 32000	

Above program from the Control Data 1604 Computer Reference Manual, page 4-7, Copyright 1963 by Control Data Corporation. Pub. No. 600016700.

Fifteen

To run his program on a computer in the early 1960s, for example, a programmer had two choices: he could write the program on paper and type it in himself, using a keypunch; or he could write the program on a coding form and have it typed in by a keypunch person (paper tape wasn't often used). In both cases, he would make use of a keypunch (probably made by IBM), which was similar to an electric typewriter except that it produced 80-column cards as output; Remington Rand used a different punch card format, with 90-column cards (most people used the IBM-standard 80 column cards). After the program was keypunched, he might use an IBM accounting machine, such as the model 407, to print it out and verify it. To use such a machine, he would put the card deck in the hopper and push a button. The program (or data) would be printed, and his card deck would appear in another hopper. To submit the program to be run, typically a "job" card would be placed in front of the program deck, containing an account number, estimated CPU time, and estimated pages of output. The next card would probably call in the compiler. After the program cards, another card would tell the system to execute the just-compiled program. The data, if any, would be placed after a separator card at the end of the program deck. The collection of cards would be followed by an end-of-job card. Then the user would place the deck in a tray of jobs to be run and return in a few hours to get his printed output and his card deck. This describes the Control Data 6600 batch job environment. On rare occasions, the computer operator might drop the card deck, a very annoying mistake. If the program didn't compile, the output would probably be a listing of his program and a few error messages. And if the user had lots of data or a huge program, the input would be submitted on a reel of tape, about 10" in diameter and ½ inch wide. Tapes are still used on mainframe computers, but they are now in small cartridges and often handled by robots, which retrieve the tape from a cabinet, place it in the drive and put it back when it is no longer needed. At some installations, programs were recorded on paper tape and read in by an operator or programmer. Paper tape was more likely to be used with minicomputers.

Of course, the batch processing mechanism was slow and cumbersome, which is why users started to use interactive, or time-sharing, terminals in the early 1960s. One example of an early interactive terminal was the Teletype, a kind of electric typewriter on a stand, which was used for input and output. One used by this author ran at 110 baud, or 11 characters per second. The terminal would also include a modem (modulator-demodulator) and a dial, for calling the computer. The modem was required (actually at both ends of the line) to convert digital data to audio pulses and back to digital again at the other end. This process was very similar to how the Internet is accessed today, for dialup terminals. Later, in the 1970s, terminals running at 300 baud and 1200 baud became common. Some terminals were hard-wired, so no dialup process was needed.

Time-sharing was typically used to type in and run shorter programs. The user would typically save his program on the computer's disk drive. He could later recall the program, edit it and run it again, as often as desired. In addition to text editors, compilers, interpreters, and link-editors were typically available to time-sharing users. Programs that were very long or used lots of machine time were more likely to be run in batch mode.

Sixteen

Thomas Watson, Senior

Thomas Watson, Sr. was born in Campbell, N.Y. in 1874. His father was a lumber dealer. Tom got his start in business selling sewing machines, and then became a salesman at National Cash Register (now called NCR Corp.) in Buffalo, N.Y. NCR was headed by John Patterson, who wasn't known for his ethics. Watson was one of their best salesmen; he later became general sales manager. He worked hard to force NCR's competitors, selling used machines, out of business.

Watson, Patterson and 29 others were found guilty, in 1912, of violating federal antitrust laws.[1] Watson's sentence was one year in jail and a $5,000 fine. He was released on bail, and the sentence was dropped a few years later. Patterson kept his distance from Watson after the conviction, and Watson left NCR voluntarily in 1913.

He married Jeannette Kittridge in 1913; they had four children, including Thomas, Jr. and Richard, who both became IBM executives. Thomas, Jr. succeeded his father to become CEO, and Dick became the head of the IBM World Trade division. The daughters were Jane and Helen.

Late in that decade, Watson bought an expensive house near Manhattan, for $19,500. He had renovation work done for three months, before the family moved in.

Watson liked to play with his children. Some family films show him playing games with his kids. But he was a strict disciplinarian, at home and at work. He would sometimes get angry at the kids.[2]

In 1919, Watson's house burned to the ground. No lives were lost. He rebuilt on the same site. He was very particular about how the house was built. So, construction took more than a year.

Watson was named general manager of the Computing Tabulating Recording (CTR) firm in 1914.[3] Watson met Charles Flint, the CEO of CTR, in 1914, through a mutual friend. Watson's pay was $25,000 per year, plus stock options.[4] The company was made up of three small firms that made computing scales, tabulating equipment and time-clock recorders. The firms' names were: Computing Scale, Tabulating Machine Co., and International Time Recording Co. The CTR firm was founded by Charles Flint. CTR executives were concerned about Watson's conviction, which is why they didn't name him CEO at that time.

In 1915, the CTR board named Watson president; he was no longer being prosecuted at that time.[5] The NCR verdict was set aside that year by the feds.[6]

Watson was concerned with his own image. He joined the Short Hills Episcopal Church and a tennis club.

In the 1917-1921 era, Watson added to his roster of CTR executives. He promoted them from within. When he was advised to hire from outside, Watson replied, "That's not my policy. I like to develop men from the ranks and promote them."[7]

One of Watson's executives was Otto Braitmayer, an assistant general manager, who developed CTR's engineering labs and traveled to other countries, at Watson's direction, to increase sales and expand markets.[8]

Other executives he promoted included Samuel Hastings and A. Ward Ford. From the outside, he hired Fred Nichol, who was originally Watson's secretary at CTR. Nichol thought of Watson like a father.[9]

Growth was rapid in the tabulating equipment industry until 1920. Revenue for CTR grew from $4.2 million in 1914 to $14 million in 1920. But competitors were closing in. One of them was the Powers Accounting Machine Company.

Watson responded by setting up an engineering lab, headed by Eugene Ford. A guy named Fred Carroll built the Carroll Press, for producing punch cards quickly. CTR also hired James Bryce, who eventually was granted over 400 patents.[10] Watson used cash to motivate his engineers, giving them $5000 bonuses, or ¼ of their annual salary.

CTR's customers were only allowed to rent the firm's tabulating equipment and had to buy blank punch cards from CTR. Of course, the rental policy reduced the competition from used machines. Watson was hoping for fast growth in the 1920s. But CTR's revenue dropped 30% in 1921.[11] There was a recession in 1920 and 1921. Watson responded with layoffs and salary reductions.

Watson imposed his own culture on CTR/IBM. He liked to work in his office wearing fine, expensive suits. He wanted his sales people to dress like their customers. But he didn't want the customers to concentrate on the salesmen's clothes. He wanted them to pay attention to the sales talks.[12] Soon the company's white-collar workers were mostly wearing conservative business suits.

The economy started growing again, in 1922. Watson exuded optimism, hoping other executives would notice and maybe start using his products.

Watson didn't like employees drinking, especially during working hours; he had had at least one bad experience with alcohol before joining CTR. But the firm sent a mixed message on that topic. Wine was served at CTR's conventions. But Watson's subordinates enforced a ban on drinking on the job. The firm allowed drinking in private, such as at home, but executives frowned on it.

Consistent with his distaste for alcohol, Watson also preached healthy living, including exercise and a good diet. He also preached optimism.[13]

Watson soon realized that tabulating equipment was where the growth was for his firm, so he sold off the other two divisions in a few years. He renamed the Canadian subsidiary International Business Machines in 1917. He renamed the Latin American subsidiary in 1923, using the same name. Then, in 1924, he renamed the U.S. firm International Business Machines.[14] The firm's stock started trading on the NYSE that year. The firm's revenue was only $11 million in 1924.

Watson was named chairman of the board of IBM in 1925.[15] The board met in Endicott, N.Y. The previous chairman was George Fairchild, who had died recently. After the recession, the 1920s were a period of tremendous growth in the U.S.

IBM had acquired many patents, via Bryce's lab and by buying small competitors. IBM's punch cards were another key to the firm's success. The cards didn't work on other firm's machines. Also, the customers had to buy punch cards from IBM.[16]

IBM under Watson was known for its company songs, its strict dress code and pep talks from the CEO. He also originated the "Think" slogan.

In 1935, the new Social Security law increased the need for accounting machines by the federal government and by businesses. Of course, this was good for IBM's revenues. They increased from $19 million in 1934 to $21 million in 1935. They grew to $25 million in 1936, $31 million in 1937, and they kept growing steadily.[17]

Watson did well in the 1930s. He was the country's best-paid CEO in 1935, making $365,358 that year. Newspapers commented on the "$1000-a-day man". Watson felt that he had to justify his high pay, and he did so in a speech.[18] Part of his pay was from profit-sharing.

IBM also prospered in the 1930s. Their revenue grew from $21 million in 1935 to $38 million in 1939. Probably some of this growth was due to the new Social Security law. In that period, IBM opened new factories in Europe.

Watson tried to help at least some of the people in need who wrote to him during the Depression. He would send out checks for $25 or $50.

The author of The Maverick… described a typical day in Watson's life. He mentioned Watson's clothing and his breakfast, usually oatmeal. A chauffeur drove him to work. He would get to work in 15 minutes, at IBM's world headquarters. He would walk by five male secretaries. He thought pretty young women were distractions. He said to his subordinates, "[Y]ou must have male secretaries."[19] Watson also drank lots of coffee and ate lots of junk food. He would occasionally take the train to Endicott, where a factory was located.

The author of The Maverick…[20] stated, "Watson's psychological ruthlessness was his way of getting things done." He would push people hard, to their limits. In meetings, Watson would often talk for 50 minutes, leaving ten minutes for subordinates to talk.[21]

Watson's views on the Nazis and Mussolini were controversial. For example, he visited Berlin in 1937 and met with Nazi officials. He didn't seem to be worried about the Nazis at that time, like other people were.[22] He visited Italy and gave a speech praising Mussolini.[23] Watson "felt ambivalent about the Nazis" in 1937.[24] Watson was awarded the Cross of Merit medal by the German government.[25] The author of The Maverick... stated, "Certainly neither Watson nor IBM actively collaborated with the Nazis."[26]

But IBM continued to do business with Germany until 1940. IBM owned 90% of its subsidiary, Deutsche Hollerith Machinen Gesellschaft, or Dehomag. According to The Maverick..., "He [Watson] didn't work with the Nazis, but he failed to work against them." [27]

Watson apparently started to have a guilty conscience in 1940, for he sent back his medal, given to him by the German government, in June of that year. Most likely, Watson was glad to be rid of the medal. He sent a letter with the medal, which read in part, "In view of the present policies of your government, which are contrary to the causes for which I have been working and for which I received the decoration, I am returning it."[28]

IBM built an exhibit at the World's Fair, in May, 1939. May 4 was declared "IBM Day." IBM showed off some of their machines. There were 4000 invited guests for IBM Day. Then the 4000 guests attended a banquet at the Waldorf-Astoria hotel in New York City.[29]

There was even a second IBM Day at the World's Fair, on May 13, 1940. It was a bigger event than the first. On that day, 30,000 people saw a shows from IBM, including a symphony and opera stars. The World's Fair finally closed, in September, 1940.[30]

IBM experienced a surge in demand in the early 1940s due to the war effort. The federal government ruled that, "...all new or refurbished IBM machines must go to the military or to companies connected to the war effort."

Endicott was still IBM's manufacturing center in that era. They built new factories there.

Nearby was IBM's Country Club and the Homestead; it was a lodge. "The Country Club became the employees' social hub."[31] Watson staged the Hundred Percent Club convention at the Country Club and at the Homestead.

Watson really liked the Homestead. But by the 1990s the Homestead and the Country Club fell into disuse. So IBM put the Homestead building up for sale. The Country Club is no longer used by IBM.

In the summer of 1940, Watson staged a concert in the area for 15,000 people, at his En-Joie Park.[32]

Watson liked to keep in touch with people he met and worked with. He knew Alfred Sloan, John D. Rockefeller, Eddie Rickenbacker and other famous people. His secretaries kept track of his friends and acquaintances.

At one meeting, Watson discussed the more important duties for executives: (1) employ men, (2) supervision, (3) promotion, and (4) discharging, or firing. At the end of the meeting, Watson emphasized his management philosophy: "Give people a chance to do their best; be open to innovation and new ideas; fire people when you have to; get out in the field as much as possible; and above all, be outstanding citizens.[33]

In the Endicott, N.Y. area, Watson became aware of George Johnson, who ran a shoe factory in the area. IBM also had a factory in that area. Johnson was a popular manager with his employees, because of free meals, free medical care and other benefits.[34] Watson had problems retaining his employees, but he learned from Johnson. He increased pay, offered two weeks of vacation and built a golf course for employees. He also built a facility for training employees. Watson and Johnson became closer friends in the 1930s. In 1938, Johnson said he "loved" Watson.[35]

Watson's most important subordinates were: Fred Nichol, George Phillips, and Charles Ogsbury.

Watson was an authoritarian manager. Even though he was often critical of subordinates, they accepted it because they wanted to work for Watson.[36] As the author said, "Few other American companies offered the promise and excitement of IBM—or such an opportunity to get rich...Many felt blessed to be able to follow Watson."[37]

The CEO didn't like to surrender control, but he often gave credit to others, such as in speeches. But his speeches were often boring and lacking in humor.

Watson wasn't good at setting up a management structure for a big firm.[38] Too many decisions went through him. The management structure was like a spider's web. Watson was the spider in the web.

Watson's wealth was growing in 1927. That year, he bought a horse for $500 and a Stutz Speedster for $4300.[39]

The author of The Maverick...[40] describes some of IBM's songs, including one sung to "Over There" and another sung to "My Bonnie Lies Over the Ocean." A third was sung to "Auld Lang Syne." But the songs faded out by the late 1950s.

The 1929 stock market crash worried Watson and his executives. But publicly, he was optimistic. He said, "I see absolutely no reason why the public should be alarmed over the situation, nor get the idea that a money or business panic might be impending."[41]

Watson and his wife Jeanette had a puzzling marriage. She seemed to be afraid of him, but at times she could control him, tempering his bad habits, such as speaking too long. The author of The Maverick...[42] stated that she wasn't very pretty. She was thin most of her life, and she said little in public. She also did some of the repairs around their house; her husband wasn't very handy.

Jeanette would often watch Watson to prevent small mistakes, and "She ran the household and did the majority of the day-to-day parenting.", according to the author of The Maverick...,[43] Watson, Jr. said, "She was much more accessible than father, and always made us feel protected and loved." Watson, Sr. would sometimes give orders to his wife, like he did to others at work. His wife resented that behavior. She also didn't like the way her husband reprimanded Tom and Dick. At one point, Jeanette told her husband that she wanted a divorce. He was devastated. So she decided not to pursue it.[44]

The feds filed their first antitrust suit against IBM in 1932. The firm was charged with, "... abusing a dominant market position and engaging in anticompetitive tactics to maintain that position".[45] The Supreme Court ruled against IBM in 1932; they could not require their customers to buy blank punch cards from IBM.

The economy got much worse in the early 1930s. But Watson retained his optimism. He decided to keep his factories running, without layoffs. He also increased spending on research and development. In early 1932, he announced that he would spend $1 million on a new research lab, at Endicott, N.Y. Watson even increased IBM's manufacturing capacity over 30%. The new lab was completed in 1933.[46]

IBM announced many new products in the 1930s, including a new accounting machine, new punch card machines and new machines for banks. But the new machines didn't help. Revenues didn't grow and profits were elusive. The author of The Maverick...[47] stated, "IBM edged toward insolvency." The firm's stock price languished.

Watson helped women to advance when he kept 25 female employees after finishing an IBM class. He fired most of a class of 67 young men, to make room for the women.[48]

During the War, IBM had to devote its full resources to the war effort. They even built guns and ammunition. A July, 1940 headline read, "IBM Offers Its Full Facilities for the War Effort."[49]

Senior found a place to build the gun factory, in Poughkeepsie, N.Y. He had a 140,000 sq. ft. factory built there, which produced guns and cannon for aircraft. He called it the Munitions Manufacturing Company.[50]

The military used lots of IBM's punch card machines during the war. They were used to keep track of troops and equipment.

Watson Sr. lost one of his best executives to a "physical breakdown." He found a replacement, Charley Kirk, who started in sales but later moved to manufacturing. Kirk did very well during the war.[51]

Senior held a meeting with his executives in June, 1943, to discuss new products. One was the Radiotype, which connected two typewriters by short wave radio. That product was popular with the military, but not in the commercial market.

IBM was often short of engineers, but they didn't try to recruit female engineers. The author of The Maverick...[52] stated, , "IBM's male engineers never pursued the hiring of women engineers with conviction."

IBM decided to slow down its machines after the war. Many machines would be returned by the military and by defense contractors. So IBM wanted to rent the machines, at low rates, to small businesses.

The firm had lots of factory space, to meet new demand, after the war. They had 2-½ times as much factory space as they had in 1940. Demand in other businesses grew rapidly after the war, so those firms had to lease or buy IBM accounting machines. [53]

Electronic calculators began to appear around 1939. They would eventually become a threat to IBM's punch card technology, but Watson wasn't concerned about the threat. He thought customers wouldn't need to "…process data thousands of times faster."[54]

But IBM funded a new calculator anyway. It was Howard Aiken's calculator, which he built at Harvard. It was called the ASCC/Mark I. IBM invested $500,000 in the machine, plus weeks of IBM employees' time. But Watson didn't see any practical use for the machine. It was completed and working in Jan., 1943. [55]

Watson learned about the Eniac machine (see Eckert and Mauchly section of this chapter) when the inventors, Eckert and Mauchly, asked IBM for help with their digital computer. IBM developed a machine to read cards containing data for their computer. Of course, they also learned about Eckert and Mauchly's electronic computer. Watson showed no interest in the Eniac, but his son Tom Jr. did. He and Charley Kirk went to see it in March, 1946 at the Univ. of Pennsylvania. They decided that the Eniac wasn't reliable or practical. [56]

In 1946, IBM announced their first electronic product, the IBM 603 electronic multiplier, a calculator with 300 vacuum tubes. It only did multiplies. [57] An employee named Halsey Dickinson developed it. It was introduced in Sep., 1946 at the National Business Show.

Watson Sr. reportedly said in the late 1940s, "There would only ever be a market for five computers." But there is no proof that he actually made that statement. [58]

IBM then developed the IBM 604 Electronic Calculating Punch. It contained 1400 vacuum tubes.

Watson Sr. met with Eckert and Mauchly and offered to set them up in a computing lab at IBM. But they wanted to sell their company, possibly to IBM. But IBM refused.[59]

IBM's next electronic product was the Selective Sequence Electronic Calculator (SSEC), which was 250 times faster than the Mark I. The SSEC was still primitive, because it stored information on punch cards. Magnetic tape was more efficient.

The markets were becoming more difficult for IBM, starting in 1950. Competitors like Univac were developing electronic digital computers, which wasn't an IBM strength. Watson found out that 14 competitors were developing digital computers, and all were backed by the U.S. government.[60]

In 1950, Remington Rand bought the Eckert and Mauchly firm. They were testing the first Univac computer (Univac I) in the summer of 1950. They delivered it to the Census Bureau in 1951.[61]

IBM's first true electronic computer, a response to the Univac machine, was called the Defense Calculator, because it was meant for the military. The Defense Calculator was later renamed the IBM 701, the first in a series of computers. The first Univac computer was delivered in 1951[62], but the IBM 701 was introduced in Jan., 1953[63]. The 702 model was announced soon after the 701. They also developed the TPM, the Tape Processing Machine.

Watson's biggest mistake in the technology area, at that time, was that he misjudged magnetic tape and magnetic storage.

Watson Sr. and other executives visited Scotland to find a location for a new factory. They visited several sites, but Watson decided that he preferred an unlikely site, a farm called Spango. Scottish officials didn't like that location; it wasn't zoned for an industrial site. But the factory was built there anyway. It was dedicated in July, 1954, by Dick Watson.[64]

The Justice Dept. filed an antitrust suit against IBM in 1952. The complaints were that IBM required customers to buy IBM punch cards, that machines could only be leased, preventing a secondary market in used machines, and that IBM controlled patents on its machines, preventing other firms from making their own machines, etc. The suit was filed by H. Graham Morison, head of the anti-trust division.[65]

The antitrust suit was settled in early 1956, with a consent decree, which restricted IBM's practices[66]. They had to make their machines available for sale, and they had to license patents. They also had to reduce their share of punch card sales below 50%.

Watson, Sr. turned over his role in IBM to his son, Thomas, Jr., on Jan. 15, 1952, according to an announcement on that date. But Watson, Jr. had actually taken over months earlier[67]. The son had much more interest in electronic products.[68] His father's specialty was punch card devices.

Some readers may think that IBM sold the first digital computers in the U.S, but that was not the case. Univac, a division of Remington Rand Corp., sold the first digital computer, the Univac I, in 1951[69]; it was also installed in 1951. IBM introduced its first digital computer, the 701 model, in April, 1953 at their head-quarters. This model was followed by the 702 (early 1954), the 704, the 705, the 709 and the 305[70]. The 704 model was derived from the TPM machine. IBM wasn't as innovative as their competitors in the computer industry. One reason probably was that they wanted to continue selling lots of tabulating equipment. Except for Remington Rand, their competitors weren't selling tab equipment.

In June, 1953, Watson Sr. sailed for Europe on the S.S. United States. He was there for two months to promote the IBM World Trade division.[71] He lived in luxury. After returning from Europe, Watson slowed down, but he didn't retire. His 80th birthday was celebrated in 1954. Watson cut back on his workload in 1954. He left a bunch of mementos in an envelope. He effectively resigned in February, 1956. Starting at the end of March, "Watson Sr. rarely went into the office."[72] In May, 1956, Watson Sr. finally turned everything over to Tom Jr. Other executives congratulated Watson Sr. via telegram.

Watson Senior's health deteriorated rapidly after he gave up control. He died on June 19, 1956 at the age of 82. He was buried in the Sleepy Hollow cemetery, near Tarrytown.

IBM experienced tremendous grown under the elder Watson. By the time he died, IBM had 60,000 employees, compared to 235 in 1914. Jeannette Watson died in 1966, also at age 82.

The author of The Maverick...[73] describes Watson Senior's legacy: (1) He turned information into an industry; (2) Watson discovered the power of corporate culture; (3) Watson was the first celebrity CEO.

Some of IBM's songs are available on the Internet, at http://www.users.cloud9.net/~bradmcc/ibmsongbook.html.

Thomas Watson, Jr.

Thomas Watson, Jr. was born in Jan., 1914 in Dayton, Ohio. His father was unemployed at the time. He was the first of four children. Watson Sr. had two daughters and another son, Arthur (Dick), who was the youngest of the four. Junior married Olive Cawley in 1941. A few months after Junior was born, Watson Sr. got his new position at CTR.

Thomas Watson, Jr. often worked in the shadow of his more-famous father when he was at IBM. In the late 1940s, Watson, Sr. felt that his Tom, Jr. wasn't ready to be CEO yet. In May, 1947, Tom Jr. toured Europe together with another executive, Charley Kirk. But Kirk died suddenly in Europe of natural causes.[74] Kirk was replaced by George Phillips. Watsons Sr. and Jr. would often fight. The senior Watson didn't like some of Junior's decisions. Tom Jr. was less polite than his father. Watson Sr. didn't like debt, but junior thought it was essential for growth[75].

About that time, Tom Jr. was becoming anxious to be named CEO. But his father thought Tom Jr. wasn't yet ready. Kirk was a mentor to Tom.

Tom Jr. thought the firm was falling behind in electronics in the late 1940s, so he appointed a new director of engineering, Wally McDowell. McDowell then hired hundreds of electronics engineers. Tom Jr. also hired some new executives about that time, including Al Williams (finance), Red Lamotte (sales) and Vin Learson (punch card sales). Watson Sr.'s man Phillips was the only old guy left.

Watson Jr. became known as "Terrible Tommy Watson," according to the author of The Maverick...[76] Watson Sr. let his wife discipline Tom Jr. Watson Sr. paid little attention to Dick, the other son. Senior had his secretary, George Phillips, look after Junior when he was away. When his father was away, Junior tried to become an athlete at the various schools he attended, but he failed at many sports. His grades were average at best.

Tom later transferred to the Hun school, a college prep school for Princeton. But he spent a lot of time partying, and his grades stayed about the same—just above passing. Tom Jr. had a problem with depression, at the Hun school.

Watson Jr. described himself, at 21, as "…an aimless playboy who had spent a lifetime getting into trouble." Junior's grades were poor, and he had switched schools several times, to find one that was a good fit. Tom also had some health problems, including depression.[77]

Tom Jr. realized his father wanted him to be CEO some day, but this caused him a lot of anxiety.

Junior tried to get into Princeton. Senior talked to the dean there, who said, "Mr. Watrson, I am looking at your son's record, and he is a predetermined failure."[78] But his father was able to get him admitted to Brown University.

During his Brown U days, Junior got an allowance of $300 per month. This was to pay for his social activities. That was more than the income of most families. Tom's grades at Brown were erratic.

Junior tried a new activity while he was at Brown, flying. It was a way to get away from his father.

Senior wasn't grooming any other successors at IBM. He was grooming his son as the next CEO.

Junior was able to get a job at IBM. He started by attending the IBM Sales School in Endicott. He was elected class president. The author of The Maverick… didn't say if his father had a hand in that result.

Tom Jr.'s income was high during the Depression: $15,772 in 1937 and $17,687 in 1938. In 1940, Junior was assigned to the New York sales office. Big, profitable accounts were transferred to him, apparently by his father. So, Tom Jr. met 169% of his sales quota in April, 1940.

Junior met his future wife, Olive Cawley, in 1939. He proposed to her in Nov., 1941. They were married the next month. They had a son in Dec., 1942, but the baby died, apparently from SIDS.

Watson Sr. created a new division for his other son, Dick. He called it IBM World Trade, which was started in 1949[79]. It handled IBM's international business. That business grew faster than the domestic business after the war.

The Japanese used IBM as a model in the 1950s. The author stated, "When we started to rebuild Japan in the 1950s, we looked around for the most success-ful company we could find. It's IBM, isn't it?"[80]

Tom Jr. didn't like the idea of a separate World Trade division, and he let his father know it. But Watson Sr. helped World Trade to grow. By 1953, that divi-sion had 15,000 employees, or about half the size of the parent firm in the U.S.

In the spring of 1951, Watson Sr. noticed that Tom Jr. was getting upset with having his decisions reversed. So Watson Sr. decided to make Tom Jr. president. The actual announcement was made in Jan., 1952.

In late 1956, Tom Jr. reorganized IBM into six divisions and World Trade. Subordinates described Tom Jr. as "not a nice man."[81]. IBM grew very fast, starting in the late 1950s. The firm had just over $1 billion in revenues in 1957 and over $5 billion in 1967. The firm's revenues again soared, from $7.5 billion in 1970 to $26.2 billion in 1980. Employ-ment grew from 269,000 to 341,000 in that period.[82]

Tom Jr. suffered a heart attack in Nov., 1970. He retired from IBM in June, 1971. Vin Learson and Frank Cary took over after Tom left. IBM's revenues soared from $7.5 billion in 1970 to $26.2 billion in 1980. Employment grew from 269,000 to 341,000.[83]

Tom Jr. died from the effects of a stroke in Dec., 1993. He was 79.

Thomas Watson's son Dick was born in April, 1919 in Summit, N.J. Dick was not a good student. He also had behavior problems in school when he was a teenager.

Dick attended Yale University, where he got adequate grades.

He actually did some manual labor, working on a milling machine at IBM's Endicott factory one summer when he was a Yale student.

Dick served in the Army during World War II, starting in 1941. He was discharged in 1947. His father decided in 1948 that Dick, fluent in four lan-guages, should run the World Trade Division. It would be independent of the main company.

Dick met and married Nancy Hemingway. They were married in June, 1948. Then they went to Europe immediately, as requested by Dick's father. The new-lyweds weren't pleased with the assignment, but they went to Europe anyway.

Eckert and Mauchly

Eckert and Mauchly designed and built the first general-purpose electronic digital computer, a machine that was very primitive and slow by today's standards, but very fast and very advanced for its time. The British claim to have built a digital computer, called the Colossus, earlier than Eckert and Mauchly's machine. But it was dedicated to code-breaking;

Encyclopedia Britannica describes it as "The first code-breaking machine..."

John Mauchly grew up in the suburb of Chevy Chase, Maryland. As a boy, he liked to experiment with electrical devices. He wired up an intercom system to communicate with the neighbor boys, and he set off fireworks by remote control. He got excellent grades in high school, and he did well in math and physics.[84]

Mauchly received a scholarship to Johns Hopkins, to study engineering. But he got bored with the field in his second year, so he switched to physics, where he studied at the graduate level. His specialty was molecular spectroscopy. For his calculations, he used a Marchant calculator, an electro-mechanical device that performed the four arithmetic operations. Mauchly obtained his Ph.D. in 1932. He had earlier married Mary Walzl, in 1930. They later had two children.[85]

He first did some research work and later obtained a teaching position at Ursinus College, in Collegeville, Pennsylvania. The salary was only about $2160 per year.

Mauchly taught lower-level courses, but he soon became known for his flamboyant teaching style, such as demonstrating angular momentum while wearing roller skates.[86] He also did research on weather forecasting. Mauchly had help from Ursinus students in that area. But he soon realized he didn't have enough computing power, due to the quantity of data.

Mauchly learned about vacuum tubes, used in cosmic ray research at Swarthmore College. He noticed that the tubes were used as on/off switches, but he assumed that they could do more. He thought they could be used as counters, and maybe in calculators. So, Mauchly decided that he needed to learn more about electronics; he took a night course in electronics, in 1939.

This was a learning period for Mauchly in other ways. He visited Dartmouth College in 1940 to attend a meeting of the American Mathematical Society. He saw a new device there, called the Complex Number Computer, invented by George Stibitz. He also talked with Norbert Weiner, a mathematician, about computers. They agreed that electronic computers were "the way to go."[87]

The next year, 1941, Mauchly met and talked with John Atanasoff, a professor who taught at Iowa State University. Professor A. had been working on a digital electronic calculator. Most of the larger universities, at that time, had been working with analog computers, such as the Bush Differential Analyzer, which solved differential equations. Mauchly tinkered with Atanasoff's electronic calculator for a few days, but then he had to leave to start an electronics course at the Univ. of Pennsylvania's Moore School. His lab instructor for that event was Presper Eckert, who had only a bachelor's degree—a 1941 graduate. This was the first time he and Eckert met.

Eckert grew up in a wealthy family in Philadelphia. His father was a real estate developer. Presper was "a genius, in his own right,"[88] He attended an exclusive school as a child and was driven to school by a chauffeur.

Eckert built electrical and electronic devices as a teen-ager, including radios and amplifiers. He did very well on the math portion of a college entrance exam and was accepted at MIT. But his father had other ideas, so Presper had to attend the Wharton School, part of the Univ. of Pennsylvania. Eckert soon got bored and tried to switch to a physics major, but found there was no room. Then, he tried the electrical engineering dept, which had spaces. He started in that program, in 1937.

While he was a student, Presper invented the Osculometer, for measuring the intensity of a couple's kiss. If the kiss was very intense, ten light bulbs would light up. He also used a method for recording sound using a light beam on film.

Eckert also worked on radar improvements at the Moore School. He and Mauchly worked on lab assignments together and often talked about computers during the lab time. They would also talk at a nearby restaurant, often making sketches on napkins.[89]

They talked about building an electronic calculator, with no moving parts. Eckert continued producing inventions, and Mauchly did more research on digital devices. He wrote a paper on electronic calculation in 1942, emphasizing the high-speed calculations. But the other faculty were working on their analog computers, including the Differential Analyzer. So Mauchly's ideas were ignored.

A Ph.D. in math, Herman Goldstine, had the mundane assignment, in 1943, of producing firing tables for big guns for the Army. He was working at the Aberdeen Proving Ground in Maryland. Women and calculators were producing the needed tables, but it took over a month for each table, much too long.

But then Goldstine heard about Mauchly and his proposal for an electronic calculator. He was working on table calculations at the Moore School. So he went to see Mauchly about his proposed calculator. Mauchly realized that the Army might fund his new project.

Goldstine brought Eckert and Mauchly to a meeting, with other officials, to ask for funding for the calculator. An advisor to the Army, Oswald Veblen, a mathematician, like the idea and said, Col. Simon, head of the Ballistics Research lab, should fund the project.

The project got $61,700 in funding from the Army for the first six months.[90] It was called Project PX. It was given the name Eniac, for Electronic Numerical Integrator and Computer.

They decided that their machine would have three major parts: (1) separate units for each arithmetic operation, (2) there would be memory units to hold data and instructions, and (3) a control unit to give orders to the other units. The latter was called a "master programmer."

Data was entered into the Eniac with using punch cards and switches. The machine had many units, which were wired together with cables.

Work on the machine began in July, 1943, with 12 faculty members; none were senior faculty. They were able to use a room in the Moore School. Each of the 12 worked on a separate part of the machine, using designs from Mauchly and Eckert. People worked on the project day and night, seven days a week, because of the urgent needs of the war. Lt. Goldstine, representing the Army, was always working with Eckert and Mauchly.

They did a lot of research on electronic counters, visiting RCA Corp., known for its vacuum tubes. RCA provided assistance, but they didn't want to be a sub-contractor. They felt it wasn't realistic to build a machine with so many vacuum tubes, which would burn out at random. Eckert and Mauchly soon found a reliable counter design, which they called a "decade counter ring"[91] It used ten flip-flop circuits; a flip-flop is a circuit with two stable states, which can change based on the inputs.

Of course, many people thought that vacuum tubes were too unreliable for use in such a large machine. This was a big worry for Eckert, who looked into various ways of making them more reliable, such as using them at very low voltages.

The Eniac project kept growing because of the army's requirements. It grew from ten accumulators to 20 and from 5,000 vacuum tubes to nearly 18,000.

Eckert had a lot of energy, and he would constantly monitor the work, such as soldering. He would sometimes get upset about a problem, but would soon calm down. Eckert was the engineer. Mauchly was more of a people person than Eckert. He was more of a talker and a social person. The Eniac book describes him as, "...the lovable intellectual who charmed and always kept an eye on the big picture".[92] Mauchly was an idea man who wanted others to carry them out.

In June, 1944, the Eniac people got major parts of the machine working; they were two of the accumulators. Col. Goldstine worked hard to get the needed parts, including steel for the cabinets. The Eniac had a clock cycle of 5,000 hertz (5,000 cycles per second). The machine did arithmetic in simple ways: multiplies with repeated adds and divides with repeated subtracts.

Setting up (writing) a program for the Eniac required one to two months[93]. Getting it into the machine took one to two days. The Eniac book stated, "The Eniac was a son-of-a bitch to program,"[94] according to Jean Bartik; she was one of the six original programmers.

In 1945, just after the war ended, the Eniac was ready to use. It had consumed enormous resources: 200,000 man-hours and $486,804[95]. It occupied 1800 square feet of floor space and was 1000 times faster than any other digital calculator. It consumed 174 kilowatts of power, or $650 per hour, for the electricity. As described in the Eniac book[96], it included 17,468 vacuum tubes, 70,000 resistors and 10,000 capacitors.

After the war, the Army decided to use the Eniac for nuclear weapons work. We still don't know exactly what the Eniac did, but it was related to simulating nuclear explosions. The simulations were related to the weapons work of Edward Teller, the physicist.

The Eniac was shown to the media in early 1946. It ran a demo program which calculated a trajectory. There was a press release from the War Department which credited Eckert, Mauchly and Goldstine as the principles on that project.

The Eniac was later moved to the Aberdeen proving ground[97], where it was used for weather forecasting (one of Mauchly's goals) and for more ballistic tables.

In early 1944, Eckert started designing a second machine, later called the EDVAC, or Electronic Discrete Variable Calculator. In late 1945, the army funded that project, for $106,000.

Goldstine met John von Neumann in mid-1944 at the train station in Aberdeen. Goldstine invited him to see Eniac, then being built at the Moore School. von Neumann soon got involved in the Edvac project. He did much of the design work on that machine. He wrote a 101-page paper, titled "First Draft of the Report on EDVAC," which was published in June, 1945. It wasn't classified, and it circulated widely, even overseas.

Eckert and Mauchly didn't do much writing on their projects. But they did write their own paper on Edvac, in Feb., 1944. That paper was marked Confidential by Goldstine.

Von Neumann's paper caused a flurry of activity. Computers were built at many universities in many countries. Contrary to some reports, von Neumann wasn't the father of the stored-program idea[98]. Eckert and Mauchly proposed the idea, in their 1944 paper.

Von Neumann got much of the credit, from people at other universities who built new digital computers, due to his 101-page paper; Goldstine helped to distribute copies of the paper. "...Eckert and Mauchly never forgave von Neumann—or Goldstine—for the 'First Draft...' distribution.", according to the Eniac book[99]. Eckert was still bitter about it in a 1991 speech. According to a classmate of Eckert's, "Von Neumann had very little impact on what we were doing."

Eckert and Mauchly resigned from their positions at the Moore School in March, 1946, due to patent disputes. This was just five weeks after Eniac was shown to the media.[100]

The pair decided to go their own way. IBM tried to lure them, in 1946. They said no.

They both taught a computer class in July and Aug., 1946, at the Moore School. Goldstine also gave some of the lectures.

Eckert and Mauchly were able to get a contract for a new machine, the EDVAC II, from the National Bureau of Standards, part of the Commerce Dept. The contract was for $270,000, over a two-year period.[101]

The pair then formed a new company, called the Electronic Control Company, after raising some money on their own. Mauchly was the CEO.

Eckert and Mauchly started working on their new machine, in Aug., 1947, at their new firm with a new staff.[102] The machine was renamed the Univac. The firm was located in Philadelphia.

Eckert, at that time, was often talking of new technologies, including printer tech-nologies, new input and output devices and faster memories. Eckert would occasionally have steak fries at his house, to help the staff relax.

Mauchly married for the second time, in early 1948. He married Kathleen McNulty, one of the six original programmers of the Eniac.

Grace Hopper, later known for her work on the Cobol language, joined the firm at that time.[103] She helped to develop the new instruction set for the Univac; she had previously been at Harvard.

In late 1947, the firm was running out of money, so they agreed to develop another machine, called the Binac, which would be a tandem machine, with two processors. It was built for the Northrop Corp. They also agreed to sell it for $100,000, which was probably too low. The Binac had a delay line memory, containing 512 words.[104]

Also in late 1947, they incorporated under a new name, as the Eckert-Mauchly Computer Corp. The firm's financial problems at that time were due to fixed-price contracts, and the prices they charged were too low. The Univac price was only $270,000, but it cost EMCC $900,000 for the first one. The Binac was completed in Aug., 1949; the test was successful.

In Feb., 1950, Remington Rand bought 60% of the EMCC stock, investing $538,000 in all. Eckert and Mauchly got salaries of only $18,000.

They got their first Univac machine running in Mar., 1951. It had fast magnetic tape drives and 5,000 vacuum tubes, less than one-third of the tubes the Eniac had. The Univac machine later became famous, in 1952, for correctly forecasting the presidential election. It forecast the electoral college results and was 98% correct. They built 46 Univac machines in all.

Remington Rand bought the Engineering Research Associates firm in 1952.[105] The ERA people didn't get along with the Eckert-Mauchly people. William Norris was the CEO of the ERA firm at the time.

About the same time as the Binac project, the Whirlwind computer was being developed at MIT. One author summarizes the project: "Under the leadership of Jay W. Forrester, a young engineer who had spent the wartime years in the MIT Servomechanisms Laboratory, Project Whirlwind had its origins in a program, begun in late 1944, to develop an analog system to simulate airplane-flight characteristics."[106] But Forrester decided to switch to digital technology for the Whirlwind project in Jan., 1946. Fifty people worked on the Whirlwind project in 1947.

The Whirlwind machine used a number of innovations. Some of them were: magnetic core memory, an advanced computer language, software utilities for programming, and graphical output. After studying various memory technologies, Forrester decided to use magnetic cores for the fast memory in the Whirlwind machine. Whirlwind contained 5000 vacuum tubes and had a word length of 16 bits. It could do a multiply in 16 microseconds.[107]

Seymour Cray

Seymour Cray was born Sept. 28, 1925 in Chippewa Falls, Wisc. His father was a civil engineer.

In his early years, he showed an interest in photography. He built a darkroom in the basement, where he developed film and made photographic prints. Soon he developed an interest in electronics. He learned Morse code and persuaded his sister to learn it, so he could send messages to her by wire at night, when he was supposed to be sleeping.[108]

During summer vacations, his favorite pastimes were swimming, boating, fishing and kite-flying.

Seymour developed an interest in science. His father bought him a chemistry set, which he would work on sometimes late at night. His high school classmates noticed his interest in science. One classmate wrote in Seymour's yearbook: "As science is becoming more and more important each year, many students are needed in this field. Seymour Cray has received the science award. He has been very much interested in this work through high school days. If anyone were to predict his future, I dare say it would be along the science line."[109]

He graduated from high school in 1943 and joined the U.S. Army, specializing in radio communications. He served in Europe and later in the Pacific theater. He married Verene Voll, a nutritionist, in 1947. They had been childhood friends, and both families expected that she would marry Seymour.[110] Verene's job initially provided most of their income. They later had two children.

Cray and his wife initially attended the University of Wisconsin at Madison, but Seymour decided that the University of Minnesota had a better electrical engineering program, so the two moved to the Minneapolis area after a year in Madison. He enrolled at the University of Minnesota and obtained his B.S. degree in electrical engineering in 1950 and a masters in applied math in 1951.[111]

After graduation, he repaired radios and televisions for a time. He was looking for something better, but he wasn't finding any leads for an engineering position. Then he ran into one of his professors at that time, who suggested that he apply at Engineering Research Associates, which occupied an old glider factory in St. Paul. Seymour filled out an application there. An author describes Cray at that time: "To the personnel manager there, Cray looked average in every way. Youthful and fit, with close-cropped dark hair, Cray at first glance looked like any of a hundred other former soldiers at the glider factory. He was also an electrical engineer, a University of Minnesota grad, and a kid at heart with a passion for radio technology. That made him even <u>more</u> like the engineers at the glider factory— so much so that they hired him."[112]

His first project was the Atlas II computer, which had already been designed. Seymour made some improvements anyway. He was soon put to work on the ERA 1103 computer, successor to the original 1101 computer, which was developed under a Navy contract. He worked on the control system for the 1103, a difficult assignment. The control system decodes and executes each instruction, such as an integer add. One author commented: "Designing the 1103 control system from scratch was one of the first major proofs of Cray's innate talent. A complex device, the control system analyzed each software instruction and built a sequence of operations to execute it. An instruction might say, for example, to add two numbers and then put the result back in the computer's memory."[113] Cray was soon promoted to senior engineer.

The ERA firm was later bought by Remington Rand and became part of the Univac division, along with the Pennsylvania-based Eckert-Mauchly Computer Corp. Like IBM, Remington Rand was in the tabulating equipment business at that time.

Another project Cray worked on was the successor to vacuum tubes. At Univac, the candidates they tried were magnetic switches and transistors; the transistor had been invented in 1947. Two groups of engineers were involved; each group built a computer using one of the technologies. Both technologies had some advantages. An author describes the result: "Transistor technology was in its infancy, they said, and was destined for dramatic improvement...So after members of the group finished scribbling the logical pros and cons, they followed their instincts. The consensus turned, and they bet their future on the transistor. Seymour Cray, sitting quietly at the back of the room, nodded in concurrence."[114]

Ironically, the other half of Univac, the Eckert and Mauchly group in Pennsylvania, decided that magnetic switches were the better technology. They built a computer using that technology, called the 409-3. It was developed for the Air Force.

William Norris was the head of Univac in the 1950s, having originally been with the ERA firm. Norris grew increasingly frustrated with the lack of resources his division needed to compete with IBM and other competitors developing digital computers. He asked Harry Vickers, the head of Sperry Corp. (Univac's parent firm), for more funds to do research and development. But he and his colleagues provided little help.

Norris grew increasingly annoyed with Sperry's executives, so he and some colleagues met to discuss starting a new company. They were Frank Mullaney, Arnold Ryden and Willis Drake. The idea for a new firm came from Ryden. Norris resigned from Sperry in July, 1957. Mullaney and others followed his lead.

Norris called a meeting at his house for people interested in starting a new computer company. He describes the turnout: "And I was absolutely flabbergasted at the number of people that came. The neighbors thought there was a funeral."[115]

They decided to call their new company Control Data Corp. It was started with $600,000, raised from selling common stock. Willis Drake did most of the work needed to sell the shares.

Norris wanted Cray to work at the new company, but the Navy wanted him to finish work on one of their projects first, which would have taken about six months. So Cray stayed at Univac until the critical work was done, about two months later. Then he called Norris to say he would be starting work at CDC. Norris was worried about the Navy's reaction, so he told Cray to wait. Cray responded, "I don't care about the Navy. This job's far enough along they can do it and I want to come to work next week. Well, do you want me or not?" Norris responded, "Well hell yes, Seymour."[116]

CDC's headquarters were initially at 501 Park Ave., in downtown Minneapolis. The firm began business on July 15, 1957, according to Norris.

Norris wasn't sure which types of products his firm should produce first, so Cray decided to develop digital computers. He was quoted as saying, "All I know is how to build computers, so I'll do that."[117] The first machine Cray and other engineers developed was the 1604 model, an all-transistor computer.[118] They used cheap, poor-quality transistors to develop that machine. Money was tight at the new firm. Seymour got some of the transistors he needed at a neighborhood electronics shop, where he found some for 37 cents each. He bought all the store's inventory of that product. None of the transistors was fast.[119]

Seymour developed a new circuit that would work with the slow transistors he was using. It used two transistors rather than the usual one, with good results.[120] The number 1604 came from the old 1103 model + the 501 in the firm's address. The 1604 was pretty advanced for its time, with a clock speed of 200 kilohertz, or five microseconds per cycle. It was developed for scientific use.

The 1604 contained 25,000 transistors and 5000 diodes. It was a 48-bit machine, with a 15-bit address, and a memory of 32,768 words, made from ferrite cores. The 1604 was often connected to a Control Data 160 or 160A model minicomputer (with a 12-bit word), which handled the input and output.

CDC's engineers were impressed with Cray's new computer. "Within Control Data, engineers were in awe of Cray's achievement. ...At the time computer engineers knew that the construction of a big machine required talented teams with individuals who understood processors, memories, power systems,...and architecture...; mastery of all of them was next to impossible. Yet somehow Cray had mastered all of them; his instinct in all of those areas was what enabled the 1604 design to work...By 1960, when the 1604 reached the market, it was the fastest machine in the world..."[121]

CDC's next machine was a business machine, the 3600 model, which wasn't Cray's project. Norris wanted to build a business-oriented machine, to compete with IBM in that area. But Seymour's next machine was a much faster model, the 6600, which he expected would be 50 times faster than the 1604—an aggressive goal even for Seymour.

Seymour didn't care much for meetings or memos. When asked to elaborate on his goals, he wrote: "Five-year goal: Build the biggest computer in the world. One-year goal: One-fifth of the above."[122]

Seymour and his crew of engineers moved to another location, the Strutwear Building, also in the Minneapolis loop area, to design the new machine. But he soon found the new location to be inadequate. He decided to build a new design and development lab. After scouting several locations, he decided on a familiar one—Chippewa Falls. Another CDC executive thought Cray's moving to Chippewa Falls was a terrible idea. But William Norris responded to Cray thusly: "Do what you have to do, Seymour."[123] Seymour was behind schedule with his new machine at that point. He knew he needed the quiet environment and isolation from CDC's meddling management. Cray and his group moved to the new building in Aug., 1962. The engineers in Cray's crew found some advantages in the move to Chippewa Falls. They could afford bigger houses, on bigger lots. And they could join country clubs, which were now affordable on their meager salaries, $8000 or $9000 per year.[124]

Their 6600 project had some serious problems that they worked on at the new development lab. One was putting lots of circuitry into a small space. The circuit density had to be at least ten times that of the 1604 machine. They were able to cram 6700 circuit boards into the small space allowed, over 400,000 logic gates in all. With that amount of circuitry, a new cooling system was needed. An engineer named Dean Roush developed a new system, using the Freon refrigerant (like old air conditioners). Seymour liked that idea, but CDC headquarters did not, saying it was too expensive and risky. (Computers were normally cooled by air in that era.) Cray said to ignore them.[125] One author described Cray's view of management: "It was obvious that Cray had no intention of listening to management on any matters."[126]

The new 6600 model was demonstrated to the press in Aug., 1963. As Seymour predicted, it had a clock speed of 10 megahertz, 50 times faster than the 1604. It executed three million instructions per second and cost $8 million.[127] The three million figure was the average speed. The 6600 could start a new instruction every 100 nanoseconds, if the appropriate functional unit was available. It had functional units for integer add, floating divide, etc.

Thomas Watson Jr., president of IBM, wasn't pleased with the 6600 machine. In a memo written a few days after Cray's 6600 unveiling, he wrote:

"Last week Control Data had a press conference during which they officially announced their 6600 system. I understand that in the laboratory developing this system there are only 34 people, including the janitor. Of these, 14 are engineers and 4 are programmers, and only one person has a Ph.D., a relatively junior programmer. Contrasting this modest effort with our own vast development activities, I fail to understand why we have lost our industry leadership position by letting someone else offer the world's most powerful computer."[128]

Seymour reportedly had a one-sentence response to Watson: "It seems like Mr. Watson has answered his own question."

Seymour designed more large machines at CDC: the 7600, introduced in Dec., 1968, and the 8600 model, which never worked as expected. Cray expected it would have a clock speed of eight nanoseconds, almost four times faster than the 7600. It was to be built with discrete components, and the first machine generated a lot of heat. Cray had also designed the 8600 to contain four processors, compared to one in the 6600. On top of the 8600's other problems, Cray's development lab budget was cut by 10% at that time, in mid-1971.[129] CDC was funding another supercomputer at that time, the Star-100, developed by a different group, led by Jim Thornton.[130] Control Data never got the 8600 working properly while Cray was with the firm.

Cray announced to Norris that he was leaving CDC, in Feb., 1972. Norris described his reaction, when another executive asked him what he planned to do about Cray's resignation letter. "Hell, there's nothing we can do about it. It's his life. He's got every right to start his own company."[131]

Norris knew that Cray's departure would leave a big void at CDC, but he tried to put the best face on it. Norris and a few other executives attended a going-away luncheon at a Chippewa Falls restaurant, Reiter's Steak House. Seymour had actually invited Norris to visit him in Chippewa Falls on that occasion, a rare occurrence. The six CDC employees who were leaving with Seymour also attended. A few of the men gave speeches on that occasion.

Cray then started his own firm, Cray Research, that year with the six other CDC employees. Norris decided that CDC should actually invest in Cray's new firm, a likely competitor. They invested $250,000, but the other executives didn't like the idea.[132] Cray's first project was the Cray-1, which was like the 8600 in some ways, but more advanced. The newer machine used integrated circuits, unlike the 8600. Cray had learned at least one important lesson from the 8600 project: integrated circuits are better. The 8600 used discrete components, which produced too much heat and used too much power.

Cray's new machine had a clock speed of 12 nanoseconds vs. 8 nanoseconds for the 8600.[133] The slower speed was still a very ambitious goal at that time; no competing firm had come close to the 12-nanosecond speed. His new machine would still be the fastest in the world. The Cray-1 had Freon cooling, with the coolant flowing through bars, which carried the heat away from the circuit modules. Ironically, the work on the new machine was done at a new lab, completed in 1972, just a few hundred yards from his old CDC development lab, in Chippewa Falls.[134] Meanwhile, CDC engineers got management approval to finish the 8600 project.

The Cray-1 was completed in 1976. Two U.S. government labs tried to get the first Cray-1 machine, Serial One; it was a status symbol. They were the ERDA and Los Alamos. The dispute was finally settled when Cray's company gave away the machine for six months, to Los Alamos. Seymour said, "We'll give you the machine. You can keep it for six months, then you can decide whether to buy it or lease it or give it back. But we've got to get this machine installed."[135] It was a great PR move, because the next customer to buy a Cray-1 called them (NCAR in Boulder, Colorado).

Print reporters sometimes asked Cray's associates about the details of his life. One detail that surfaced was Seymour's habit of digging tunnels, near his home in Chippewa Falls. One author said that Cray dug a tunnel near his home, which measured eight feet by four feet and was supported by wood timbers.[136] He also got a divorce after almost 30 years of marriage.

Cray and crew started on the Cray-2 in 1978, which was completed in 1985. He planned for it to have a clock speed of four nanoseconds (four billionths of a second), but it isn't clear if Seymour achieved that goal. The Cray-2 was a different kind of machine. It had 64 processors, compared to the usual single processor in large computers. With this new architecture, Seymour assigned one of his engineers, Steve Nelson, to write a compiler designed for the new architecture.[137] With a system like that, it is difficult to keep all the processors busy. One-processor machines tend to be more efficient. Seymour soon decided that the customers wouldn't want 64 processors, so he returned to his original design, with four processors. The clock speed remained the same, four nanoseconds. Two years into the Cray-2 project, Seymour felt that his group had mostly wasted the last two years, and they still didn't have an adequate cooling system.[138]

Seymour would often work on the Cray-2 project at home, where he had a Data General computer and CAD (computer automated design) software. He also used some personal computers at home, to help with his design work.[139]

At that time, Seymour decided that he needed another group designing supercomputers, which would be called Cray Laboratories and was located in Boulder, Colo.. It was called Cray Laboratories, and it was headed by G. Stuart Patterson, who was previously with the National Center for Atmospheric Research in Boulder. Their first project was reverse engineering a Cray-1, and redesigning it using the latest VLSI (Very Large Scale Integration) chips.[140] The Boulder facility had hired some engineers, but they needed more employees. However, they could only get two people to move there from the Chippewa Falls design lab.[141] Cray Laboratories was shut down in 1982.

Seymour moved on to the Cray-3. But that project didn't go well, so he decided to start his own firm, in Colorado Springs, a move he announced in Aug., 1988. It was called Cray Computer Corp. The first Cray-3 was finished in 1993. Seymour gave it away.[142]

His next machine was, as you would expect, the Cray-4, a project which went much faster. One reason was that he used circuits that contained many more components than those in the previous machine. The clock speed on the Cray-4 was confirmed at one nanosecond, in 1994. Engineers at his firm started work on more-advanced machines, the Cray-5, with a cycle time of one-half nanosecond and the Cray-6, with a quarter-nanosecond cycle time.[143] But Cray Computer, the new firm, ran out of money in March, 1995. The firm shut down at that time. Cray and several executives continued to work at that location for several more months.[144]

Cray was seriously injured in a car accident in Sept., 1996. Another car collided with his SUV. He died two weeks later, without regaining consciousness; he was 71 at that time. His associates were devastated. But he had just finished designing a new machine, which contained up to 512 Intel microprocessors. This was the first time Seymour had designed a supercomputer using microprocessors. Its speed was estimated at a trillion floating-point operations per second. It was to be built by a new firm, SRC Computers, using Seymour's initials.[145]

The original Cray Research firm still exists, with a new name, Cray, Inc., located in Seattle. Their latest product is the Cray CX1, a small machine that can be bought for as little as little as $25,000. It uses Intel microprocessors and a version of Windows, called HPC Server 2008.

Cray is called by some, "The Father of Supercomputing," according to the Cray, Inc. firm.

There were several organizations that used Cray's name in their title, including: Cray Research, Cray Computers, SRC Computers, Cray Laboratories, and Cray, Inc.

John Rollwagen was an early CEO of Cray Research. He was previously a salesman for International Timesharing Corp. Rollwagen had an engineering degree from MIT and an MBA degree from Harvard. Seymour offered him the position of vice president of finance, in 1975. Rollwagen accepted the offer and immediately started to work on the firm's biggest problem, a shortage of cash. They were unable to get a $5 million bank loan that they had been seeking. Rollwagen soon sold $600,000 worth of bonds and obtained a bank loan for $1 million.

But Seymour didn't like debt. He told Rollwagen to sell stock in the firm, rather than using borrowed money. Rollwagen went to New York City to make sales pitches for Cray's new stock offering. Again, Rollwagen was successful. In March, 1976, 600,000 shares of Cray Research stock were sold in an Initial Public Offering, generating $10 million for the firm. The firm put the money to good use, finishing development of the Cray-1 and starting construction of a new building in the Chippewa Falls area.[146]

Les Davis was often Seymour's right-hand man on computer projects. They had worked together since Cray's early days at ERA, starting in 1955.[147] They also worked together on the 6600 project at Control Data.[148] According to one author, Davis had better people skills than Seymour. He was gentler with people and not as abrasive as Cray sometimes was. He was better at listening to engineers than Cray and less likely to reject their new ideas. When an engineer wanted to talk to Davis, he would listen intently and take notes. Davis would sometimes bring up the new ideas when he and Seymour had lunch together at a nearby restaurant, The Flame.[149]

Davis was one of the first people to learn about Cray's resignation from CDC and his goal of starting a new company, Cray Research. Davis helped Cray to set up his new firm, which initially had only $2.5 million in starting capital. The two of them knew that $2.5 million wouldn't go far, so they decided one option was to do research for other computer companies (explaining the firm's name). Davis wasn't pleased by the prospect of the 25% pay cut required at the new company. He had a family of six to support, on a salary of $18,000.[150]

Davis and Cray worked together also at Cray's new firm, on the Cray-1 and other machines. According to one author, there was a saying at Cray Research: "When Seymour drops the design out the window, Les catches it."[151] That author also summarized Davis' responsibilities at Cray Research: "He oversaw the design for the memory, disk drives, input/output, cooling, and virtually every other aspect of the machine. In his soft-spoken way, Davis blended talent, handled egos, and built confidence, and it was Davis, the street-smart engineer, who made the machines go."[152] Davis eventually retired from Cray Research in 1995.[153]

———◆———

How would Seymour Cray have loaded his new operating system, COS, into the 6600's memory? This is an exercise for computer science students. Others can read on.

I have found nothing in writing on this topic, but this may be how he did it. Cray wrote the operating system in machine language, probably in octal.

It is likely that there was a utility program written for the CDC 160 model minicomputer, which would read and process machine language, punched into cards; CDC had been producing the 160 model (later the 160A) for several years at this point. This program could have been modified to run in a 6600 peripheral processor, which I believe was a modified 160, a 12-bit machine. It could have read in and processed location and data statements, recording the location for placing the code in central memory. The data statements would have contained 20 octal digits (a 6600 word), which would have been moved to the 6600's central memory; each peripheral processor had its own memory. This process may have been repeated for each data statement, until all the data (Seymour's machine language code) was in central memory, starting at the specified location. Code for the peripheral processors, at least initially, would likely have been written using the OSAS (One-Sixty ASsembler) assembler. (Utility programs, such as for input, output and the system's console displays, ran in the peripheral processors.) Then the operating system would be ready to use. Without the peripheral processors, it would have been much more difficult to place the new operating system into memory.

Alan Turing

Alan Mathison Turing was born in 1912 in Paddington, England. He had an older brother named John. Alan was the son of a British civil servant, who had worked in India. He was born just after his parents returned from India.

Turing's father arranged for the boys to be raised, at least for a few years, by a retired couple, Colonel and Mrs. Ward, while the Turing parents went back to India to resume their work. The Wards also had other children to raise, including their own four daughters.

One of the schools Alan attended was St. Michael's, where he learned Latin. Then he attended Hazlehurst, a small school, along with this brother John. John liked Hazlehurst, but Alan did not. Alan also attended Sherborne school.

The First World War had little effect on the Turing family.

Alan Turing studied mathematics from 1931 to 1934, completing his degree in 1934 at the University of Cambridge. He later obtained a Ph.D. at Princeton University, in the field of mathematical logic, in 1938. His adviser was Alonzo Church.

His main areas of expertise were cryptanalysis, computer science and artificial intelligence. He also worked on probability theory. During the World War II, starting in 1939, he worked at Bletchley Park, part of the Government Code and Cyber School. While at Bletchley, he was the principal designer of the "Bombe," a machine that decoded German messages created with their Enigma machine.

The Bombe, a type of analog computer, decoded thousands of German messages per month. He was the best cryptographer in England during the war.

After the war, he worked at the National Physical Lab and designed a type of electronic digital computer called the ACE, or Automatic Computing Engine. The NPL eventually built a smaller version of the ACE, called the Pilot Model ACE.

Turing also contributed to computer science. He is famous for his Turing Machine (hypothetical), which gets its instructions from a paper tape, which also contains data. The machine can write on the tape, move it and erase squares on the tape. It was meant to be a digital computer.

He is also known for the Turing Test, which is used to decide if a person sitting at a terminal is communicating with a human or a machine. The test also includes a time limit.

Turing died in 1954, in England, of an apparent suicide.

Seventeen

William Norris

William Norris was an important figure in Minnesota's computer industry, which was mostly located in the Twin Cities area.

William Norris grew up on a farm in southern Nebraska. He received his degree in electrical engineering in 1932 and returned to the family farm.[1] Times were tough then. It was early in the Depression, and there was a drought in the Midwest. The corn they were growing wasn't adequate to feed their cattle. So, Norris had an idea. He decided not to sell the cattle, because prices were so low. Instead, he fed them Russian thistles, a type of tumbleweed. Their neighbors didn't approve of the idea, but Norris didn't care.

He hired a group of vagrants to help him stack the thistle plants on the farm. Norris' plan worked, for two winters. He was then able to sell the cattle for higher prices.

His first job after graduation was as a salesman for Westinghouse for $160 per month. His home base was Chicago sales office. He would travel throughout the Midwest, selling medical and industrial X-ray equipment.[2]

When the war began, Norris decided that he wanted to do engineering work. So he went to work for the Bureau of Ordnance, doing design work. Later he went to work for the Naval Reserve, at the CSAW group (Communications

Supplementary Activity-Washington) He worked on identifying the source of messages from German U-boats (submarines). Scientists were skeptical of Norris' techniques. The CSAW group had good luck in locating German submarines. One reason was that their coded messages included the sub's location. They were able to crack the German Enigma code.[3]

After the war, Norris was looking for commercial applications for the codebreaking machines. The Navy brass wanted to keep Norris and his colleagues together, working on codebreaking devices. Even Admiral Nimitz got involved. Discussing the project with John Parker (owner of Northwestern Aeronautical), he said, "There's a job I'd like you to do."[4]

Norris and colleagues started a new firm in Jan., 1946 called Engineering Research Associates. Their goal was to produce codebreaking computers for the navy. His colleagues were Howard Engstrom and Ralph Meader. They set up operations in a glider factory in St. Paul, which was run by Northwestern Aeronautical, a firm that produced gliders during the war.

Their first customer was the Naval Computing Machines Lab.[5] ERA's factory was nothing to brag about. It had shabby furniture, unpainted walls and uncovered floors. The engineers liked working at ERA; "It was, in short, an engineer's paradise."[6] ERA soon had sixty employees working at the old glider factory.

Willis Drake started work at ERA in 1947. He would later be one of the founders of Control Data Corp., along with Norris.

The machines ERA was producing no longer used relays, like some of the older computers. They used vacuum tubes, the technology of the late 1940s.[7] This was familiar technology to many of the engineers, who had experimented with vacuum tubes when they were kids, working on radios.

Another technology that ERA worked on was the magnetic drum, a type of memory.

Of course, it was relatively slow as a memory device, but it worked. Magnetic core memories would come later. Their drum held one million bits of data. It was a type of random access memory, like today's hard drives. It could be used to hold programs or data, and programs could alter themselves on the drum, if needed.

Norris decided in 1949 that it was time to start commercializing ERA's technology. The drum was one of those technologies. He was able to sell ERA's first drum for $5000, to Automatic Electric Company. The price was somewhat arbitrary and was determined by one of the ERA salesmen, William Butler.[8]

In 1950, ERA started building a new computer that they called Atlas. But their first commercial computer was called the 1101.

In Dec., 1951 ERA was sold to Remington Rand. ERA's engineers didn't like the idea. Norris didn't like the idea either. Remington Rand's principal products where typewriters and shavers, which had little to do with computers, as the engineers noticed.

Remington Rand had earlier bought the Eckert-Mauchly computer firm, showing some kind of dedication to getting into the digital computer industry.

The idea for the Univac 1103 model was spawned when J. P. Eckert visited the ERA division to discuss a new commercial computer. But the ERA people had nearly completed the design for the new machine.[9]

Norris was named the general manager of the Univac division of Remington Rand. He had a sarcastic comment for the Philadelphia people. He said, "The difference is that you [Philadelphia] people run a laboratory, and ERA runs a business."[10]The Philadelphia people had a habit of spending way too much developing new computers, such as the Univac I.

Norris asked Willis Drake to oversee the installation of the first Univac I, at GE's Appliance park facility. in Louisville, Kentucky. It was a disaster. Drake found that many of the parts were missing. The parts didn't even exist in Philadelphia. Some of the peripheral devices, like the printer, were still in the development process. GE's Appliance Park manager was disgusted. He said, "Either this equipment is going to be here on this date, or all this stuff is going to be out in the middle of the street, and I'm not kidding you."[11] Despite the many problems, Drake finally saw the installation to completion—two years after he first arrived in Louisville! He finally got everything working.[12]

Norris grew increasingly annoyed with Remington Rand's management. He decided to start a new company, in 1957, which was called Control Data. Norris and others raised $600,000 in starting capital. The firm began operations in July,

1957 at 501 Park Avenue in the Minneapolis loop area. Seymour Cray left the Univac division a few months later to begin work at Control Data.

Norris wasn't sure at first what the new company should build. But Cray had an idea. He said, "All I know how to do is build computers, so I'll do that."[13] Cray's first project became the 1604 computer. It was made from poor-quality transistors that cost 37 cents each. They started selling the 1604 model in 1960. It had a clock rate of 5 microseconds. So, a simple instruction like an integer add would take that much time, giving a speed of 200,000 instructions per second, which was fast for that era. The 1604 was the fastest machine in the world when it reached the market.[14]

The Stein and Munro book, Computer Programming,[15] includes an extensive discussion of the 1604 and its instruction set. That book was used as a textbook in some computer programming classes. The University of Minnesota bought a 1604 for academic use, in their Numerical Analysis Center, later renamed the University Computer Center. The UCC also wrote their own Fortran compiler for the 1604 and a statistics package, which they called Umstat.

They later wrote another Fortran compiler, for 6600 users, called MNF, Minnesota Fortran.

Norris acquired many small firms early in CDC's history, including Cedar Engineering, the computer division of the Bendix Corp., the Control Systems Division of Daystrom and Meiscon Engineers. The 1960s were an era of tremendous growth for CDC. That was also when they started moving into services, such as renting out time on its large computers.

Control Data's next big computer was the 3600 model[16], which was more business-oriented, at Norris' request, than the 1604. But Cray didn't work on that model. His next machine was the 6600, the first supercomputer. His goal was to build a machine fifty times faster than the 1604! He achieved that goal. The 6600's cycle time was 100 nanoseconds, or 10 megahertz in today's terms, 50 times the speed of the 1604. That meant that a new instruction could start every 100 nanoseconds. Usually an instruction would require 300 nanoseconds or more to complete. The machine had ten functional units (such as long add), so if the required unit was free, the instruction could start immediately. Another reason for the machine's speed was the ten minicomputers built in, which were called peripheral processors. They handled the mundane tasks, such input, output, memory management and console display processing. The 6600 was demonstrated to the media in Aug., 1963, at Cray's lab in Chippewa Falls, Wisc.

IBM had a response to the powerful 6600 machine. They announced the 360/90 model, which they said would be several times faster than the 6600. It soon affected sales of the 6600 model. Norris was angry. He told a group of executives to start gathering evidence against IBM and about the new model, which was only in the design stage. Norris decided to sue IBM. Their board of directors thought it was a terrible idea. One of the board members said, "I think it's a bad idea. They'll kick the hell out of you."[17] But Norris persisted. He was afraid IBM would harm sales of the 7600 model also, when it came out. He hired antitrust lawyers to help with his case.

In December, 1972, IBM's CEO, T. V. Learson, agreed to settle with CDC, for $150 million. Norris said it wasn't enough. Later Learson called Norris and agreed to a $200 million settlement, which included turning over IBM's Service Bureau Corp. division. CDC also received $15 million for its legal costs.[18]

Cray went on to develop the 7600, another supercomputer which was nearly four times faster than the 6600, with a clock speed of 27.5 nanoseconds, or 36.4 megahertz. The design was very similar to the 6600's design. The 7600 was announced in Dec., 1968.

But, at that time, there was a shortage of money inside CDC for developing new products. As one author stated, "Engineers couldn't get enough development money to fund their projects. A decade of dramatic growth had strained the budget in ways that no one had foreseen."[19] New products that came out around that time included the 900 series machines, the 800 series, the 6400, the Star supercomputer and the 8600. The author continues, "The computer group [management] was irate. Because they saw themselves as the creators of the company's wealth, they couldn't understand why they now had to struggle for funding. . . . There were people from peripherals, government services, software, and data services—all of which had products they wanted to develop, too."[20]

Despite CDC's rapid growth, Norris didn't get a huge salary. In 1965, it was under $40,000 per year.[21] But he did own 90,000 shares of stock at that time, which were worth about $27 million.

Cray soon started work on his next machine, the 8600, which never worked as expected. He admitted as such to Norris. Cray decided it was time to leave Control Data and soon started his own firm, Cray Research. He redesigned the 8600 using integrated circuits and called the new machine the Cray-1. Norris didn't complain about Cray's borrowing the 8600's design.

CDC later created a new division to produce supercomputers, called ETA Systems and located in St. Paul, Minn.[22] They produced and sold a new supercomputer, the ETA-10, but they lost money and were eventually shut down.

Norris became a philanthropist late in life, which didn't help Control Data. They needed those resources for research and development. According to one author, "Now seventy-one, he was known for eccentricities that equaled those of Seymour Cray. Under Norris, the company [Control Data] invested in such dead ends as wind power and tundra farming. ...He invested in the revitalization of ghetto areas..."[23] He also started the PLATO division, which later became a separate company, which developed hardware and software for computer-based education. Norris was also known for his hydroponic gardening project, with gardens visible on the roof of the old company headquarters. He also rented cars to ex-convicts. But the cars sometimes disappeared, along with the ex-cons.

CDC was split into a services division, Ceridian, in 1992 and a hardware division, Control Data Systems, which was later acquired by another firm. Norris had retired by that time.

In retirement, Norris founded the William Norris Institute, a charitable organization.

Norris died in Aug., 2006, according to the Minneapolis Star-Tribune (Aug. 21, 2006). He died at age 95, from Parkinson's disease. At the time of his death, Norris had a wife, Jane, and eight children.

Jack Kilby

Jack Kilby was born in Great Bend, Kansas in 1923. He was the son of an electrical engineer. His father ran a small electric utility, supplying electric power to customers in western Kansas. The younger Kilkby showed an early interest in amateur radio and in electronics. He attended the University of Illinois, where he obtained his BSEE degree in 1947. He started working at Centralab, in Milwaukee, Wisconsin soon after graduation. He continued his studies and obtained an MSEE degree from the Univ. of Wisconsin in 1950. Kilby started working with transistors at Centralab in 1952. The transistor was invented at Bell Telephone Labs in 1947, by Shockley, Bardeen and Brattain. Centralab had obtained a license to manufacture transistors. In 1958, Kilby left Centralab to work for Texas Instruments in Dallas, Texas. He had previously written letters to various firms which he knew were working on solid-state electronics. One of his letters caught the attention of Willis Adcock at TI. Adcock decided to hire Kilby, even though he didn't have the required Ph.D. for TI's research work.[24]

Jack Kilby invented the integrated circuit while he worked at Texas Instruments in 1958. Kilby got the idea of putting additional components, such as resistors, beside transistors on a single piece of germanium, less than a square inch in size, by adding impurities. They had some germanium bars in their lab. Silicon was expensive and not very common at that time. Kilby and his technicians were able to include resistors and capacitors on the germanium. They made six circuits in all, figuring that one might not work. Kilby assumed that integrated circuits could also be made from silicon, if he could get them to work with germanium. Centralab had previously done some work on depositing components on circuit boards.[25] Despite such innovative processes, Centralab also sold storage batteries, similar to car batteries, to Sears.

On July 24, 1958, Kilby wrote down an important idea in his notebook: "The following circuit elements could be made on a single slice [of semiconductor material]: resistors, capacitor, distributed capacitor, transistor."[26]

Another way of stating his idea was, according to the Microchip book[27], was "The essence of his idea—that if you make all circuit elements out of the same type of semiconductor material, you can make them all on a single piece of that material—required him to accept that other circuit components, not just the transistors, could also be made out of semiconductor." The book goes on to add [28], "According to the conventional wisdom, the idea was ludicrous." That was because resistors and capacitors were very cheap at the time, so why go to the extra expense and bother of putting them on a semiconductor? Kilby further explained, "At that time, the amount of silicon required to make a resistor would have made a silicon transistor that you could sell for ten dollars. So making resistors was not an obvious thing to do."[29] Of course, now resistors are much cheaper and millions of them can be placed on a tiny chip of silicon, when making a microprocessor.

Kilby's first integrated circuit was described as a phase-shift oscillator.[30] It converted direct current into alternating current. He tested the circuit's output with an oscilloscope, which showed the expected sine wave output.[31] That was on September 12, 1958. TI filed a patent on that integrated circuit in 1959. Robert Noyce of Fairchild Semiconductor Corp. filed a patent on a similar device a few months later. The courts awarded Kilby the credit for inventing the integrated circuit. Kilby and several other inventors (but not Noyce) received the Nobel Prize for inventing the integrated circuit in 2000. The integrated circuit revolutionized the computer industry, making possible much smaller and faster computers.

The Air Force was interested in integrated circuits. TI was awarded two contracts from that branch of the services. One contract, overseen by Kilby, was to create a production line for integrated circuits that could "turn out 500 integrated circuits daily for at least ten consecutive days."[32] Kilby also developed military devices using integrated circuits.

The other contract required TI to build a computer entirely from integrated circuits. That project was headed by Harvey Cragon. The resulting computer was about the size of a paper-back book. Cragon described it: "It was a tour de force that was made to impress people." [33] It contained 300 integrated circuits. The computer performed only simple calculations, like the four arithmetic operations. TI called the device the Experimental Molecular Electronic Computer. The "Molecular" part of the name came from the Air Force, which was interested in molecular electronics in that era. After they got the device working, TI people showed it off in three cities.[34]

After that triumph, TI was awarded other contracts for devices using integrated circuits, including one to monitor radiation in the Van Allen radiation Belts and another for computers for the Minuteman series of missiles.

Of his Nobel prize, Kilby said, speaking of integrated circuits, "Humankind would have eventually solved the matter, but I had the fortunate experience of being the first person with the right idea and the right resources available at the right time in history." Of Robert Noyce, he said, "I would like to mention another right person at the right time, a contemporary of mine who worked at Fairchild Semiconductor… If he were still living, I have no doubt we would have shared this [Nobel] prize."[35]

Kilby went on to say, "People often ask me what I'm proud of, and, of course, the integrated circuit is at the top of the list. I'm also proud of my wonderful family. I have two daughters and five granddaughters, so you could say that the Kilbys specialized in girls."

From 1978 to 1984, Kilby was a professor of electrical engineering at Texas A & M University. Kilby obtained over 50 patents in his lifetime. He died in 2005, in Dallas, Texas.

Noyce and Gordon Moore would later start Intel Corp., in 1968. Intel produced the first microprocessor, the 4004, a type of integrated circuit, in 1971; it contained only 2300 transistors. It was developed for a customer to use in a calculator. Today microprocessors contain millions of transistors.

Grace Hopper

Grace Murray Hopper was born in New York City in 1906. She graduated from Vassar in 1928, with the Phi Beta Kappa honor. She then went to Yale, where she got a master's degree in math and physics. She later obtained a Ph.D. in math from Yale, in 1934. She joined the U.S. Naval Reserve during World War II and was assigned to the Bureau of Ordnance computation project at Harvard. He first project was the Mark I computer, working with Howard Aiken at the Cruft Laboratory, according to a Yale University article. She became a programmer on that very early computer. She continued to work on the Mark II and Mark III machines at Harvard after the war. She married Vincent Hopper in 1930; they didn't have any children. Her husband died in 1945. She taught at Vassar College.

In 1949, she joined the Eckert and Mauchly (see their story above) company to work on the much faster Univac I machine, which was originally called just the Univac. She did a lot of the design work on that machine. Ms. Hopper developed the A-O compiler for the Univac machine. According to the Yale Univ. article, "The A-O series of compilers translated symbolic mathematical code into machine code, and allowed the specification of call numbers assigned to the collected programming routines stored on magnetic tape. One could then simply specify the call numbers of the desired routines and the computer would 'find them on the tape, bring them over and do the additions. This was the first compiler,' she declared." She stayed with that firm after it was acquired by Remington Rand and then by Sperry Corp., making it the Univac division of Sperry Rand (Sperry later merged with the Burroughs company to form Unisys).

For Univac, her next project was the B-O compiler, later called the Flow-Matic, which later became the Cobol language. She was an advisor to the Codasyl group, which created the Cobol language, in 1959. Ms. Hopper often gave speeches where she persuaded managers to use English-like languages like Cobol. She retired from the Navy in 1966 but was asked to return as an advisor. She worked at that time for the Naval Data Automation Command. Grace Hopper was promoted to rear admiral in 1985. She retired again in 1986. It was a major event, held on the USS Constitution in Boston. She died in 1992.

John Backus

John Backus was the father of the Fortran language; he also wrote the first Fortran compiler. He had graduated from Columbia University in 1949 and began work at IBM in 1950 as a programmer. His office was in New York City. IBM's first digital computer was the model 701, which was announced in 1953. Backus and his co-workers developed the Fortran language in 1954 and produced the first Fortran compiler in 1957. It ran initially on the IBM 704 model.

The Fortran language and his compiler are described in the article, "The Fortran Automatic Coding System,"[36] written by Backus, et al.

An article from IBM[37] describes how the Fortran inventors began their work. "They were an eager, absorbed young group that spring of 1954: three IBM computer programmers and a former U.S. Foreign Service employee hired to do technical typing. Their offices were tucked away on the 19th floor of the annex to what was then known as IBM World Headquarters—down the block from

Tiffany's on the busy corner of Manhattan's 57th Street and Madison Avenue. Far below, in the ground-floor display center, was the machine they were trying to improve upon. It was the IBM 701 computer, which, only the year before, had launched the company into a new world of electronic data processing."

The article goes on, "By November, they were ready with a preliminary report. Based on what the group's manager, John Backus, then 29, calls more faith than knowledge. It stated that the programming language for the new 704 [model] would enable it 'to accept a concise formulation of a problem in terms of mathematical notation and to produce automatically a high-speed 704 program' for its solution. The report suggested that the automatic program would run as fast as a program painstakingly coded by a human programmer. Months of testing would prove them right. They named the language FORTRAN, for FORmula TRANslation."

Backus, in his own words, said he had "a checkered educational career." He attended a prep school starting in 8th grade and then attended the Univ. of Virginia for six months until he was drafted into the Army.

According to an article from IBM, Backus didn't start out to become a mathematician. In the Army, he was interested in becoming a doctor. So he studied premed and went to New York Medical College. But he decided there was too much memorization required. Backus said, "I had visions of right away doing research on the functions of the brain. But at medical school, all they wanted you to do was memorize, memorize, memorize. By the time I got out of the Army, my one ambition was to build a good hi-fi set." So he switched to electronics. He went to a radio technician school, paid for by the G.I Bill. Of course, in that program, he had to learn some math. He went on to Columbia University, to get a masters degree in math. One day he saw IBM's SSEC, which was on display at IBM's headquarters at 57th St. and Madison Ave. It was installed there in 1948. The SSEC was one of IBM's earliest electronic products. He was able to talk with the SSEC's co-inventor, Rex Seeber. Backus stated, "I had holes in the sleeves of my jacket and my shoes needed shining, but she [IBM systems service rep] got me an interview then and there." He had to take a test, but he did adequately and was hired.

After designing the Fortran language, Backus stated in a paper that Fortran would allow a computer to "accept a concise formulation of a problem in terms of mathematical notation and to produce automatically a high-speed [model] 704 program" to solve the problem. Backus is also known for Backus-Naur Form, a language for defining the syntax of programming languages.

In his early days, Backus thought of the programming process as tedious. He said, "Much of my work has come from being lazy. I didn't like writing programs, and so, when I was working on the IBM 701, writing programs for computing missile trajectories, I started work on a programming system to make it easier to write programs for the 701. And that wound up as something called Speedcoding [an early programming system]." Backus was able to convince the hardware designers for the 704 to include some of the features that were provided by the Speedcoding system.

Backus also stated, "From then on, the question became, what can we do for the poor programmer now? You see, programming and debugging were the largest parts of the computer budget, and it was easy to see that with machines like the 704 getting faster and cheaper, the situation was going to get far worse."[38]

Consequently, Backus wrote a letter to his manager, Dr. Cuthbert Hurd, proposing an automatic programming system for the 704. Hurd liked the idea and approved it.

Further, Backus said, "Most people think Fortran's main contribution was to enable the programmer to write programs in algebraic formulas instead of machine language. But it isn't. What Fortran did primarily was to mechanize the organization of loops."

One result of the Fortran language and compiler was a big increase in programmer productivity. The IBM article stated, "What previously had taken 1,000 machine instructions could now be written in 47 statements."

Backus lamented, in recent years, the complexity of new programming languages. He said, "I just got sick of seeing more and more new programming languages—what I call von Neumann languages. They've just become so baroque and unwieldy that few of them make programming sufficiently cheaper to justify their cost. Fortran started the trend. You see, all programming languages are essentially mirrors of the von Neumann computer. Each one may add a gimmick or two, to automate some of the dirty work. But it's usually done at the price of a much more complicated language. Today's programming manuals are that thick [holds up a thumb and forefinger]. Some of them have 500 pages. It's just a vicious circle, because language designers design to fit the computer, and computer designers think they must design to fit the languages."[39]

Backus described digital computers as two boxes, is to one being memory and the other the central processing unit, or CPU. He said the purpose of a program, in his view, was "to make a big change in the store [memory]." He went on to say,

"But how does it do it? By huffing and puffing words [32 or 64 bits long] back and forth through the tiny passage between the store and the CPU. One word at a time."

In his later years, Backus was working on a new programming system: "What I want to do is come up with a computing system that doesn't depend on memory at all, and combine that system, in a rather loose fashion, with one that has a memory but keeps the simplicity and the algebraic properties of the memoryless system. Then, hopefully, the process of algebraically speeding up programs can be mechanized so that people can write the simplest programs and not have to care whether they are efficient or not. The computer will do the hard work. And, more than that, perhaps a lot of programs can be written simply by describing the program you want with an equation."[40]

Backus wrote papers on Speedcoding, Fortran and the Algol language. John Backus died at his home in Ashland, Oregon in March, 2007.

Bill Gates

In an interview (Smithsonian interview), Bill Gates said he got started in computers at age 12, when he was attending Lakeside School, a private school. He and his friends used a time-sharing system, typing in programs with a Teletype machine and running them on a GE computer. Later, the school obtained a DEC PDP-8 minicomputer. Gates said he and his friends would type in their programs off-line, saving them on paper tape. He wrote a program in Basic to play tic-tac-toe and he wrote a few other programs. They also used other languages, including Fortran and Lisp.

Later they got free time on a PDP-10 machine, in return for fixing bugs in that system. Gates and his friends formed a company when he was in 11ᵗʰ grade, called the Lakeside Programming Group. Paul Allen, later a Microsoft founder, was one of the members.

Gates also described the PDP-10 machine: he said that it had a 36-bit word (unusual at the time), and 18-bit addresses. They would use octal numbers, such as when working with machine language. Some of DEC's later machines had other word sizes, including the PDP-11 and the VAX. They used the PDP-10 for time-sharing.

One of the Lakeside Programming Group's early projects was a payroll package, which they wrote in Cobol, also on the PDP-10. That group also got involved in processing road traffic data, which came in on paper tapes and had to be analyzed.

Gates graduated from Lakeside School and went to Harvard for a time. He said he didn't get involved with computer people there, because they weren't as interesting as the people he had been working with. Gates took a few computer courses, and he liked economics, but didn't say if he took any courses in that subject. It was about that time that he and Paul Allen decided that they should start their own company.

Gates and Allen were interested in the new 8080 microprocessor that had come out about that time. Allen wrote a simulator, to process the 8080 instruction set, which ran on the PDP-10.[41]

The MITS Altair was introduced in Dec., 1974 when an article in Popular Electronics magazine described it. It was designed by H. Edward Roberts, who some authors credit as the inventor of the personal computer.[42] However, it was just a box. A picture of the device does not include a keyboard, a video monitor or any diskette drives. It was meant for hobbyists, who presumably would find ways to connect those devices to the Altair. Indeed, it is described as the "world's first minicomputer kit."[43] The kit cost only $400. Fully assembled, it would cost $498. But there was a long wait for the assembled kits. The wait for an assembled version was about one year.[44]

A group of Altair hobbyists in Kansas City found a way to store programs on cassettes, which would allow Altair owners to exchange programs with one another.[45]

Later Gates and Allen started experimenting with the Altair machine. They offered to write a Basic interpreter for the Altair, using only 4K bytes, for the program and data. The Altair people didn't offer them any money, but Gates went ahead anyway. But they only had the Altair's instruction set. They didn't yet have an actual Altair to work with. They wrote everything but the input and output subroutines. Then they went to visit MITS, in Albuquerque. They got it working in short order. The Altair people were impressed. Gates said, in his interview, "He [Paul] and Roberts, the head of this company, sat there and they were amazed that this thing worked. Paul was amazed that our part had worked, and Ed was amazed that his hardware worked, and here it was doing something even useful. And Paul called me up and it was very, very exciting." Gates said his Basic was modeled on the Dartmouth Basic interpreter. His Basic came out in 1975, according to Gates.

They also wrote Basic interpreters for other machines and had started on a Fortran compiler. Gates said Paul had worked for MITS, the Altair people, for a short time, but quit to work for Microsoft.

Gates said that Microsoft was founded in 1975 and was located in Albuquerque from '75 to '78. They had about 16 employees at the end of that time. Paul Allen was one of the founders working there. Most of the employees were programmers, but they had a technical writer, Andrea, and an accountant, Marla. Gates did a lot of the sales work. At that time, many new computers were coming out, which increased the opportunities for the new firm. He said they would often commit to deadlines and had to work long hours to finish a project on time. They moved to the Seattle area in '79.

New machines, such as the TRS-80 and Commodore Pet, were coming out about that time ('75 to '78). Some of them had their own Basic interpreters, but Gates said his Basic was better. He said, "Well, our BASIC was fairly deep. The BASIC they first put in this machine [TRS-80 and Pet] was really, really limited. It just wasn't going to be expandable. And they wanted to put on graphics. They wanted to put on a disk. They wanted to have sound. And we knew how to do those things. We went in and showed them that we could help them design new machines, really work in partnership with them. And do it even less expensively than what they could in trying to manage software development themselves." Gates said they worked with Steve Wozniak at Apple to produce the Applesoft Basic. They also worked with Commodore on software for their Pet machine.

Gates said they also wrote languages [meaning language processors] to work on the CP/M machines, using the operating system from Digital Research. Then they started working on a word processor and a spreadsheet product called Multiplan. They were competing with the Lotus 1-2-3 product at that time. But, Gates said, Multiplan didn't do well versus 1-2-3: "Multiplan…was essentially passed by with the work that Lotus did on 1-2-3." They didn't want to have just a single product, which could become obsolete. He said they continued to develop more language processors for PCs, including Cobol and an assembler. Another of their competitors was WordStar, with their word processor of the same name. Gates said they also developed some games; one was called Adventure, which ran on the TRS-80. They had a Consumer Products group at that time to develop games. They also developed the Flight Simulator product.

About that time, Gates decided to switch to 16-bit software, which would be more powerful. The 8086 microprocessor from Intel was their preferred environment for 16-bit software. They did some custom work for Intel at that time; they had earlier produced a Basic for Intel.

Gates said he moved to Seattle in '79, and he also hired Steve Ballmer in that year. Ballmer was good at hiring people, he said, so the company doubled in size every year for about the next five years. Gates said he stopped writing most of the code himself at that time. He started doing more monitoring of the development groups. They hired a sales person, a finance person and a consumer products manager at that time, for retail sales. The company also started going international.

Gates also discussed the Microsoft Way of development: hire smart people (high I.Q.s), use small teams, and provide great tools. He also said they put a lot of documentation in the source code. He and Paul Allen owned most of the firm, until 1981. But they had given a small percentage to Ballmer by that time.

He said the firm had some early problems, such as customers that went bankrupt and couldn't pay. He also wrote most of an APL interpreter, but they didn't ship it to customers. They developed another interpreted language called FOCAL, but didn't market it. They also developed a Cobol and a Fortran. The firm wrote a product (not specified) for Texas Instruments, but they later got out of the PC business.

Gates decided that he would let Lotus dominate in the old DOS environment, and his firm would move on to the Windows and Mac environments. Multiplan was part of the DOS environment.

He learned about Japan from Kazuhiko Nishi, who helped his firm learn to use Japan's first popular PC, the NEC PC-8000. Bill said that his vision of the future was that the PC would become a very important tool, processing text, numbers and later full-motion video. He shared the firm's vision with competitors, but not their schedule for developing important products.

Gates talked about their important competitors of that time, including Digital Research, VisiCorp, Wordstar and Ashton-Tate, which developed the dBase product. Some other companies were writing applications, such as games and payroll.

Another project Gates discussed was his work on the TRS-80 model 100, which had a new, larger screen than older models; it sold for only $500. He developed a type of user-friendly system for that model, which included a text editor and a file-management system. His product was kept in a 32K ROM chip.

Gates also discussed early storage media that he used, including paper tape, which he would sometimes use to distribute software, cassette tapes and then the diskette. At that time, during the interview, he said the paper tape he was holding was really the beginning of Microsoft—his Basic interpreter. Much of the early software was written in that Basic, he said.

He said that when the new IBM PC came out, the other personal computers faded away pretty quickly. Gates said they were writing 16-bit software for the 8086, which was used in the first IBM PC. He said they worked with a software firm called Seattle Computer Products, which wrote a version of the DOS operating system. Of course, the IBM PC became the standard machine in the early 80s. Microsoft worked with IBM on the Basic for that PC, which was discussed in computer magazines, including PC Magazine. Other firms brought out 8086-based machines around that time, including Victor.

IBM executives were frustrated that they were taking five years to bring out a new machine. But they found an internal group that could get it done in two years and possibly less. They saved time by buying parts from outside firms, including Intel for the microprocessor and Microsoft for the software. They signed the contract with IBM in December of 1980, according to Bill, but they had done some work on the IBM PC before that. The new IBM PC came out in August or September of 1981, Gates said. Microsoft supplied a Basic in a ROM and the operating system, which was SCP-DOS, which Microsoft had just purchased from Seattle Computer Products. That became MS-DOS on the IBM PC. IBM had earlier looked at the CP/M operating system for their new machine. Gates said his firm also supplied a few Basic application programs that ran on the first IBM PC.

Jobs and Wozniak

Steve Wozniak grew up in southern Calif. and Sunnyvale, starting at age 7. His father was an electrical engineer, at various firms, including Lockheed, the defense contractor. Steve learned a lot about electronics as a child. One way he learned was from an electronics hobby kit, which he received when he was in the fourth grade.[46]

Woz loved electronics and spent a lot of time designing circuit boards. He did well at science and math in high school, but did poorly at other subjects. Woz had friends in the neighborhood. One of his friends, Alan Baum, helped him design a new computer in the summer of '69. They spent several months designing it and built it out of surplus parts.[47] Bill Fernandez helped.

Steve Jobs (now deceased) was born on Feb. 24, 1955, in San Francisco, Calif. His mother didn't want to keep her new baby and gave up custody to a couple in the area, Paul and Clara Jobs. Steve was their only child. Steve's new father Paul served for a time in the U.S. Coast Guard. After World War II, he met and married Clara, in 1946. They moved to Indiana, where Paul got a job with International Harvester, as a blue collar worker.

In 1952, Paul and Clara decided to move back to California. They moved to an apartment in San Francisco. Paul got a job collecting auto loans. As part of his job, he sometimes had to repossess cars.

After adopting Steve, they moved to a house in South San Francisco. Steve was a bright boy, but he often got into trouble. One day, he had to be brought to a hospital after he swallowed ant poison. As a child, he watched a lot of television, probably more than he should have.

Steve was also a curious boy, who liked to experiment with gadgets. One of them was a carbon microphone, which a neighbor had given him. In school, he wasn't well-liked by his classmates. One classmate described him as a "loner, pretty much of a crybaby."[48] Jobs would sometimes get bored in school, sometimes skipping assignments. Speaking of his school days, he said, "I turned into a little terror." He eventually caused so many problems in school that he was expelled. He skipped fifth grade and enrolled in Crittenden Middle School, in Mountain View. But that school was too tough for him, so he decided not to return the next year.

That caused a problem for his parents, who had to move to get him into a new school, Cupertino Junior High.[49]

At Cupertino, Jobs met Bill Fernandez, another student who also had an interest in electronics. The pair tinkered with electronics in neighborhood garages. Steve Wozniak, with his family, lived across the street from the Fernandez's. Woz was a freshman at the Univ. of Colorado at that time. He was a prankster who liked to play computer pranks. The dean had enough of his pranks, and he was expelled at the end of his freshman year.

Bill Fernandez invited Jobs to see the computer that he and Woz built in the summer of '69. This was the first time Jobs met Woz.

Woz was a member of a neighborhood group, called the Electronics Kids. One of their projects was a group intercom, which connected their houses. He also built lots of his own electronic projects, until the eighth grade. He also built a ham radio transmitter and a receiver, but he soon got bored talking to adults on his ham radio.[50]

Woz built science projects in grade school, such as a project showing how carbon rods conduct electricity and another one demonstrating electronic structures of atoms. He also built AND and OR gates, which were used in computers.[51]; today they are built into microprocessors. In the eighth grade, he built an adder/subtracter, which did arithmetic like a computer.

Woz was a shy boy, but he would often break the ice by pulling a prank on someone. Later, in the mid-1970s, he joined a neighborhood group, called the Homebrew Computer Club, which he attended for two years. They paid a lot of attention to the Altair PC, a product for hobbyists.

A teacher, Mr. McCollum, taught him a lot about math and electronics in high school. The teacher got him a part-time job, at Sylvania, doing programming in Fortran. Starting in 12th grade, Woz got manuals for many minicomputers. He would use them to redesign many of those machines, using fewer components. He tried to use as few chips as possible, sometimes half as many as in the original machine.[52]

Woz attended the Univ. of Colorado as a freshman. But he couldn't resist pranks. One of the things he built there was a TV jammer, a pocket-size device for jamming TV signals[53]. He used it in a student lounge, to fool people. The students thought the TV was failing. He also used the device to jam signals in a closed-circuit TV class.

Woz rarely got into trouble for his pranks, but he did get in trouble at Boulder for "computer abuse." He used too much time and paper to print out numbers he had computed, such as powers of 2. Woz thought he shouldn't have been charged, maybe because the work was valuable, in his opinion.

On his own, Jobs went on to build a frequency counter and a Blue Box, for making free, illegal, long-distance phone calls. He did get some help from Woz on the Blue Box. They made some more Blue Boxes, charging $150 each when they sold them; the parts cost $40. Jobs was making so much money from the sales that he decided not to finish high school.

Steve enrolled in Reed College in Portland, Oregon, with his parents paying the bills. He got poor grades, and he dropped out after one semester. He soon moved back to his parents' house, in the spring of 1974. He tried to find work as an electronics technician at the Atari firm, which hired him.

In 1975, Woz joined a new club in the neighborhood, the Homebrew Computer Club, to share information. He built new circuit boards, called "breadboards," which were experimental PCs. Jobs was impressed. They decided to start a new company to manufacture the boards and called it Apple Computer (now Apple, Inc.).

Apple Computer was founded on April 1, 1976, with Jobs and Woz each getting 45% of the stock, and Ron Wayne, a Jobs friend, got 10%. See Apple Computer story in "Computer Companies" chapter.

Of course, Steve Jobs got much more attention in the media than Wozniak. He was the CEO of Apple and was often given credit for the success of Apple's products. Many of their recent products were successful, at least partly due to Jobs. One author describes him thusly: "Jobs is a control freak extraordinaire. He's also a perfectionist, an elitist and a taskmaster to employees."[54] Another reason for Apple's success is copying. Jobs said, "And we have always been shameless about stealing great ideas."[55] One of the greatest ideas they copied was the icon-and-mouse invention from the Xerox PARC, a research lab. The idea was first widely used in the Macintosh computer and later in Windows.

Another reason for Apple's success was Job's policy of only hiring the best and firing the bozos. As one author stated, "Job's strategy is to hire the smartest programmers, engineers and designers available...Jobs is an elitist who believes that a small A team is far more effective than armies of engineers and designers. He has always sought out the highest quality in people, products and advertising."[56] One more reason for Apple's success was apparently Job's micromanagement. Of course, he was also known for his temper, which might have something to do with the firm's success. As one author stated, "Critics have compared Jobs to a sociopath without empathy or compassion. Staffers are inhuman objects, mere tools to get things done." [57] But Jobs was known for getting the best out of his people, despite his temper.

Many Apple employees, including executives, tried to avoid Steve, because of his temper. As one employee stated, "Like many people, I tried to avoid him as much as possible. You want to stay below his radar and avoid him getting mad at you."[58] He typically didn't interact with lower-level people. But he sometimes visited departments at random and asked employees what they are working on. Jobs sometimes praised employees, but not very often.[59] If Jobs encountered a prototype product he didn't like, he sometimes used an expletive to describe it.

Jobs organized his first A team to work on the Macintosh, in 1980. Some of the members were Bill Atkinson, Andy Herzfeld and Burrell Smith. Steve also recruited other members himself, from the Silicon Valley area. They actually flew a pirate flag over their building to set them apart at Apple.[60] The Mac group was a separate division of the company. Jobs isolated them from the bureaucrats at Apple, who were more interested in enhancing the Apple II, the firm's most important product at that time. Steve wanted to keep the Mac team no larger than 100 people, so it wouldn't become too difficult to manage.[61]

Steve didn't like complex products; they should be simple for the customer to use. "Jobs pares down the complexity of his products until they are as simple and easy to use as possible."[62] This is contrary to the preference of many software developers, who want to load up new products with as many new features as they can think of, resulting in a very complex (and hard to use) product. Apple also makes lots of prototypes for a new product, such as the Mac OS X, before deciding on the best one. The OS X was much different from the old Macintosh operating system. Jobs and his crew spent 18 months perfecting the OS X software interface for the users.[63] As one author stated, "Under his [Job's] guidance, products are developed through nearly endless rounds of mockups and prototypes that are constantly edited and revised. This is true for both hardware and software."[64] Possible results are a redesign from the beginning, or the product might be scrapped.

An additional reason for Apple's success was Job's interest in aesthetics, which began with the Apple II product. The Apple II was the first packaged PC. Jobs stated, "My dream for the Apple II was to sell the first real packaged computer... I got a bug up my rear that I wanted the computer in a plastic case."[65] Up to that point, personal computers were sold as kits that were hard to use. Jobs developed an interest in industrial design. He decided to hire an actual industrial designer in early 1982, Hartmut Esslinger. Esslinger was actually the winner of an Apple design contest.[66] Jobs has also been influenced by Edwin Land, inventor of the Polaroid camera, who Jobs thinks of as a hero. The first Henry Ford was another of his heroes.[67] Another excellent industrial designer Jobs hired was Jonathan Ive. Ive later became head of Apple's design department.[68]

Not all of Apple's products have been hits with consumers. One example is the Power Mac Cube. The critics, like the WSJ's Walt Mossberg, loved it. But it didn't sell well. "Apple had hoped for sales of 800,000 the first year, but shipped fewer than 100,000 units."[69] Apple decided to end sales of the Cube.

Apple is considered one of the most innovative companies in the digital device area. Business Week in 2007 "named Apple as the most innovative company in the world, beating Google, Toyota, Sony, Nokia, Genentech, and a host of other A-list companies."[70]

Apple's most innovative products include: the Apple II; the Macintosh, with its graphical user interface (icon and mouse); the iPod, with its Internet music store, iTunes; the iPhone, which is also a computer; and the iPad, the first popular tablet computer. Now most new cars have iPod connectivity.[71]

An author goes on: "Apple produces blockbusters like the iMac, iPod and iPhone, but there's also been a long list of smaller yet important and influential products like the Airport and Apple TV. Apple's Airport is a line of easy-to-use WiFi base stations that enabled Apple's laptops to be among the first wireless notebooks, a trend that later went thoroughly mainstream. The Apple TV is a streaming set-top box that links the TV in the living room with the computer in the den."[72]

Jobs hired John Sculley as CEO from the Pepsico firm, to help Apple manage its growth.. One of the ways Jobs persuaded Sculley to come to Apple was the line, "Do you want to sell sugar water for the rest of your life, or do you want to change the world?"[73] Sculley later decided to fire Jobs, but Steve resigned first. One author described the situation: "In 1985, Jobs was effectively kicked out of Apple for being unproductive and uncontrollable. After a failed power struggle with then-CEO John Sculley, Jobs quit before he could be fired. With dreams of revenge, he founded NeXT with the purpose of selling advanced computers…"[74] At that time, Apple was in serious trouble. "Apple was in a death spiral. The company was six months from bankruptcy."[75] Jobs returned to Apple as CEO in July, 1997. He took over from the previous CEO, Gilbert Amelio, who resigned.

Steve's response to the crisis was to scrap dozens of Apple's products that he thought weren't needed. He looked at every product. Jobs allowed each product group to decide which products to cut and which to keep. Each group had to sell the CEO on any products they wanted to keep.[76] Jobs even killed the Newton PDA product.[77]

Another thing that changed with Steve's return was the firm's culture. He banned dogs and smoking at work. And employees put in longer days, ending their preference for arriving late and leaving early.

Another aspect of Job's life was the Pixar firm, which he bought for $10 million from George Lucas in 1986.[78] Steve pumped $60 million of his own money into the firm for ten years, until it produced its first hit. Jobs was CEO of Pixar for some years, but he was a hands-off manager at that firm, perhaps because animated movies weren't his specialty. He mostly worked behind the scenes, such as when he negotiated deals. Jobs made a comment on Pixar to the press. He said, "If I knew in 1986 how much it was going to cost to keep Pixar going, I doubt if I would have bought the company."[79] Eventually, Pixar was sold to Disney for $7.4 billion.[80]

Steve also started the NeXT firm after he was forced out of Apple while CEO. NeXT was not very successful. But eventually Apple bought it for $427 million.[81] Apple used some of the NeXT firm's technology in the Mac OS.

Probably everyone by now has heard of Steve's cancer. It was a form of pancreatic cancer, which was cured by surgery. The specific type of disease was islet-cell cancer, or neuroendocrine cancer. The surgery he had is called the Whipple procedure. Jobs appeared emaciated at times, despite the cancer cure.[82] When Steve wasn't around, Tim Cook, now the CEO, was in charge. Cook started at Apple in 1998 as senior vice pres. of operations. His specialty is manufacturing.[83]

Cook's personality is different from Job's. He doesn't get angry like Jobs did. As one author wrote, "But where Jobs is emotional and volatile, Cook is quiet and soft-spoken. ...He has reportedly never raised his voice in anger—an incredible claim, especially given Jobs's reputation for having a nasty temper."[84] Cook is also known for his humor and is a workaholic, like Jobs.[85] Cook previously worked for Compaq computer and started at Apple as chief operating officer. His first assignment was to simplify Apple's supply chain management. He reduced the number of suppliers from over 100 to about 24. He also greatly reduced the amount of inventory, from about 70 days to 7 days, that Apple kept on hand.[86]

Another of Apple's innovations is their own stores. To avoid getting burned in that new venture, Jobs hired Ron Johnson in 2000. Johnson was an executive at Target Corp. Apple opened their first store in May, 2001. They located their stores in high-traffic malls. Apple apparently learned from Gateway's stores, which located its stores where real estate was cheap, in remote parking lots; Gateway closed all of its stores in April, 2004.[87] Getting back to Apple, they only had four products to sell when they started to open their stores, so they decided to sell the Apple life style, or "customer experience."[88] Apple even built a mockup store in a warehouse, to try out their ideas. Apple decided to include a Genius Bar in their stores, where customers could get answers to their questions and get their Apple products repaired in a few days, rather than the usual weeks.[89] The Genius Bar was one of the four parts of their stores. The other parts were devoted to products, music and photos, and accessories.[90]

Hewlett and Packard

David Packard met Bill Hewlett in the fall of 1930, when they were freshmen at Stanford University. Packard first worked for General Electric after graduation. The pair started planning their own company in the summer of 1937. They called it the Engineering Service Company.[91] The firm actually started in 1938, in the famous garage (now a historic landmark) in Palo Alto. They first did custom engineering work, such as control equipment for air conditioners. Their first product was an audio oscillator.[92] They sold an improved version of that product to the Disney Studios; eight of them were sold for $71.50 each, much less than the cost of a competing product.

In 1964, Hewlett-Packard started to develop its first mini-computer, the 2116. It was meant to be a controller, but it became popular as a stand-alone computer.

HP started to develop another computer, a 32-bit machine the called the Omega.[93] But they decided the project would consume too many resources, so the project was cancelled. A scaled-down version of the Omega machine was later developed, a 16-bit mini, called the Alpha, or later the HP-3000.[94] Its operating system was called MPE. The HP-3000 and its later versions were very popular.

HP later became an innovator in PC printers, including ink jet.[95] and later laser printers. They also produced some of the early pocket calculators, the HP 35 for example, which was introduced in 1972.

An Wang

An Wang is best known as the founder of Wang Laboratories, which produced minicomputers. He also invented magnetic core memory in 1948, which was widely used in the computer industry in the 1960s, before semiconductor memories made it obsolete in the 1970s. Magnetic core memory typically consisted of thousands (sometimes millions) of small, donut-shaped hard ferrite cores, with wires going through each core, which were used to read the magnetization, one of two directions, and write a new magnetization. Each core was one bit of memory.

An Wang came to the U.S in 1945. He was born in China. He enrolled at Harvard University and obtained his doctorate in physics in 1947.[96] He soon began working at the Harvard Computation Laboratory, working for Howard Aiken. Wang's first assignment was to find a way to store information in a computer. In 1948, he found a way. It was magnetic core memory.

He founded Wang Laboratories in Boston, Massachusetts in 1951. Magnetic core memories were their first product. They later produced electronic calculators, in the 1960s.

The firm produced several models of calculators. The first was the LOCI, or logarithmic calculating instrument. It sold for $6500, a high price for a calculator at that time, 1965. The firm modified it, renaming it the 300, which sold for $1700. They later came out with an improved calculator, the 700, in 1969. All three of those models were programmable, meaning computers in disguise. As Dr. Wang commented in his autobiography, "[I]t is a lot easier to sell a calculator—even an expensive one—than it is to sell a computer: For one thing, we could sell a calculator directly to the user, and we were good at that. In contrast, in the late 1960s and early 1970s, the decision to buy a computer would involve top management at most corporations …There would be committees and meetings with the company's data processing people and a great deal of deliberation…"[97]

This author once used one of Wang's electronic calculators. It looked something like a tower PC, with a box containing the electronics on the floor and a head on the table, with a cable connecting them; the head consisted of a keypad for entering numbers and a nixie-tube display, which displayed the result. I believe it cost around $2000. Wang later produced typesetting machines[98] and word-processing systems, which used a minicomputer and terminals.

After much experimentation, the firm (specifically Harold Koplow) decided to produce a new type of word processing system, using intelligent terminals containing the Intel 8080 microprocessor and a server, a minicomputer, which handled the file processing and printing. Their Word Processing System came out in 1976. There was a small version which could support three terminals and several printers. A more-powerful version could support 14 terminals.[99]

The firm folded in 1990, after the founder died.[100] The author of Microchip explains why the firm folded.[101] "Soon, Wang's premier office machines were eclipsed by personal computers that were more multifunctional. With software to program them, they performed word processing in addition to loads of other tasks. The labs had no new products to answer the challenge. Instead it merely attached itself to the [IBM] PC development, bringing out an IBM-like product of its own." Dr. Wang wrote an autobiography, titled Lessons,[102] published in 1986.

Edgar Codd

Edgar Codd is known for creating relational databases. He wrote an important paper, published in June, 1970 "A Relational Mode of Data for Large Data Banks," in the Communications of the ACM. His paper proposed replacing the then-common hierarchical structure of databases with rows and columns, which would reside in tables.

Codd was a native of England, where he attended Oxford University, obtaining degrees in math and chemistry. In 1967 he get his doctorate in computer science at the Univ. of Michigan and later moved to San Jose to work for IBM.

An article from IBM describes how relational databases would work: "Ted's basic idea was that relationships between data items should be based on the item's values, and not on separately specified linking or nesting. This notion greatly simplified the specification of queries and allowed unprecedented flexibility to exploit existing data sets in new ways," according to Don Chamberlin, the co-inventor of SQL. "He believed that computer users should be able to work at a more natural-language level and not be concerned about the details of where or how the data was stored."

Chamberlin continues, "Codd had a bunch of fairly complicated queries, and since I'd been studying CODASYL (the language used to query navigational databases), I could imagine how those queries would have been represented in CODASYL by programs that were five pages long that would navigate through this labyrinth of pointers and stuff. Codd would sort of write them down as one-liners...[T]hey weren't complicated at all." Chamberlin went on, "I said, 'Wow.' This was kind of a conversion experience for me. I understood what the relational thing was about after that."

IBM's first attempt at a relational database system was called System R, which IBM developed at their San Jose research lab, starting in 1973.

Included in System R were these features: (1) Structured Query Language, (2) a cost-based optimizer, which creates an execution plan, (3) a query compiler, (4) query formulation and execution, and (5) online data definition.

System R worked as expected and led to IBM's first relational database product, SQL/DS, in 1981. Another relational system, DB2, was announced in 1983. IBM stated that one feature of DB2 is that it could store data on any size machine, from handheld devices to large mainframes.

One of Codd's co-workers, Chris Date, said, "Codd's biggest overall achievement was to make database management into a science. He put the field on solid scientific footing by providing a theoretical framework –the relational model—within which a variety of important problems could be attacked in a scientific manner."

An IBM manager, Janet Perma, said, "Codd will be forever remembered as the father of the relational database...perhaps his greatest achievement is inspiring generations of people who continue to build upon the foundations he laid. Database professionals all over the world mourn his passing."

Besides System R and DB2, other successful relational database systems in that era include Larry Ellison's system, from Relational Software, Inc. (later renamed Oracle) and Ingres, developed at Univ. of Calif.-Berkeley, by Mike Stonebraker. Newer relational database systems include Sybase and SQL Server.

Codd died in April, 2003. (From htttp://www-03.ibm.com/ibm/history/exhibits/builders. [103])

William Shockley

William Shockley is best known for inventing the transistor, at Bell Labs, in 1947. He worked with John Bardeen and Walter Brittain on that project, and the three were later awarded the Nobel prize for that invention. He was born in London, England, in 1910. His father was a mining engineer.

Shockley obtained his Ph.D. from the Massachusetts Institute of Technology in 1936. His first job after that was with Bell Labs in Murray Hill, N, J. He started out doing R & D work on vacuum tubes, but soon switched to solid state electronics.

In 1956, he left Bell Labs to start his own company, Shockley Laboratories, in Palo Alto, California. Jeffrey Zygmont describes the Shockley of that era: "He was irresistibly appealing. When he wasn't theorizing or inventing, he performed legerdemain. He pulled practical gags. He climbed mountains. He raised ants, constructing elaborate obstacle courses equipped with fulcrumed teter-totters. To youthful and aspiring chemists, physicists, engineers, and other science-guild members, going to work for Bill Shockley was like taking a bit part alongside James Dean."[104]

Some of Shockley's employees developed a strong dislike for the man. Eight of them left his firm in 1957 to start their own firm, Fairchild Semiconductor. Two of the eight were Gordon Moore and Robert Noyce, who later founded Intel Corp. Probably the last straw for the eight was Shockley's request that they all take a lie detector test. He had also decided that his firm would make diodes, not transistors.[105] Gordon Moore described the environment before he left Shockley's firm: "Working for Shockley proved to be a particular challenge... [H]e developed traits that we came to view as paranoid. He suspected that members of his staff were purposely trying to undermine the project and prohibited them from access to some of the work."[106]

Shockley's firm was acquired by a firm called Clevite Transistor in 1960. His laboratories shut down in 1969.

Late in life, Shockley became controversial for his views on genetics and human intelligence. Shockley died in San Francisco in 1989. He was married twice and had three children.

The Microchip[107] book has an excellent summation of his life: "Technoscenti who encountered him even briefly while he lived remain awed to this day by his brilliance and sparkle."

James Rand, Junior

James Rand, Jr. was born in Nov., 1886 in North Tonawanda, New York. His father was James Rand, Sr., who invented an office filing system and founded the Rand Ledger company to manufacture filing products. The senior Rand developed a serious illness in 1910 and turned over control of his firm to his son, James Jr. By 1915, the father had recovered and resumed control of the ledger firm.

The junior Rand followed his father's advice to make his own living and founded a similar firm, called American Kardex, in 1915. They produced filing products. The firm grew rapidly and in five years had about the same revenues as Rand Ledger. The firms were competing intensively, but Mary Rand, the mother of James Jr., persuaded Rand Jr. and Sr. to combine their firms. American Kardex bought Rand Ledger. The new firm was called Rand Kardex. Rand Jr. became president, while his father became chairman.

The new firm went on an acquisition binge. They bought, for example, Safe Cabinet Co., Library Bureau and Dalton Adding Machine. Then they merged with the Remington Typewriter Company in 1927. The firm's named was changed to Remington Rand.

The junior Rand became chairman of Remington Rand in 1929 and also became president in 1931.

The firm had some serious problems in the 1930s. The Depression was a big blow, causing their revenues to drop by 75% by 1931. The firm was later hurt by a strike in 1936, which ended in 1937. Then, in 1939, they were sued by the U.S. Justice Dept. for violating the antitrust laws.

During the War, Remington Rand became a defense contractor, building bomb fuses and a pistol, and other products. James Rand, Sr. died in 1944.

After the War, the firm expanded rapidly. They purchased the Eckert-Mauchly Computer Corp. in 1950. They later bought Electronic Research Associates of Saint Paul, Minn. The firm's computer division was renamed the Univac division, which combined the two firm's operations. Remington Rand merged with the Sperry Corp. in 1955. James Rand, Jr. became vice chairman.

Rand Jr. died in 1968 at the age of 81.

Eighteen

Many operating systems have come and gone in the computer industry. So only a few examples will be discussed here: OS 1100, System/360 OS, CP/M, Unix, DOS, and Scope. A characteristic of all these systems was that they all processed text commands, such as for copying files. The icon-and-mouse came later. Of course, the latter mechanism meant the systems were much easier to use.

OS 1100 was developed for the Sperry-Univac 1100 series of mainframes. It was written in assembly language. It had the typical features of early operating systems, including commands that started with the @ character, or the @@ combination. The double @ commands were transparent, so they could be processed while the system was compiling a program, for example.

The symbol after the single @ would be the name of a program, such as FOR to call the Fortran compiler, or CTS to call the Converstaional Time-Sharing system. Input/output on the 1100 was done by executive requests, such as the assembly language instruction: ER IOW$, meaning perform the I/O (specified in a packet parameter) and wait for completion. Some typical commands were: @ASG, to assign a file; @COPY, to copy a file; @PRT, T to display the table of contents of a file (i.e., list the programs); and @PMD to perform a post-mortem dump.

CP/M was an early system, for personal computers, developed before the DOS system, by Digital Research. MP/M (also from Digital Research) was a more advanced version of CP/M, which allowed multiple users to access one machine, via terminals. CP/M's commands were similar to DOS commands, and it used the same type of three-character extension that is used in DOS and Windows. CP/M had a command prefix, such as "A>", which showed which disk drive was in use, and the ">" prefix invited the user to type in a command. Some typical CP/M commands were: DIR, list files in a directory; ED, call the text editor; TYPE, display a text file; ERA, erase a file; and SYSGEN, copy CP/M from one disk to another. In the CP/M days, computers didn't hard drives; they had two diskette drives. So, the user had to specify the correct drive, A or B, before executing a command for the appropriate diskette. When hard drives arrived, PCs where built with just one diskette drive, usually called A. So, the B drive was missing and the hard drive was (and is) called C. CP/M is now obsolete. Its users have likely switched to DOS or Linux, similar to Unix.

Unix was written at Bell Labs by Ken Thompson and evolved from the older Multics system, which Thompson had worked on. Dennis Ritchie, developer of the C language, also worked on Unix, which they developed on a PDP-7 mini-computer. Unix was developed in the early days of time-sharing, which many people preferred to batch processing. The Unix OS was written in assembly language, but Unix applications were in other languages, including B, the predecessor to the C language. By 1973, Unix was rewritten in the new C language. Of course, Unix now completes with the free Linux system, which is very similar to Unix.

DOS is another early operating system for PCs. It was purchased from Seattle Computer Products (called SCP-DOS) and enhanced by Microsoft and now includes dozens of commands. Some sources say the original name for DOS was QDOS, meaning quick and dirty operating system. The enhanced DOS came to have various names, including IBM Disk Operating System, MS-DOS and PC-DOS. IBM included it on their early PCs. Of course, most users have switched to Windows. But DOS can still do some things that Windows can't; for example, the command DIR *Steve*.* will display all file names in the current directory containing the name Steve, regardless of where the five-character name appears in the file name, and regardless of the extension. The COPY command and some other commands also accept that type of syntax. DOS survives as a command-prompt window in current Windows systems. Of course, DOS has the commonly-used commands DIR, COPY, DEL (for delete), MD (make directory), CD (change directory), REN (rename), and FC (file compare). It also has some lesser-known commands, including ERASE, EDIT, REM (for comments), FORMAT (for formatting a disk), DEFRAG (defragment a disk), and RD (remove directory), and HELP (explain a command).

COS (Chippewa Operating System) was the first operating system written for the Control Data 6600, the first machine in the 6000 series. Seymour Cray wrote it in machine language. It wasn't widely used outside of Control Data. The widely-used systems for the 6000-series machines included Scope and Kronos. Another system, NOS, came along later. Scope was used mainly for batch-processing, and Kronos was used for time-sharing. Mace was the basis for Kronos and was mainly used internally. The name Mace (from Supermen book) stands for Mansfield and Calander Executive. Some typical commands in Scope were: RUN, call one of the Fortran compilers; UPDATE, call the Update program to edit source programs; COMPASS, call the Compass assembler; COPY, copy a disk or tape file; COPYSBF, copy a text file to create a file for printing. The 6600 and 7600 operating systems were quite a bit different from other operating systems in one respect: they had slave computers, small minicomputers, to do most of the work. Those minicomputers were built into the system. Typical tasks for the minicomputers included input, output, memory management and handling the system's console displays and commands. This architecture freed up the main processor for the important tasks.

Nineteen

These types of storage media were in use on digital computers, up to 1981. Some of these media were in use for years after that.

1) Paper tape: Paper tapes are the oldest storage medium, since they were initially used with teletype systems, in the mid-19th century. The early tapes had six holes across the tape, with one of the holes used to hold the tape in position. They were later used in other equipment, including Linotype machines, manufacturing machines and then computers. Some teletype machines could read and/or punch paper tapes. Paper tapes would often break, but the breaks could be repaired, and editing of tapes was possible, with the appropriate machine.

2) Punch cards: The 80-column punch cards were invented by Herman Hollerith, which he patented in 1887; they came into use after paper tape. They were initially used with tabulating equipment, for the 1890 U.S. Census, which Hollerith also invented. Punch cards in later years measured 3-1/4 by 7-3/8 and had 80 columns. The size was standard for decades. The holes punched in the cards were originally round, and were punched manually in the early years, using the Pantographic punch. Later IBM, in the late 1920s, came out with a standard card, which was

punched with rectangular holes. Hollerith's firm was later acquired by the IBM Corp., which was originally called the CTR company. When computers came into wide use in the 1950s, punch cards were used for recording programs and data. Many computers had fast card readers and card punches. Even the 1940s Eniac machine had a card reading device, provided by IBM Corp. Remington Rand used 90-column punch cards, which had two rows of 45 columns each. Those cards were punched with round holes.

3) Fixed disks: Fixed disks came into use in the late 1950s, and were available on some IBM mainframes of that era. Their principal advantage was the direct-access feature; i.e., records could be read, updated and re-written quickly, regardless of their location on the disk. With a tape drive, the computer might have to read to the end of a long tape to access a record, a time-consuming process.

4) Removable disks: These were an improvement over the fixed disk drives, since the disk packs, as they were called, could be stored for safekeeping.

   IBM introduced their 1311 series of removable disk drives in Oct., 1962. Each disk pack had a plastic cover, included multiple platters, and could easily be moved from one disk drive to another. Also it could be sent to another site or placed in storage. Typical capacity was two million characters per disk pack, according to IBM.

5) Floppy disks—three sizes: Floppy disks were common on minicomputers and on PCs and came in three sizes: 8 inches, 5-1/4 inches and 3-1/2 inches.

   They were called floppies because they were flexible—at least the older ones were flexible. Capacities varied, and the 3-1/2" disks came in capacities up to 250 megabytes, from Imation. They consisted of a disk of plastic coated with magnetic oxide, in a plastic cover. Floppies aren't used much today, since flash drives have much higher capacities. Writable DVD disks or CDs are an option for some people.

6) Magnetic tapes: These consisted of long spools of magnetic tape, usually ½" wide and 10-1/2" in diameter, which were accessed by read and

write heads. The data was recorded as seven to 13 bit groups or characters laterally and was grouped in records, with a gap after each record.
More modern tape drives use cassettes, which are higher density and
don't need to be threaded onto a takeup reel.

7) Metallic tapes: One of the earliest tape drives used by the Univac
machines used metallic tapes, ½" wide. The tape was nickel-plated
phosphor bronze, 1200 feet long. Data was recorded on 8 channels.
That tape drive was called the Uniservo and was used on the Univac I
machine.

8) Magnetic drums: Magnetic drums were similar to fixed disk drives,
which were stacks of metal disks covered with magnetic oxide and
accessed with read and write heads for each disk. The drums consisted
of a rotating metal cylinder, also coated with magnetic oxide, which
were also accessed with read and write heads. The cylinder rotated at
high speed, up to 24,000 rpm.

Twenty

The Bunch

"The bunch" is an old term which refers to five companies that made mainframe computers. The industry mainly consisted of The Bunch and IBM, which had the largest market share in the industry. The combined sales of The Bunch were much less than IBM's by 1960. The five letters in the word stood for Burroughs, Univac, NCR, Control Data and Honeywell. General Electric and RCA also made mainframe computers, but later abandoned that line of business.

Burroughs Corp.

The Burroughs firm, founded in 1886, produced calculators and was originally called the American Arithmometer Company, later changed to Burroughs. It was founded in St. Louis by William Seward Burroughs, who invented and patented their first adding machine. Mr. Burroughs was born about 1855 and got his first job of note as a bank clerk in Auburn, New York. He moved to St. Louis for health reasons. He developed his adding machine in a machine shop and obtained a patent for it in 1888. Then his firm had to convince banks and other firms to buy his adding machines, which wasn't an easy task at the time.

From St. Louis, the firm moved to Detroit in 1904. The next year they changed the company name to Burroughs Adding Machine Co. They also made other products, including typewriters and check protectors. The firm grew rapidly.

During World War II, the firm obtained some government contracts. They continued getting government contracts after the war and later in the 50s.

The firm started moving into computers and changed the name to Burroughs Corp. in 1953. They were producing mainframe computers at that time, but like the other Bunch companies, were much smaller than IBM, based on revenues. They sold a lot of their products to banks. They were still selling calculators in the 50s. Some of the Burroughs computer models were the B5500, B6500, and the B7500, which used their MCP operating system. Languages available included Algol, Cobol and Fortran. Burroughs also developed a systems programming language called ESPOL. They also sold the TC500, a terminal, for use with that series. They acquired some expertise in electronic digital computers when they bought Electrodata Corp. in 1956.

Other machines that they produced included the B1700, the B2000 and the B700. In the early 1980s, Burroughs began producing PCs, called the B20 and B25 machines.

In 1985, talks began with the Univac division of Sperry Rand about a merger. The merger was completed in September, 1986. The merged company was renamed Unisys.

Remington Rand

Remington Rand Corp. began as the Remington Arms Company, in 1828. Later, in 1873, they bought the rights to the new typewriter invention. They also acquired or merged with five other typewriter companies over the next 20 years. They later went into the electric razor business, and they made sewing machines.

In 1927, James Rand, Jr. merged his firm, Rand-Kardex, with several other firms: Remington Typewriter (the original Remington firm), Dalton Adding

Machine Co., Powers Accounting Machine Co. (a competitor of IBM), and the Safe Cabinet Co. He called the new firm Remington Rand Corp.

Univac

The Univac firm was part of the Remington Rand Corp., founded by James Rand, Jr. It was a conglomerate, which also made typewriters and electric shavers. The firm got into computers when they bought the Eckert-Mauchly Computer Corp. in 1950 and then Engineering Research Associates in 1952. The Univac name, short for UNIVersal Automatic Computer, came from one of the computers developed by Eckert and Mauchly.

The Rand people contacted the ERA management about the possibility of buying the firm. ERA's John Parker was the main contact.[1] But many ERA employees wanted the firm to stay independent. As Willis Drake, an ERA employee, stated, "We could be employees of someone we didn't even know; shavers and typewriters [Remington's products] were not our bag. So it turned out to be a very bitter fight internally. John [Parker] tried to persuade us."

The two firms were combined to form the Univac division of Remington Rand. The Univac division became part of Sperry Rand when Sperry Corp. and Remington Rand merged to form Sperry Rand, in 1955. The Sperry Corporation was formed from the merger of Curtiss-Wright Corporation, North American Aviation Company, and Sperry Gyroscope in 1933. The Sperry Gyroscope company was founded in 1910 by Elmer Sperry

Univac was the leader in computers in the early 1950s, but they let IBM take the lead in that decade.

The firm's computer division expanded in 1971 when Sperry Rand acquired RCA Corporation's computer division, for $490 million. Sperry Rand changed its name in 1979 to Sperry Corporation.

William Norris said[2], speaking of Univac, "We sat there with a tremendous technological and sales lead and watched IBM pass us as if we were standing still." Late in his term at Univac, William Norris wasn't pleased with his superiors and called a meeting, at his house, for all those who wanted to start a new company.

Norris stated[3], "And I was absolutely flabbergasted at the number of people that came. The neighbors thought there was a funeral. And one of the young guys that came there I didn't know, [was] Seymour Cray." Norris left Univac in July, 1957, and Cray left in September of that year, after he finished work on a Navy project. Sperry Rand later merged with Burroughs Corp. to form Unisys Corp., which still exists.

Univac's Early Days

David Lundstrom, in his book about the early days of Univac and Control Data, describes his experiences at the ERA firm, which later became part of Univac. The cover of the book shows the console of the ERA 1101 computer, ancestor of the Univac 1103 and later 1100 series models.

His assignment was to work on the Univac II hardware, after learning the Univac I. He was in charge of testing the Univac II hardware. The Univac II was a vacuum-tube model.[4] The now-famous Seymour Cray also worked there at that time.

He describes Seymour: "Although a relative newcomer to ERA, Seymour Cray was already regarded as one of the top, if not the top computer designer in St. Paul...he had taken to computer design like one born to it.... Of medium height and absolutely average appearance, Seymour Cray was normally soft-spoken but capable of biting sarcasm when confronted with foolishness."[5]

One of Lundstrom's activities was to learn the details of the Univac I model, at the former Eckert-Mauchly computer firm. He drove there in his car. As part of the class, he also learned about the latest tape drive for the Univac II, called Uniservo. Soon the Uniservo I models were replaced by the improved Uniservo II models. Lundstrom met Presper Eckert at the Philadelphia location.[6] Back at ERA, he and co-workers were completing five Univac II machines.[7]

The author described the first attempt to power up a Univac II machine, at the ERA location. It didn't work the first time.[8] The engineers blew dozens of fuses the first time they turned on the machine. He describes what followed: "There was nothing we could do but trace through the wiring of the entire machine, checking for the proper voltage on every chassis pin."[9]

Lundstrom continues his narrative by describing how a drum printer works. That was one of the peripherals used with mainframe computers. He describes it as a horizontal cylinder with 120 or more sets of vertical characters on the surface. The cylinder rotates ten times per second. There is a print hammer, for each set of characters, which is used to push the paper and ribbon together at the right instant to print the character. These types of printers were big, noisy and expensive. They also developed band printers, where the characters moved horizontally in front of the paper, which made the printed characters more legible.[10] Of course, that was before the era of ink jet and laser jet printers.

He also describes card-to-tape converters, which were used to replace key-punches. They recorded typed data directly onto a magnetic tape, which would eliminate the need for punch cards. Univac's parent firm, Remington Rand, also produced punch cards and related equipment. He describes their punch cards: "These used round holes and stored ninety characters on a punched card, as opposed to IBM's rectangular holes and eighty character cards. The Remington Rand cards never caught on in the marketplace although they were superior from a strictly technical standpoint."[11]

Another data entry machine was produced by the Eckert-Mauchly firm. They called it the Unityper. It recorded each typed character on a magnetic tape, one character at a time. Of course, that device was not as efficient as some later machines, which kept many characters in memory, allowing some corrections and editing, before writing them out to a tape as one record.

Another peripheral device from the Eckert-Mauchly firm was the Fastrand, which provided long-term storage, like today's hard disk drives. It was a magnetic drum, consisting of two rapidly-rotating horizontal cylinders which were read and written by one magnetic head, which moved between the two cylinders. Magnetic drums never became very popular in the computer industry, probably because they used a lot of space, compared to the equivalent disk drives.

At the ERA location, engineers had developed a disk drive, which was not removable like some later models.

Lundstrom also described the Uniservo II tape drives, which used the vacuum-column technology, as opposed to the older technology, described by that author as the "pulley-and-fishing-line buffer loops" in the Uniservo I model drives.[12]

The ERA people also developed the Univac File Computer, which was a vacuum tube computer. It used magnetic drums developed at ERA and was used for inventory management. Those machines were used by a few airlines for seat reservation systems.[13] The ERA firm also worked on so-called thin film memories, for the U.S. Air Force, which were similar to magnetic core memories. That latter type of memory came into use in the early 1950s, replacing the older Williams-tube and mercury-delay-line memories.

Lundstrom writes about what it was like when colleagues resigned to start the Control Data firm, just across the river in Minneapolis. William Norris, the head of the Univac division, was one of them, and so was Frank Mullaney.[14] There was a lot of speculation about what would happen next. Willis Drake, one of the Control Data founders, held a meeting at his home, to sell stock in the new firm, for one dollar per share. Drake discussed, in general terms, what the new company was planning to do, and he emphasized that it was a speculative stock.[15] Lundstrom stated that he bought 200 shares. Soon Seymour Cray and Bob Kisch, another Univac employee, left to work at Control Data.[16]

A new manager was named to head the St. Paul Univac division, named Bob McDonald, who was previously with Northwest Airlines, which had a local headquarters.[17] Now the St. Paul operations of Univac needed more managers, so some people were moved there from the Philadelphia operations of that division. They did provide the needed help, such as on the Univac II problems. One person from the Univac II group of engineers was assigned to each of the five current customers, to assist with the computer's installation.

Another project at the ERA facility was the NTDS, or Naval Tactical Data System, which used a new computer, built with transistors (not vacuum tubes), called the M-460. Lundstrom stated that the machine was to be used on board Navy ships. The M-460 had 32,000 words of 30-bit magnetic core memory. Magnetic cores were the newest memory technology at that time, for the fast internal memories.

Transistors were the latest circuit technology, replacing vacuum tubes. The M-460 was cooled by circulating air. He stated that the M-460 used magnetic tape drives on board ships, but it didn't use magnetic disks or drums. They were thought to be incompatible with the difficult environment at sea.

Univac in that era had a hard time retaining talent. Many of its engineers quit to work at Control Data, across the river. They also lost engineers to RCA and General Electric, which had computer divisions at that time. Many small companies were founded in that era, by former Univac and Control Data people. Some examples include: Data 100, Data Display, and Lee Data.[18]

Lundstrom described how it worked with Sperry Rand hired a new vice president for the Univac division. He said he and his co-workers would first read about the new V.P. in the *Electronic News*, a periodical for engineers. None of them had any computer experience, he said. But they would tour the plants and offices, and they would never be seen again. Each V.P. would just fade away, in effect. He described what happened: "Then Electronic News would have a photo and a short news article on the next messiah [vice president]. The former messiah, proven false, would fade away with no announcement of his destination, and the new man, hailed by all as the true savior, would make his ritual tour of the plants."[19] That problem might explain how IBM was able to gain a much bigger share of the computer market, by 1960, than Sperry-Univac, even though Univac produced the first mainframe computer, two years before IBM's first computer.

Lundstrom stated that his Univac division had to compete for development funds with the Sperry Gyroscope division, which actually tried to develop its own digital computer.

That author describes how they tested the first prototype of the NTDS computer. He wrote that it was "...not nearly as exciting at the first Univac II power-up [described above]. No fuses blew and no smoke arose. Of course, there were no printed circuit cards in the machine for the first power-up."[20] He stated that the cards were tested slowly. Finally, after six weeks, the NTDS machine was running programs.

Their work for the U.S. Navy went well. He stated, "Univac established a reputation for quality shipboard computers that has kept them a favorite supplier of the Navy to this day. Univac has won follow-up contracts for shipboard computer equipment totaling hundreds of millions of dollars."[21]

Lundstrom stated that the NTDS computer design was altered to create a commercial computer, called the 490, which was the first of the Univac 490 series models. The NTDS machine was also the basis for the popular 1100 series. He wrote, "This [new] design, an extension of the NTDS computer in the general direction of the Univac 1103 [a commercial computer] was built instead of the formally planned computer. It became the Univac model 1107 computer."[22] Of course, there were later extensions of that line, including the 1108, the 1106 and the 1110. The line actually began with ERA's 1101 model, which wasn't a commercial machine.

Univac never had a designer as good as Seymour Cray, but they did produce the LARC computer, which was fast for its time.

The A Few Good Men... author described his visit to a Control Data peripherals factory, at the invitation of Dick Clarke, an engineer he had worked with at Univac. He saw many different type of peripheral devices under development, including a card reader, a printer, drums and disks. Lundstrom filled out a job application at that time. He received a job offer a few days later, which included a raise. The author accepted. His view of the Univac division was that the accountants seemed to be running the company. About Control Data, he stated, "At Control Data it was clear that the *engineers* were running the company, with spectacular results. I could hardly wait to join the first [Control Data] team."[23]

NCR Corp.

NCR Corp. was originally the National Cash Register Corp., founded by James and John Ritty. John Patterson was running a dry goods store at that time and had a problem with sales that weren't recorded. He had heard about a firm that made cash registers, for recording sales and holding cash. So, he ordered two of the machines. He liked the machines so much that he bought some stock in the Rittys' company. Patterson joined the board of directors; he bought more stock and, by 1884, had control of the firm. As president, he decided to emphasize sales over manufacturing. Consequently, sales of his machines doubled by 1886. He also started print advertising, using direct mail and other means.

Patterson hired Thomas Watson in 1895 (later CEO of IBM), who worked hard to reduce the number of competitors, sometimes with unethical means (see The Maverick and His Machine); he was very successful in that venture. By 1900 NCR employed nearly 2,300 people. An NCR employee, Charles Kettering, designed a low-cost cash register, the Class 1000 machine, in 1906. By 1911, NCR had sold a million cash registers. Kettering later left NCR to work in the auto industry.

In 1912, the federal government filed suit against NCR for violating various laws, relating to trade violations. The president, Watson and other officers were found guilty in three of the 32 cases. Watson soon left the company, after he lost favor with Patterson, and started work at the Computing Tabulating Recording company, the predecessor to IBM.

In the 1920s NCR started to produce accounting machines. One example was the Class 2000 Itemizer, which was a type of cash register that provided 30 different totals.

During the Second World War (1942), NCR was ordered to stop making cash registers to save on metal. But they rebuilt and sold old machines as well as making parts such as bomb fuses for the war effort. NCR also built a code-breaking machine to counter the German's Enigma machine. It was an electro-mechanical machine reportedly called "The Bombe."

It entered the computer industry when the firm purchased the Computer Research Corp. in 1952. NCR expanded to foreign countries after the war, including the U.K., Australia. Japan and Canada. NCR produced an electronic accounting machine in the late 1950s and later introduced the Century series of computers. They produced a solid-state computer, the 304 model, in 1957. In 1960 NCR produced its first small computer, named the 390 model. It was actually manufactured by Control Data Corp.

In the late 1960s, NCR came out with their Century Series of computers, which included some business applications software. NCR was known in that era as part of the BUNCH, meaning Burroughs, Univac, NCR, Control Data and Honeywell. They were called the BUNCH because they collectively were smaller than IBM, their chief competitor in business computers.

NCR joined with Control Data to start a computer peripherals company in 1971. In 1972 NCR started a microelectronics division. NCR moved aggressively into computers in the early 1970s. But their technologies were aging, and a three-month strike at their Dayton, Ohio plant cost the firm millions of dollars. A weak U.S. economy and worsening inflation in the early 1970s also caused some problems for NCR. Their computer business finally showed a profit by the end of 1974, after losing money for several years.

After appointment of a new president in 1976, Charles Exley, the firm announced a new series of computers, the 8000 series, which they soon enhanced. They also moved into new products via acquisitions, including systems for factories and microcards. Their core product lines at that time were for banking and retailing.

They also produced the Tower Unix machine. NCR was not very successful when they competed with IBM, so they got out of the mainframe computer industry. NCR Corp. was owned for about fie years by AT & T, but is now a stand-alone company, with over $6.5 billion in annual sales. They mostly make ATM machines, retail terminals and products for various industries, including financial services, hospitality, travel and gaming.

(Most NCR material from FundingUniverse.com company histories.[24])

Control Data Corp.

Control Data was founded in 1957 by William Norris (head of Univac), Willis Drake, Frank Mullaney and several other people who left the Univac Division of Sperry Rand; Norris became the first CEO. Their initial capitalization was $600,000 (600,000 shares at $1/share), according to Norris.[25] The money had to be raised only from Minnesota residents, to satisfy the authorities.

The state Securities Commissioner, a Mr. Hull, gave his opinion of the new firm: "But you don't have any products, you don't have any plant, you don't have any machines, you don't have any customers, you don't have any money." According to Drake,[26] "Once we had the money it was microseconds before we got hit with a lawsuit from Sperry charging all kinds of terrible things." CDC was located at 501 Park Avenue in the Minneapolis loop area. Other employees who started that year were Seymour Cray and Bob Kisch. CDC sold stock in the early years to investors in the Twin Cities area. Much of the $600,000 was used to fund the 1604 project.[27]

Norris recalls the first month of CDC[28]: "Well, we opened the doors to the company, as I remember, the 15th of July. Hell, I put in $25,000, enough to get the thing started and we raised the money as we were going along." The interview stated that the initial capitalization was $600,000. Willis Drake[29] decided that they needed to issue 600,000 shares at $1 each. He led the group that raised the funds. Drake said that part of the prospectus was written on his kitchen table.[30] Norris described CDC's plans at the beginning, "They didn't have any plan. They had, Arnie Ryden had one sheet of paper." Norris explained[31] what happened next, "Well, we committed a good piece of it [the $600,000] to the 1604 and hoped that we could get contracts and that we could get additional financing, which we did." Seymour Cray joined the firm very early, in 1957, and started designing large, scientific computers. His first machine at CDC was the 1604, a solid-state machine with a clock speed of 200 kilohertz, or 5 microseconds per cycle. Control Data produced many other products, including the 6600 (the first supercomputer), the 7600, the 3000 series, the 160A minicomputer and peripheral equipment, including tape drives, disk drives, card readers and software, such as compilers and operating systems for their computers. The company was later restructured, exiting the mainframe computer industry, with the Ceridian firm and Control Data Systems remaining as two of the largest pieces. Both of them were acquired by different firms, and the Control Data name no longer exists. Control Data was renamed to Ceridian in 1992, according to Robert Price, the CDC CEO until 1990. Ceridian still exists, as part of another company.

Norris[32] describes the initial planning at CDC: "It wasn't a question of somebody else planning it. They didn't have any plan. They had, Arnie Ryden had one sheet of paper."

Ryden was one of the founders, according to Norris. Willis Drake, in a CBI interview[33], stated that there was more detailed planning: "...there evolved then a business plan for this hypothetical new company which was simply reduced to paper in a readable, logical, sequential way, a written plan, which explained what the objective of the company would be, what areas of business it would expect to pursue, and what kinds of people were required in order to pursue these business objectives." The plan became more detailed, according to Drake:[34] "And the result of the prose business plan then, of course, lead to the translation of that plan into money terms, budgets. What's the magnitude of the investment required; and what is the application of these funds? And parallel to that the development of sales and earning's forecasts and cash flow requirements that flowed from tracing the expected time tables, objectives, sales, and earning's results of executing the plan." The CDC executives discussed various products that they might build, but decided on one type of product, according to Drake[35]: "The one area that was most real in the whole thing, then, was the one that you'd expect, that's just a direct extension of earlier efforts at Univac and ERA before, and that's the development of a new large scale computer, the digital computer which was a success. And that is the product that ultimately launched the company."

Drake[36] describes the initial company structure at CDC: "Bill Norris was clearly to be the CEO and President. Bud [Ryden] was to be a chief financial officer of the company, vice president of finance. My job was to be director of marketing, and everybody else was going to be developmental engineer or something related to that; there were people who knew something about manufacturing obviously, but the task was--nothing to build yet, so it was basically developmental engineering."

Drake stated that CDC had a credibility problem at the beginning, because they didn't have a factory, and they didn't have tangible products that they could sell. Drake stated[37], "Gee, we've got to have some credibility; we gotta be making and shipping something; and we got to do it before we've gone broke--while there is still asset and financial resource here. So we acquired a company called Cedar Engineering, which had a factory, and it was making electro-mechanical products ... It was profitable and it had been around a long time, run by a seasoned old hand in the business. That became the Cedar Engineering Division of Control Data Corporation. We were able to take people on the plant tour and we had revenues and receivables and manufacturing employees, space." Drake later founded the Data Card Corporation.

David Lundstrom wrote about his years at CDC[38]; he started there in early 1963. He said the firm had about 3000 employees by that time, showing its fast growth. Two of the earliest products were the 160 minicomputer (which looked like a desk) and the 1604 mainframe, which was completed in 1959. Cray worked on the 1604 model. The 3600 model was designed by early 1963; it was adapted from the 1604 model.

Seymour Cray set up his famous Chippewa development lab in 1962, giving him a quiet environment to design his 6600 computer. James Thornton was part of the crew; he later designed the Star-100 supercomputer for CDC. Seymour Cray and crew finished development work on the new 6600 supercomputer in Aug., 1963, when Seymour introduced it to the press, at his Chippewa, Wisc. lab. The 6600 is described elsewhere in this book. Cray moved on to design the 7600 at his lab. Cray also designed the 8600 (a discrete component machine), successor to the 7600, but it was never sold to the customers. The 8600's main problem was overheating. Cray left CDC in 1972 to start his own firm.

Control Data created the Cyber 70 and 170 series as successors to the 6600 and 7600. The 70 series used old technology. The 170 series used new technology, integrated circuits and semiconductor memory. Later they developed the Cyber 180 series, which was designed to run in the old 60-bit mode (as in the 6600 and 7600) or in 64-bit mode, using the 8-bit ASCII characters. The latter mode was more suited to business data processing.

Control Data acquired many small companies, in its early years. Two of them were Rabinow Engineering and Cedar Engineering. Cedar made electromechanical devices.

The 1604's peripherals were purchased from outside suppliers. CDC manufactured the 1604s themselves. They were able to recruit engineers, to develop peripheral devices, from Univac. Those engineers became very productive. Lundgren described Univac management as "...inept and confused...". Over at CDC, he wrote, it was clear that engineers were running the company, with spectacular results. Lundgren described problems that CDC had with their tape drives, made by the Peripheral Equipment Division. CDC had the 3M company make their tapes, which became the CDC brand.

The Lundgren book describes some of the products he worked on at CDC. The 405 model card reader[39], for example, was excellent, he wrote. It read every card twice, compared the results and kicked out cards that didn't read the same both times. He also worked on optical character reading (OCR) machines, which were the specialty of Rabinow Engineering.

OCR equipment wasn't as popular as keyboard-to-tape machines and keyboard-to-disk machines. These became popular because they allowed customers to avoid using the fragile, bulky punch cards as a storage medium.

Another project at CDC was called SPIN, which was a large, fixed disk system used on the 6600 and 7600 systems. In 1980 sales of CDC's peripherals reached $1 billion per year. [40]

CDC spun off its ETA supercomputer division, located in St. Paul, in 1983. ETA was given the Cyber 205, a newer version of the Star-100, as a product they could sell. ETA produced and sold the ETA-10 supercomputer, but the firm was shut down in 1989 after unsuccessful attempts to sell it.

Due to financial problems, Control data began restructuring in the late 1980s. CDC was renamed in 1992, to Ceridian,[41] which provided software and services, and Control Data Systems, providing systems integration services, was spun off. The latter was acquired by the Syntegra firm. CDC also sold off its peripherals divisions, which made tape drives and disk drives. The disk drive division was named Imprimis and was sold to Seagate Technology in 1989. The Energy Management Division was sold to the Siemens company.

Thus, contrary to popular assumption, Control Data still exists, as Ceridian.

Control Data's Early Days

Lundstrom the author started at CDC on April 15, 1963.[42] He began work at that firm on peripherals, in the Peripheral Equipment Division factory. By that time, CDC was building their new headquarters, a low-rise building, in the Minneapolis suburb of Bloomington. They later built a high-rise tower in that suburb, which still exists.

The author stated that he met William Norris, when he first visited CDC's headquarters. He knew Norris earlier, when they both worked at Univac. One of the products Lundstrom worked on was a magnetic tape drive. One of the models was the 606, which sold for $40,000. He stated that IBM had a similar tape drive, just as good, but their manufacturing cost was just half of CDC's cost. Control Data produced a more rugged tape drive, however.[43]

The above-named peripherals plant also produced the model 405 card reader, which read the popular 80-column cards (no longer in use), sometimes called IBM cards. It would read 20 cards per second, and it would verify the cards by reading each one twice. If the read results were not identical, the card was routed to a reject bin. Typically, rejected cards were damaged in some way. Lundstrom described his impression of the 405 reader: "The model 405 was the finest example of mechanical design that I have ever seen in any peripheral equipment. Its reputation with Control Data customers has won it a unique distinction: it is still listed as an active product in the sales manual."[44] Lundstrom's book was published in 1987.

Lundstrom goes on to describe how CDC tested magnetic tapes. That firm decided that the 3M Company would supply tapes, to be sold with the Control Data label on them. CDC developed their own tape testing machine, and the 3M firm liked it so much, after seeing it in use, that they asked if they could buy a few of the tape testers. CDC sold 3M about 24 of the testing machines.[45]

That author was asked by his managers to evaluate a small company, to decide if CDC should buy it. The firm was Rabinow Engineering, in Rockville, Maryland, which had developed optical character recognition (OCR) equipment. That company's founder, Jack Rabinow, had been granted over 100 patents. The thinking on OCR was that it would be faster and more efficient than reading punched cards, for example. CDC did acquire Rabinow's firm. Optical character recognition is difficult for machines, and errors often occur when reading documents. It is hard to differentiate, for example, between O and Q and 2 and Z.

Lundstrom said he enjoyed his visits with Jack Rabinow. He stated, "One of the fringe benefits of my involvement with Rabinow Engineering was a chance to make customer visits with Jack Rabinow. Jack was one of the wittiest men I have ever known, and he probably could have made a good living as a stand-up comedian."[46]

After the Rabinow acquisition, Lundstrom was asked to decide which type of optical character reader to offer as a Control Data product. It was decided that the first product would be a page reader, called the model 915 Optical Page Reader. But the sales of the 915 were less than expected. That author stated, regarding CDC's OCR products, "...[S]ales were always lower than projected [,] and costs to Control Data were always higher, so the program was never a money-maker."[47] The 915 was very fussy about what it would actually read. The color of the text and the quality of the typewriter ribbons used to create the documents had to be just right for the 915 to work properly. If a poor-quality typewriter ribbon had been used to type a document, the 915 would likely be unable to read it. The 915 model had to be connected to a minicomputer to read documents.[48]

Control Data didn't do well in the OCR business. Jack Rabinow, the OCR engineer, eventually resigned from Control Data, and the Rockville factory was closed in 1976.[49]

The author described another acquisition by CDC. It was called Bridge, Inc. It was "...a machine shop in an industrial section of Philadelphia."[50] Their specialty was card readers, card punches and combined reader/punch peripherals. One of their products became the CDC model 415 card punch. CDC transferred the development of new tape drives to the new Bridge division (later called the Valley Forge Division). The author commented on those products: "The resulting products justified their code name (Pluto, meaning the dog); they were a disaster."[51] That same division later developed a newer generation of tape drives, which were much better, according to Lundstrom.

CDC formed a joint venture in 1972 with the NCR Corp., called Computer Peripherals Inc. (CPI). It was formed from the Valley Forge Division and the Rochester Division, which produced printers of various types. An important thing Lundstrom learned in his computer career was: Technology Doesn't Transfer Well![52]

That author also described a magnetic disk project at the CDC firm, called Project Spin.

It involved large, fixed disks that were used in the 6600 and 7600 supercomputers. The large disks were 28 inches in diameter. As part of Spin, 14-inch removable disk drives were also developed. The larger disks were meant for the supercomputers. IBM had similar products, called the 1301 and the 1311, which encouraged CDC to develop competing products.[53]

Control Data formed another joint venture in 1975, called Magnetic Peripherals Inc., with the Honeywell firm. It consisted of Honeywell's plant in Oklahoma City, which produced smaller disk drives, and the Twin Cities-based Peripheral Equipment Division, which produced the larger disk drives, such as the bigger Spin drives.

Lundstrom also describes his experiences at CDC's Arden Hills plant, where they assembled their large computers, including the 6600 and the 7600 models. CDC had some big problems with the operating systems for the 6600, except for Seymour Cray's COS system. One of the systems was called SIPROS, which was written in Los Angeles, far from Cray's Chippewa Falls lab. SIPROS didn't work very well. CDC gave up on it! That author describes what happened: "SIPROS would be abandoned, and a new operating system based on CHOPS (or COS) would be written, and existing customer contracts would be renegotiated."

The COS system was apparently written by Seymour Cray. The author stated it was "...a rudimentary operating system reportedly written in octal for engineering checkout by Seymour Cray."[54] Octal numbers (base 8) were often used with scientific computers. Hex numbers (base 16) were used with business-oriented machines.

Seymour's COS system was enhanced by Arden Hills people and became the SCOPE system. It became the standard operating system for the 6000 series, replacing the SIPROS system. Other operating systems used on 6000-series machines were NOS, Kronos, for timesharing, and Mace, written by Greg Mansfield and Dave Cahlander. That author stated that Mansfield would work on his Mace system at night, at the Arden Hills plant, when it was easy to get computer time. Mansfield did his programming at the 6600 console, using an editing program, so he wouldn't have to use punch cards. Mansfield would occasionally consult with Cahlander, who had a Ph.D. in electrical engineering, on changes to Mace.[55] The University of Minnesota added to the proliferation of systems, with their own operating system, called MOMS, for Mine and Ours Mace and Scope.

The SCOPE system was enhanced by programmers in Palo Alto and was called SCOPE 3.0. Lundstrom called it "a disaster."[56] Some customers decided to go back to an older version, SCOPE 2.0. Later SCOPE 3.0 was fixed, so it became reliable.

That author commented further on the Mace system: "MACE, while lacking some of the features of SCOPE, ran customers' jobs substantially faster. It was often used to run customer benchmark programs….Inevitably, sophisticated customers demanded and got tapes of MACE, standard product or no."[57] Mace is another example illustrating this author's theory that the best software is written by small groups, meaning four or fewer people. A listing of the 6000-series Compass assembler shows that it was written by two people, at Control Data. It was a reliable product.

One of CDC's customers in Kansas City decided that they wanted to use a 6400 machine (similar to the 6600, but slower) for time-sharing, in 1967. CDC people researched the problem, there being no time-sharing features on that model. They decided that it was possible, but not with the SCOPE operating system. Lundstrom describes the situation: "The current version of SCOPE was deemed totally unsuitable. It was simply too slow in switching between jobs [which occurs often in time-sharing]. MACE, which had been kept fast and lean, looked adaptable to time-sharing. A contract was signed." An enhanced version of Mace became the KRONOS operating system. The author continues, "The KRONOS operating system worked well, the customer bought additional Control Data computers, and the KRONOS operating system became a standard product supported on a level equal to SCOPE."[58]

Lundstrom describes his visit to the famous CDC computer development lab in Chippewa Falls, Wisconsin: "The lab building was a modest, single-story structure of concrete block and brick set slightly back from the steep bank of the [Chippewa] river. Seymour's house was invisible in the thick woods on the other side of the road. The choicest view from the lab, on the side overlooking the river, was given over to a lunchroom for the employees. There was no food service in the lunchroom. Everyone brought sack lunches, but a refrigerator and a stove were provided, as well as a great view through the picture windows…Seymour, dressed in a sport shirt and slacks like the rest of the lab employees, would greet the visitors, then we would sit down for a discussion of the new machine [the 7600 model]. No formal presentations were ever given when I was present, no slide projectors or charts were used, and Seymour's comments were so understated as to be almost comic. I remember an Army colonel asking what would be the performance of the model 7600 as compared to the 6600. Seymour replied that he would be happy if it just ran! Somehow the quiet, low-key discussions were terribly impressive. The image of a man who knew exactly what he was doing came across clearly to the visitors, as they told me afterward.

"The model 7600 was a physically beautiful machine. About six feet high, it had the shape of a hollow rectangle, with an open doorway in the center of one long side, startlingly similar to the Univac I and Univac II, but the 7600 was slightly smaller and it was open at the top. It was also much better looking than the early Univac machines...The model 7600 was cooled by freon, as the 6600 was, so the computer was totally silent."[59] The 7600 model had a maximum speed of about 37 million instructions per second, and an average speed about one-third of that rate. The clock rate was 27 nanoseconds per cycle, for minor cycles.

Seymour Cray was known for admitting his mistakes. If there was a problem with a new design, he didn't mind admitting it and going in a different direction. According to Lundstrom, Cray would say, "That way was wrong; from now on we go this way."[60]

Seymour was know for his dislike of paperwork, such as memos. But he did write a long document about his 7600 model, the reference manual, which was four inches thick.[61]

Lundstrom also describes an airline reservation system that he worked on at CDC, for the former TWA airlines. Control Data, at that time, had little experience with airline systems. The author stated, "CDC knew nothing about modern airline reservations systems, and that fact would become embarrassingly obvious once we started discussions with TWA."[62] He wasn't sure why TWA wanted to work with Control Data in that area. The plan was, eventually, to have dual 7600 computers handling the reservations. The 7600 was the fastest computer in the world when it was announced, in 1968. TWA was using a computerized reservation system at that time, which they called George.[63] It used a Burroughs computer, the model D-830. But Burroughs wasn't planning any new computers in that line. That explains why they were looking at newer, faster machines.

Lundstrom continues, "The [Control Data] TWA study report had estimated that 2 ½ to 3 years would be required to implement an advanced reservation system on dual 7600 computers, so an interim system solution had also been proposed."[64] The interim solution involved dual 6000-series computers, working with the existing George system.

Another part of the project was a new airline ticket printer, which Control Data developed. There were many requirements that the new printer had to meet. Lundstrom listed all eight of them.[65] CDC eventually got the new ticket printer working, and it was tested at the Minneapolis-St. Paul International Airport by Northwest Airlines.[66] At the time, Northwest was using Univac reservations computers.

The TWA project never amounted to much, but the airline compensated CDC for the work they did on that system.

The author described the euphoria after CDC's victory, in January 1973 over IBM in their antitrust suit. He describes a party, held near the company headquarters: "...I felt confident in entering the lobby and checking for the victory party after work.... Tables of hors d'oeuvres and an open bar had been set up. Perhaps a hundred Control Data executives were milling around... One of the executives was complementing Bill [Norris] on his persistence in pressing the lawsuit. 'There are some things a man has just got to do; those bastards deserved it.' was his reply."[67]

He also describes the beginning of ETA systems, in 1983.[68] Their goal was to design and build supercomputers. The were able to produce and sell one model, the ETA-10. Lloyd Thorndyke was the head of ETA. Control Data eventually shut down the ETA firm, in 1989.

Another innovative product from CDC was the Control Data 760, which was a programmable data entry terminal.[69] It included a microprocessor, two diskette drives, a CRT display, and a dot matrix printer was available for the 760. But the product was soon dropped from the product line, because it came too late to the marketplace. But people who worked on the product were angry about discontinuing the 760.

Another terminal developed at CDC was the FTP/80, or Financial Transaction Processor for the 80s.[70] It was meant to replace the nearly-obsolete Cyberloan terminal, made by the German Nixdorf firm. An added feature of the FTP/80 model was that it could do some loan processing internally, without communicating with a mainframe computer. It would only need to communicate with a mainframe to update date files at night.[71]

Control Data had their computer-based education division, called Plato. They decided to produce their own terminal for Plato systems, the Information Systems Terminal, or IST for short. It was a plasma display terminal, originally developed by Magnavox. But CDC decided to develop its own terminal, the IST-1. Later they built the IST-2, with some funding from the Shah's Iran. The Shah at that time was interested in computer-based education.[72] The joint venture with the Iranians failed after the 1979 Iranian revolution.[73]

Lundstrom includes a quote from an ancient Roman in his book:

> We trained hard—but it seemed that every time we were beginning to form up into teams, we would be reorganized. I was to learn that later in life [,] we tend to meet any situation by reorganizing, and a wonderful method it can be for creating the illusion of progress while producing confusion, inefficiency and demoralization. (by Petronius Arbiter, 66 A.D.)

Probably Seymour Cray would have agreed with that quote.

Lundstrom discussed how IBM set up the organization that developed their first popular personal computer, in Boca Raton.[74] But the important parts were not made by IBM. That included the color monitor, the printer, and diskette drives from several companies. Of course, the microprocessor was made by Intel and the operating system, DOS, came from Microsoft. So, IBM mainly designed and assembled the PC they introduced in 1981, using parts made by other firms.

One of the important points made by Lundstrom was, "In high technology it is still true that *the individual makes all the difference* between mediocrity and excellence."[75]

He also said, about managers in the computer industry, "From where we were, senior management seemed overly political, frequently wishy-washy, and occasionally downright dumb, working against their and our own self-interests."[76]

Honeywell

The Honeywell firm was formed by a merger in 1927. The name came from Mark Honeywell, who ran a water heater company.

In the early 1950s, the Raytheon Company asked the Honeywell firm if they wanted to start a joint venture producing digital computers. Honeywell decided in the affirmative, and they started their joint venture in April, 1955. The result was the Datamatic Corp., which was owned by both firms. Datamatic's first product was the Datamatic 1000, a mainframe computer, which they started selling in 1957. That machine had 2000 words of fast memory and 32 instructions in its instruction set. The word size was 8 characters (probably 48 bits).[77]

The Datamatic machine didn't sell very well, so Raytheon dropped out of the joint venture, making Datamatic a division of Honeywell.

Honeywell decided to compete with IBM's popular 1401 model computer. The came out with the H-200 model, which was cheaper than the 1401, offered more memory and faster execution; it ran over ten times faster than the 1401. It also offered a software package called "The Liberator," which translated 1401 programs to run on Honeywell's machines. The H-200 and the Liberator debuted in 1963 and were very successful.[78] IBM's executives were shocked by Honeywell's moves.

The computer division started to show a profit in 1967. Honeywell purchased General Electric's computer division in 1970, which had 25,000 employees. The computer division was renamed Honeywell Information Systems.[79] They moved into microcomputers in the 1970s and did well in that era. But profits dwindled in the early 1980s. Consequently, the firm restructured in that period under the direction of James Renier[80], who headed the computer division; he later was named CEO of Honeywell. One of the computer division's best-known products was the Multics operating system, which was designed for remote access, provided enhanced security features and virtual memory. The division also produced languages, including PL/I, Cobol, Fortran, Basic and APL.

Honeywell sold most of the computer division to France's Group Bull and NEC Corp. of Japan in 1986, retaining a minority stake. The Bull company was formed by Frederick Bull and Knut Kreusen in 1922, with the goal of producing punch card equipment. The firm was reorganized in 1932 as Societe des Machines Bull.[81] They produced electronic calculators, starting in the 1950s, using the Gamma brand name; they produced a series of calulators. Later they moved into digital computers and produced the Gamma ET model, which used delay lines and a drum memory, in 1958.[82]

IBM

IBM was originally called the Computing, Tabulating, Recording Company, which was headed by Charles Flint. The older firm was created in 1911 by merging Computing Scale, Tabulating Machine Company and International Time Recording Company.[83] Herman Hollerith, a tabulating equipment pioneer, sold his company to CTR after he lost the 1910 U.S. Census contract. Of the three CTR divisions, the tabulating machine division grew the fastest. CTR rented the machines. Flint met Thomas Watson, Sr., in 1914 through a mutual friend. Flint offered Watson the position of General Manager (effectively CEO). This was after Watson and other NCR executives had been found guilty in a federal antitrust suit against that firm. The salary was $25,000 per year, and the position included stock options. Watson had left NCR by that time. He accepted the offer and started work on May, 1914.

In 1915, the CTR board named Watson president; he was no longer being prosecuted by that time. The tabulating machine business grew rapidly over the years, but electronic devices were on the horizon; tab machines were electromechanical.

The awkward CTR name was changed to International Business Machines in 1924, which the firm's stock also started to be listed on the New York Stock Exchange.[84] The firm's revenue was only $11 million that year.

In 1946, IBM announced their first electronic product, the IBM 603 Electronic Multiplier, a calculator with 300 vacuum tubes; it only did multiplies. They soon produced a more advanced product, actually an electronic computer, which they called the Defense Calculator, because it was meant for the military. They later renamed it to the 701, which was IBM's first commercial electronic computer. It debuted in January 1953, but it was later to the market than the first computer from Univac, which was introduced in 1951.

But IBM caught up quickly in the sales area. By 1955, IBM was leading Remington Rand, with nearly three times as many machines on order as the Univac division.

One of Watson's sons was Thomas Watson, Jr., who specialized in electronic devices.[85] His father preferred punch card devices.

The Justice Department filed an antitrust suit against IBM in 1952. The complaint was that IBM required customers to buy IBM punch cards, that their machines could only be leased, preventing a secondary market in used machines, and that IBM controlled patents on its machines, preventing other firms from making their own machines, and other charges.[86] The suit was filed by H. Graham Morison, head of the antitrust division.

The antitrust suit was settled in 1956, with a consent decree, which restricted IBM's business practices. They had to make their machines available for sale, and they had to license patents, for example.

The original CEO, Watson, Sr., died on June 19, 1956. He had earlier turned over the presidency to his son, Tom, Jr. This was announced by IBM on Jan. 15, 1952. The announcement didn't say that the son had assumed the CEO role months earlier.[87]

The 702 model was announced soon after the 701. IBM later won the government's SAGE computer contract, to guard against Soviet attacks, beating Remington Rand. A few months later, also in 1956, IBM announced another new machine, the RAMAC 305, an accounting machine.

An IBM employee, John Backus, and four colleagues invented a new language in 1954, according to an IBM web site, which they called Fortran (for FORmula TRANslation); they assumed it would greatly simplify writing programs for digital computers. They worked at IBM's World Headquarters in New York City. Backus wrote that the goal was "to accept a concise formulation of a problem in terms of mathematical notation and to produce automatically a high-speed [IBM] 704 program" for its solution. That goal was stated for the programming language, but it is better stated as the goal for their

Fortran compiler. His group also started writing a Fortran compiler, for translating Fortran into binary, in 1954. They finished it in 1957. It ran initially on the IBM 704 model. The Fortran language and his compiler are described in the article, "The Fortran Automatic Coding System," written by Backus, et al. Backus received several awards for his work on Fortran, including the National Medal of Science.

IBM employees invented several other important computer languages, including PL/I, SQL and APL. SQL was invented by Don Chamberlin and Ray Boyce, of IBM. Edgar Codd wrote a paper about relational databases and how they would work, using SQL: "A Relational Model of Data for Large Shared Data Banks." His proposed relational database structure would use a set of tables, columns and rows, which would be accessed and altered with the SQL language. According to an IBM web site, "Ted's [Codd's] basic idea was that relations between the data items should be based on the item's values, and not on separately specified linking or nesting. This notion greatly simplified the specification of queries and allowed unprecedented flexibility to exploit existing data sets [files] in new ways."

PL/I was invented at IBM's Hursley Laboratories in England and was introduced in 1964. It was originally called NPL, but the name was already in use, so it was changed early on. PL/I was an attempt to combine the best features of Cobol and Fortran.

APL was invented by Ken Iversen, who wrote a book, A Programming Language, published in 1962. Initially, APL was just a type of mathematical notation, until someone wrote an interpreter to translate and execute APL statements. APL is a powerful language, for those who know how to use its many operators. Many APL operators are non-standard characters (not in the ASCII set) and are thus hard to remember. Consequently, some APL's use a different operator syntax, which uses only ASCII characters, such as $S for set and $R for rho.

IBM was sued by Control Data Corp. in 1968, in an antitrust suit. One of the reasons for the antitrust suit was IBM's "paper" machines, 360/90 series models that were announced but not delivered for a long time. CDC didn't get even one order for its 6600 supercomputer for 18 months after the 360/90 series was announced.[88] Some of CDC's executives were skeptical of the suit, but Bill Norris, the CEO, was enthusiastic. It was settled when IBM gave CDC their Service Bureau Corp. and millions in extra money. The federal government later filed its own antitrust suit against IBM, but it was dropped in the early 1980s.

Many of IBM's computer models and its first personal computer are described elsewhere in this book.

Digital Equipment Corp.

Digital Equipment Corporation was founded in 1957 by Ken Olsen and Harlan Anderson. Olsen was the principal founder. He was born in Feb., 1926 in Bridgeport, Conn. His parents were Oswald and Elizabeth Olsen. Ken served in the Navy, where he learned electronics. He obtained a bachelors degree in electrical engineering from MIT in 1950 and a masters in that field in 1952. He married Aulikki Valve in 1950, who was originally from Finland.[89] Anderson had degrees in physics, from the University of Illinois.

Olsen later worked at MIT's Lincoln Labs, developing a computer called the Memory Test Computer in nine months, with the help of his staff. Harlan Anderson also worked at Lincoln Labs. Olsen also worked on Project Whirlwind there, a computer used in a defense project. Olsen also worked at Lincoln Labs as a liaison with IBM on the SAGE defense project.

Olsen didn't much care for IBM. He said, "It was like going to a communist state. They knew nothing about the rest of the world, and the world knew nothing about what went on inside."[90]

In 1957, Olsen and Anderson decided to start their own company. They didn't know much about management and decided to learn about that subject at a local library. The approached a venture capital firm, American Research and Development (ARD) for funding. ARD invested $70,000 for 70% of the company. That was in Aug., 1957.[91] (ARD eventually sold their 70% stake for $400 million, in 1972.)

The pair decided to locate in Maynard, Mass., near Boston. They found office space in an old woolen mill. They rented 8700 square feet of floor space and created Spartan offices. [92] They set up offices using old desks and lawn chairs, for visitors to use. They hired Stan Olsen, Ken's brother, as their first employee. He was an electronic technician. The three hired a lawyer, an accounting firm and found a bank.[93]

Ken became the CEO. Anderson did the more mundane management tasks. Stan became the manufacturing manager. They hired their first secretary, Alma Pontz, an older woman. They were very frugal, declining to install doors, even for bathrooms.[94] They couldn't afford the expenses.

They decided that they had to start producing some products. Their first products were logic modules, the Digital Laboratory Module and the Digital Systems Module. They were first delivered in early 1958. A management professor at the Sloan School of Management, Edgar Schein, commented on Olsen as CEO in 1983: "I have observed a dozen or more entrepreneurs over the last several decades and have consistently found them to be very strong-minded about what to do and how to do it. They typically have strong assumptions about the nature of the world, the role which their organizations will play in the world, the nature of human nature, truth, relationships, time and space."[95]

The new company did well in its first year, showing a small profit.[96] Their PDP-1 project was DEC's first computer. PDP stood for Programmed Digital Processor. They started on that project in the summer of 1959. Ben Gurley was hired to work on the project. The PDP-1 prototype was demonstrated at the EJCC conference in Dec., 1959.[97] Their first PDP-1 was delivered in Nov., 1960. The price tag was $120,000 and the speed was 100,000 adds per second.[98] As one author stated, "DEC's transistorized computer [the PDP-1] provided more power for the price than users ever expected from a computer."[99] It used transistor circuitry and had only 4000 words of memory. DEC used circuits similar to the TX-0 and TX-2 machines built at MIT. Olsen, Anderson and Gurley had done design work on those machines. The school's board of directors decided not to object to DEC's use of the TX-0 and TX-2 designs.[100] DEC built 53 PDP-1 machines in all.

DEC hired Gordon Bell in June, 1960. Bell may have been DEC's best computer designer. As one author stated, "Bell is a computing genius, the Frank Lloyd Wright of computers...If there were a digital hall of fame, Bell's portrait would hang just below Olsen's...His mind races far ahead of his tongue into the corners of space and time, into the microcircuits and arithmetic units that make up computers. He rarely finishes a sentence."[101]

After the PDP-1, DEC started on the PDP-2 and PDP-3, but those projects weren't completed. Then they started on the PDP-4, which was successful but didn't sell very well. Only 54 PDP-4s were sold.[102]

Their next machine was the PDP-6, with a 36-bit word, which DEC delivered in the fall of 1964. That product required a lot of DEC's resources and turned out to be unreliable. Despite its problems, Anderson and Bell supported it within DEC. The firm only sold 23 of those machines in all.[103]

Olsen created the matrix structure at DEC. It worked well for a long time, "Whatever his motivation, Olsen was given full credit for devising a business structure built for high growth."[104]

Harlan Anderson was chosen to head the PDP-6 project. It was a troubled project, and the CEO thought of it as a way to move Anderson out of the company. He finally left the company in early 1966. Anderson got some of the blame for the PDP-6's problems. Also in that year, Gordon Bell left for a sabbatical, at Carnegie-Mellon University.[105] The PDP-6 was later revised as the DEC10.

DEC's next project was the PDP-5, headed by Nick Mazzarese. The first machine was shipped in early 1964. The price was only $27,000. The machine had core memory and DEC sold about 1000 of them in all.

Olsen hired Peter Kaufmann, a manufacturing expert. He was put in charge of hundreds of employees. Olsen came to rely on him. Olsen also relied on management professor Ed Schein of MIT. He helped to improve the management structure and communication at DEC. He also helped to organize management meetings at remote locations.

Schein also helped to improve DEC's matrix management structure. Each product line had a manager, who sometimes needed resources from other groups. Schein wrote a book, Organizational Culture and Leadership, which includes some examples from DEC.

Product lines were an important part of matrix structure. A DEC vice president, Ted Johnson, stated, "The product lines had the power. He who has the gold, rules."[106]

Olsen wasn't in charge of any products in the era. But he had a lot of influence on products, so he could just hint at what he wanted to have changes made, without giving orders. [107] The Operations Committee also had a lot of power. Johnson stated, "Ken let the middle run the company, and the Operations Committee was the bank. The product lines cane for investments [funds they needed], and we on the committee would fight it out among ourselves."[108]

DEC was run as an informal organization, compared to IBM, which was more formal. DEC didn't have reserved parking spaces. DEC's office furnishings were not related to the employee's status. People who had offices with windows could have low status, for example.[109]

Another new machine the PDP-8, was announced in the fall of 1965. It was a cheaper version of the PDP-5, going for $18,000, and it sold well. DEC sold over 50,000 of the PDP-8 machines. The PDP-8 was popular, partly due to its low price tag. It sold for under $10,000.

Stan Olsen hired Edson de Castro as an engineer. de Castro later started the Data General firm, with several employees from DEC. Their headquarters was in Hudson, Mass. DG's first product was the 16-bit Nova machine. It sold well by 1969.

DEC didn't sue Data General. But Ken didn't like the new company. He said DG was an unethical enterprise doomed to failure. Speaking 20 years later, Ken said, "I'm quite serious when I say the wisest thing we did was not sue Data General. Things were pretty bad. ...Anger tears your heart out. The emotions would have been so negative, it would have torn us apart. We made computers instead."[110] DEC didn't want to be seen as the big company picking on the small startup firm.

DEC initially was not generous with stock options. But after the exodus to Data General, the firm decided to more liberal with the options. One author summarized DEC's options policy: "The people most likely to get significant stock options were, and still are, engineers. Other DEC employees displaying outstanding initiative and performance also receive small options periodically, but rarely in the amounts aimed at engineers. Engineers, in Olsen's mind, are the company's lifeblood."[111]

Maybe because engineers were treated so well, "DEC was regarded as the ultimate employer by engineers."[112] It was hard to get a job at DEC. Sometimes a candidate had to endure seven or eight interviews to get an offer.[113] DEC didn't have a history of layoffs. As the CEO said, "It's good business for our people to have confidence that we will not lay them off just to help our short-term profit."[114] He commented further on layoffs: "We never promised never to have layoffs, but it seems common sense to avoid it [sic]. When a company has to have a layoff, it's often the management's fault. So at least for awhile, we should take the licking, not the employees."[115] During lean times, some DEC employees were put to work doing menial jobs, such as sweeping the parking lot. If a new employee at DEC was struggling, the person would sometimes be shifted to a position that seemed to be a better fit.[116]

DEC's management structure was informal. There were no reserved parking spaces, and office furnishings weren't related to the employee's status. A lower-level employee, for example, might have an office with windows. Olsen wasn't very status-conscious; he didn't drive a fancy car.[117] DEC salespeople didn't work for commissions. They received a straight salary. Olsen had a "death row" for executives that had failed. They had no responsibilities. The assumption was that they would either leave the company, or that their skills would be used on a new project. If an employee quit, DEC didn't want him to return.[118] Few executives quit in the 70s, because it was such a period of rapid growth.

An important philosophy at DEC was "Do the right thing."[119] The "right thing" wasn't formally defined. It would depend on the circumstances. Olsen's view was that management should guide and advise. He thought a manager would own the problem when he makes a decision. He felt an executive can be more objective if he isn't deeply involved in the project.[120] The CEO set up an informal network at DEC to stay informed. The networks included some mid-level engineers. Presumably, Olsen thought he would get better information if it wasn't filtered through several levels of managers. Before approving a new product, Olsen looked for consensus.[121] Another management technique he used was described by a former DEC executive, "Ken keeps very tight control on that company, always has and always will."[122]

DEC engineers would work with customers to find new uses for DEC machines, including simulation and process control. Customers included AT & T, du Pont and GM.[123] But DEC didn't develop much software for such purposes. DEC opened a local headquarters in Geneva, in 1969.

Getting back to hardware, the new PDP-11 machine, with a 16-bit word, was a successor to the PDP-8. Competitors had earlier introduced their own 16-bit machines, so there was pressure on that group to get the new machine out quickly.[124] The PDP-11 was introduced in Jan., 1970 and sold at a low price, $10,800. It became very popular; over 250,000 of the machines were sold.[125]

Gordon Bell returned to DEC in 1972, as vice president of engineering. His office, at that time, was just across the hall from the CEO's office in Maynard.[126]

Michael Weinstein, an ex-reporter, started work at DEC in the early 70s. In his view, "DEC was a wild place, the Wild West. ...You could see it in the terminology—there were wizards and gurus, a whole underground of technofreaks....It was a company that captured an image and a spirit, a counterculture. ...We knew we were going to win."[127]

In 1974, Olsen wrote down DEC's fundamental values. They were in the areas of: honesty, profit, responsibility, customers, simplicity, and clarity. There was also Olsen's First Rule: "When dealing with a customer, vendor or an employee, do what is 'right' in each situation." [128]

Olsen often worked odd hours, and he would sometimes call managers at any time, day or night.

At least officially, DEC didn't discriminate by gender or skin color. But women were hired for non-professional positions, such as secretarial work. Olsen seemed to be a sexist also, such as when he said, during a demonstration, "It's so easy, even a girl can do it."[129] But women could rise to high-level positions. Mary Jane Forbes, Gordon Bell's secretary, became an expert on word processors at DEC. She became an early advocate of the DECmate word processing system and even gave seminars on word processing at DEC.[130]

DEC appointed it first female vice president in 1974, Rose Giordano.[131]

DEC was growing rapidly in the 70s. By 1974, the firm had occupied all 12 Mill buildings and was using just over one million square feet of space at the Mill complex. But it wasn't enough. After filling up the Mill complex, they created a multi-building complex called Parker Street, in the Maynard area.

Also in 1974, DEC was seeking new lines of business. They moved into computer terminals and integrated circuits. Andrew Knowles, an Operations Committee member, advocated producing LSI (Large Scale Integration) circuits. Their first LSI product, the LSI-11, was introduced in 1974.

Gordon Bell made some interesting comments on his CEO about that time: He said the average CEO is "about a one-tenth Olsen. ...Ken was the most demanding person I ever worked for, but I felt he had several blind spots. He's a very physical-thinking person. I could not communicate with him at an abstract level. ...Occasionally it was fun to build things with him, but mostly it was a pain because he would mostly resort to bossing and ridicule instead of logic to win his way ...which was often wrong."[132]

Ken respected Stan, his brother, but he was often thought of as the dumb guy. Ken didn't hire any other relatives at DEC, probably because he worried about nepotism comments. Stan pushed for a word-processing initiative in the early 70s. Stan and Jack Gilmore created the DECmate word-processing system, but it cost $22,000, a high price at that time. DEC's goal at that time was to beat Wang Labs, a leader in word processing. The DECmate was poorly marketed and didn't sell well.

DEC expanded to New Hampshire in 1975; Stan moved 650 employees to a new facility in Merrimack. The CEO thought that DEC was too concentrated in Massachusetts. Eventually, DEC had 7000 employees in New Hampshire.[133]

In 1976, DEC introduced distributed data processing, which allowed any part of an organization to access the computer power it needed. Also in that year, minicomputers were recognized as a separate industry, with revenues of $5 billion.[134] Another event that year was the introduction of the VT100, a so-called intelligent terminal that became famous in the computer industry.

In 1977, DEC's revenues reached $1 billion. At that time, the firm had 38,000 employees and 41% of the world's minicomputer business.[135]

DEC's matrix management structure caused chaos for that firm in the market place. One reason was that salesmen and engineers would contradict each other. Each group would promise different things to the customers. DEC initially didn't provide the service that other computer firms, such as IBM and Honeywell, provided to their customers.

Consequently, Jack Shields, an executive, set up a service organization at DEC, which ran at a profit. They also created a remote diagnosis system, to discover and prevent problems with user's DEC machines.[136] Shields was promoted to vice president in 1974, in recognition of his achievements in the service area.

Departments at DEC would often compete with each other, causing confusion for the customers.

DEC occasionally hired MBAs, but they didn't have the technical knowledge that was so valued at DEC, so they weren't likely to move very far up the ladder.[137] One manager described how to prosper in the matrix environment at DEC: "You don't go in at Digital, sit down at your desk and get your job done. I don't care how good the electronic mail system or the network is, you have to get out from behind your desk. You have to get face to face with individuals and groups to really make something happen."[138] Power was distributed throughout DEC. For a new product to be introduced at DEC, unanimous approval was required. Some managers had veto power.[139]

Quality was very important at DEC. Profit and growth were also important. Olsen said that innovation was also important, along with quality.[140]

The VAX (Virtual Address eXtension) was a 32-bit machine introduced in 1977. It came with a new operating system, VMS. Bell was in charge of the VAX project and originated the idea. Other senior people on that project were: Strecker, Demmer, Rodgers and Cutler. The first VAX machine was the 11/780 "superminicomputer". A DEC networking system was developed for the VAX machines. Later versions of the VAX included the microprocessor-based Microvax and the Microvax II.

Bell said, about the VAX project, "Ken had absolutely no role, as president or engineer, in VAX, beginning with its inception."[141] Of course, computer architecture wasn't one of the CEO's areas of expertise.

An important feature of the VAX is that it included the PDP-11, meaning that it could run PDP-11 programs.[142] Bell knew that this feature was needed to keep DEC's customers happy. Bell stated, "Though he strongly believed that the

PDP-11 architecture was doomed, Bell knew that thousands of [PDP-]11 users would raise Cain if they were suddenly abandoned."[143]

The new machine was called the VAX-11, to emphasize the PDP-11 feature.

Gordon Bell described the VAX strategy: It would be part of a three-tier model, with mainframes at the top, then minis, and terminals or PCs at the bottom. Departments would use minis, and all the machines would be connected to a network.[144]

Bell wanted a single VAX architecture. He wrote, in an internal memo: "The essence of the strategy is simplicity through adopting a single architecture. Although superficially it appears to be possible to have numerous architectures that are segmented by size and by market, the user requirements to cross both size and application boundaries are significant. ... The most compelling reason for basing the strategy on the single VAX architecture, besides the technical excellence of the product, is the belief that we cannot build the truly distributed computing system of the '80s with heterogeneous architectures."[145]

The first VAX machine was produced in Oct., 1977. Olsen was there, and he turned on the machine. The metal handles got hot and burned his hand. Olsen called VAX "the most significant interactive computer of the last decade."[146] Other models included the 11/780, which ran at one million instructions per second, and the 11/750, which wasn't as fast. Later models included the Microvax and the Microvax II.

Bell railed against IBM's many incompatible machines, such as the 8100. He said, "I wanted to beat the shit out of IBM—that was simple. It was going to be really easy if they didn't straighten out."[147] But DEC's other executives preferred the status quo. Many of them thought the PDP-11 was adequate and didn't see the need for a VAX family of machines.[148] But Bell wanted less investment in software for the PDP-11. He thought the resources should go into the VAX's VMS operating system.

Olsen had doubts about the VAX strategy, but it was approved by the Board of Directors in Dec., 1978.[149]

The most important feature of the VAX machines was their nearly unlimited memory. To programmers and users, the machine would appear to have an enormous amount of random access memory (4.3 gigabytes), but in reality much of it was kept on one or more fast disk drives and retrieved or written out as needed. Accessing memory on disk drives was automatic and hidden from most users. Virtual addressing and virtual memory are old concepts in computer science and aren't used much now, because of the large memories used in personal computers, servers and other computers DEC introduced a popular terminal used with the VAX models, the VT 100, a video display terminal.[150]

DEC later developed DECnet, a networking system that was used to tie DEC's machines together. It was based on Xerox's Ethernet. Bob Metcalfe, the inventor of Ethernet, commented on DEC's networking strategy: "I believe the company's focusing on networking explains DEC's success and IBM's relative failure."[151] DEC worked with Xerox and Intel on its networking systems.

An April, 1979 Fortune magazine article described DEC's problems: "To achieve its long-term goal, DEC is willing to accept some internal disorder and sacrifice immediate profits. …But in recent years, DEC has acquired a reputation for being mismanaged."[152] Data General was described in that article as a fast-growing and well-run high-tech competitor of DEC.

DEC's matrix management was causing them problems in Europe. The European offices expected headquarters to give them orders, but Olsen expected that they would decide what to do.

DEC eventually started producing personal computers after IBM, which itself was five years later than Apple getting into that industry.

DEC opened their own retail stores to sell PCs. They were called Digital Business Centers, which opened in 1978. They opened 30 of them. But Ken didn't like PCs. The DECmate did poorly competing with products from Wang Laboratories. One reason was that that model used PDP-8 technology instead of the newer PDP-11 technology. But Olsen was far more interested in funding the VAX models.[153]

Several DEC groups tried to develop PCs, including Stan (DECmate group), Knowles (Components group) and Gordon Bell (VAX group, etc.).[154] DEC developed a PC called the PDT, or Programmable Data Terminal. It was created by the Components group, led by Andrew Knowles. His terminals section invented that model, which was developed for the ADP Corp.[155]

Dan Bricklin wanted to writer a spreadsheet program, later called Visicalc, for the PDT, but he wasn't able to buy one of those machines. So he borrowed an Apple II model and wrote Visicalc, which really helped Apple II sales, meaning Apple won and DEC lost.

David Ahl at DEC proposed a new PC based on the PDP-8, but smaller. It would be in a single box and sell for $5000. That was in 1974. But Ken said, "Why would anyone need a computer of their own?...The world is going time-sharing."[156] Ken was right at that time. There weren't any user-friendly PCs available when he made that comment.

But by 1980 there were more than a dozen PC models being developed at DEC. Many of them were described as intelligent terminals.[157] Of course, this showed there was a lack of focus in the PC area.

The CEO never could decide on the one best PC model to sell. Olsen said, "The personal computer will fall flat on its face in business."[158] Of course, that seems amusing now. He wanted DEC to build mini-computers, not home computers. But his emphasis soon changed, after DEC's PC problems became public knowledge. He said DEC should make "computers for clerks and clerics."[159]

In 1979 a new employee, Avram Miller, was placed in charge of a new PC project, called KO, for Knock Out. His group developed the DEC Professional PC. Two other groups were also developing new PC models, the Rainbow and a new DECmate model. Olsen decided that DEC would sell all three PC models. But DEC didn't do well in the PC area. As Avram Miller stated, "The market figured out who was right, and it was IBM."[160]

Ken's brother Stan slowly left DEC. In 1981, he took one year off. Ken didn't object. Stan switched to the real estate business and never returned to DEC.

Ken announced three new PC models in May of 1982: the Professional (325 and 350), the Rainbow 100 and the DECmate II. Computerworld liked the new machines, commenting "Analysts are generally impressed with all the systems [PCs], finding them extremely competitive with the IBM PC in both functionality and price."[161] Unfortunately, the three PC models were incompatible with each other. The first IBM PC was announced in Aug., 1981. IBM sold hundreds of thousands of PCs in the first year after the announcement.

Another problem was that the three DEC PCs came out nearly one full year after the first IBM PC. Also, dozens of firms had introduced new PCs by the time of DEC's May announcement.

DEC was in turmoil in the early 1980s. VAX models weren't being manufactured fast enough to meet demand. DEC also had the same problems with PCs in the year after Ken's PC announcement. As one author stated, "Digital was not used to failure, and that's just what the PCs were bringing to the company."[162]

DEC reorganized again starting in July, 1982. Olsen scrapped the product lines and created three regional management centers. He also combined manufacturing and engineering. But the turmoil caused some problems. Many executives left due to the reorganization, including Andy Knowles. More than 50 managers left in all.[163] DEC lost 16 vice presidents due to the reorganization.

DECtown happened about that time and lasted several days. It was held at a convention facility in Boston. 16 new products were unveiled, but few details were revealed at that time. Consequently, the media made scathing comments about DEC.

One author commented on the reorganization: "Initially the reorganization created more chaos than the structure it replaced. ...New administrative systems weren't put in place quickly enough. Forecasting, order processing and production schedules were in turmoil." [164]

The Rainbow was the best seller among the three DEC PC models that Ken announced. Overall, DEC lost $900 million on its three PC models. One reason for that problem was that DEC's PC marketing was chaotic. The Rainbow model, for example, wasn't available at DEC's Business Centers stores. Olsen summed up the PC problems by saying, "We lost our shirt in that market [PCs]." [165]

Another perspective on DEC's PCs was given by Barry Folsom, a DEC executive in the PC area, in a memo to Olsen: "We can't fight both DEC and IBM. I want to fight IBM. Please let us." Folsom was referring, for example, to excessive time spent on getting the right colors and lettering on his marketing materials.[166]

After some assets were sold off, the remaining parts of DEC were purchased by the Compaq Computer Corp. in Jan.,1998, for $9.6 billion; by then,

DEC's headcount had fallen by more than 50% from the peak mentioned above. Compaq was later acquired by the Hewlett-Packard Corp., in 2002.

Wang Laboratories

An Wang obtained his degree in electrical engineering at the Chiao Tung University in Shanghai, China. He came to the U.S as part of a program to help China recover after the Second World War.[167] The program was sponsored by the Nationalist government of China. He had to take an exam to qualify for the program. His score put him in second place. Wang soon arrived in Virginia, in June, 1945.[168] He was scheduled to be in the U.S for two years and received a monthly stipend for his expenses.

Wang decided to go to Harvard rather than work for an American firm. He applied there, without including a transcript. He and several others from the Chiao Tung University were accepted at Harvard. Wang majored in applied physics. Harvard accepted Wang, and he started classes there in September, 1945.[169] He completed his masters degree in 1946. He started working on his Ph.D. in February, 1947. Wang was awarded his Ph.D. in applied physics in 1948.[170]

His first job was at the Harvard Computation Laboratory as a research fellow, working for Howard Aiken, who designed the Mark I, or ASCC, computer, which is described in this book. Wang started there in May, 1948. He soon produced an invention that made history and changed the computer industry for decades.

He was given his first assignment by Dr. Aiken: "...[T]he problem Dr. Aiken gave me was simple, but seemingly impossible. He wanted me to find a way to record and read magnetically stored information without mechanical motion."[171] He goes on to describe his invention: "I had resolved that the best way to store the magnetic information was a doughnut-shaped configuration called a toroid, because with this shape far less current was needed to create or reverse a continuous magnetic field."[172] But Wang realized that reading the state of the toroid would cause the information to be destroyed. He soon came up with a solution to that problem: "With the information I gained from reading the magnetic memory, I could simply rewrite the data immediately afterward."[173]

His next problem was to find the right material for the magnetic toroids and to connect them together to produce an actual computer memory. Of course, the computer would need a way to read and write the bits at random to produce a practical memory. The material he found was a nickel-iron alloy which had the trade name Deltamax. A few years later, a better material was found, ferrites. Wang's initial scheme for core (toroid) memories was similar to the mercury delay lines then in use, with cores accessed serially, but it didn't become popular.

A better way to arrange the cores was found by Dr. Jay Forrester, of MIT, who came up with the matrix invention. Wang describes the invention in his book: "Dr. Forrester's idea was to organize a number of cores into a grid, or matrix, as he called it. Each core would be wrapped around the intersection of two wires. If he ran only half the current needed to reverse the magnetic field of a core through any one wire, the only place the current would be strong enough to reverse a field would be at the intersection of two wires. There the sum of the two currents would surpass the amount needed to reverse the magnetic flux of the core. In this way, he could specify exactly which core he wanted to read. ... With a system like this, memory size could expand far beyond the few thousand bits permitted by the other high-speed systems then available. " [174] Core memories became very popular in mainframe computers, such as the IBM 360 series.

Dr. Wang obtained a patent on his magnetic core invention, which he eventually sold to IBM.

He turned in his resignation at the Computation Laboratory in April, 1951 and left his position there in June. Wang wanted to do basic computer research, which was ending at Harvard. That same month, he started his new business, Wang Laboratories. [175] He started with $600 in savings and found office space in the Boston area. As he stated, "My capital was six hundred dollars in savings, and I had no orders, no contracts, and no office furniture." [176] He decided that his first product would be the familiar Deltamax memory cores. He also contacted the Commerce Department to get a list of RFPs, so he could bid on contracts.

Later Wang cashed out his Harvard pension plan and got an additional $2000. With the extra savings, he estimated that he could he could keep going for a year, while working at his new company. [177]

Dr. Wang, at that time, was constantly thinking about new products that his company might be able to build. One example was described in a notebook he kept: "Make plans to build at least one such unit [a digitalizer and counter]...to be demonstrated at next year's IRE Convention Exhibition."[178] The IRE was the Institute for Radio Engineers. Wang started selling magnetic cores of Deltamax for $4 each, which is very costly by today's standards. At that price, one gigabyte of memory would cost $32 billion!

His first employee was Bob Gallo, who had studied advertising at Boston University. He was paid 55 cents per hour. Bob was assigned to assemble magnetic cores and to greet and talk to visitors when Dr. Wang was away.

Wang's first child, Fred, was born in 1950. He later had another son, Courtney, and a daughter, Juliette. In 1955, Dr. Wang and his wife became naturalized American citizens. They had earlier decided that they didn't want to return to China and live in the People's Republic. [179]

Another early product of his company was a digital counting device, which he priced at $4 each, or $2.90 in large volumes. He decided that digital computers were just too costly to develop. Of course, Wang Labs would later sell electronic calculators and computers.

Wang got a chance to show off his products in December, 1951 at an IRE conference in New York city. His booth got a lot of attention, and he received many orders for the products. To supplement his income from the company, he taught a course in electrical engineering at Northeastern University evening school, for $12 per lecture. [180]

Dr. Wang stated that he made $3253.60 in the last six months of 1951 working at his company, slightly more than he made at the Computation Lab in the previous six months.

In 1952, he received a contract to develop a pulse synchronizer and a counting device, for $300 per week, a big increase. At that time, Wang developed a number of products that seemed to be practical, but he couldn't always sell them. He wrote a program, for example, to display numbers on a CRT and a device to count red and white blood cells. The latter wasn't completed because it needed an advanced microscope that wasn't available.

Wang had some early encounters with IBM, because they wanted to use his core memory invention in new computers that they were developing. He obtained his core memory patent on May 17, 1955. It was Patent No. 2,708,722. The following March, IBM bought Wang's patent for $500,000, with a possible $100,000 to be paid later. IBM also bought a memory patent from another inventor, Fred Viehe, about that time. [181] Wang decided that selling his patent was prudent, because he needed to devote his time to new products. [182]

One of the firm's important products was the Linasec, a phototypesetting system. Wang developed the product, but they relied on another firm, Compugraphic, to do the marketing and selling. But Compugraphic later decided to manufacture the machine themselves. They didn't need to pay a royalty, and the Linasec was developed under a contract with Compugraphic. Of course, that was an important lesson for Dr. Wang. In his words, "I vowed at that time never again to design and manufacture a product for another company to market." [183]

Another of their products was circuit boards containing transistors, which their customers could use to build digital products. They were called Logiblocs. They also produced control units for machine tools, called Weditrol, or Wang Electronic Digital Control units, for about $700 each.

Wang's firm formed an alliance with Warner and Swasey, a machine tool maker. They provided capital to Wang Labs, but Dr. Wang decided that the alliance wasn't a good decision. In his words, "...I regretted the alliance almost at once." [184] He stated that he didn't need the money from the other firm, the alliance wasn't a good strategic move, and the venture placed restrictions on issuing new Wang stock. But the money from Warner and Swasey allowed his firm to develop the Linasec product.

Another use for that money was the development of the electronic LOCI calculator. [185] LOCI meant LOgarithmic Calculating Instrument. It used logarithms to do multiplies and divides. In other words, it added or subtracted logarithms of numbers to multiply or divide them. Wang stated that he found a simple method of producing logarithms, which he called the factor-combining method. The LOCI device sold for $6500 initially. Calculators from other firms at that time were much more cumbersome to use. But a picture of the LOCI shows that it had many keys and buttons (many more than today's calculators), so probably it was meant for scientists and engineers to use. Wang stated that the device was programmable, like some of today's calculators.[186] He also stated that he applied for a patent on the LOCI, in 1964.

Wang soon developed a new calculator the Model 300, which was smaller and easier to use. A picture shows that it only had a few keys, about one-third as many as the LOCI model. Regarding the LOCI, Wang also stated: "When business people multiply, they do not want to deal with work registers, logarithmic registers, and accumulators; they want to type in the figures and read the result on the display."[187]

Their new model, the 300, eliminated some of the problems of the LOCI. They priced the new device at $1695, close to what the competition was charging. An improved design and better engineering allowed them to price the 300 model for much less than the LOCI. The Wang firm had subcontractors manufacture the circuit boards, and Wang employees assembled them, at their Tewksbury facility.

The 300 produced profit margins of 65 percent or more. It 300 was a popular product. Wang commented that they had to hire many new employees to expand their line of calculator products. As he stated, "From thirty-five employees in 1964, we grew to more than four hundred in 1967."[188] Wang thought of the 300 model as more powerful than a slide rule but not as powerful as a minicomputer. He commented on the product's usability: "This was the first product made by Wang laboratories whose end user could be just about anybody."[189]

Wang came out with new calculator models based on the 300. There was a version for scientists and engineers, a version for finance people and a version for statistics people. They created application packages for various industries.

Wang Labs opened foreign offices about that time, in Britain, Belgium and Taiwan. Dr. Wang thought of the U.K. as "…a natural market for a calculator developed in the United States."[190] That was because of the shared language and his familiarity with that country. He liked Belgium because it was an entry point to the EEC (today the EC), with no additional tariffs to sell products in other European countries. Wang liked Taiwan because it was a new market and because they could assemble products there at low cost. One example was the magnetic cores that they had made in that country.

Dr. Wang decided to take his firm public in 1967. The idea came from their banker at the First National Bank of Boston, who thought they were borrowing too much, compared to the net worth of the company. The Tucker, Anthony firm was hired to manage the offering, along with the White, Weld company. The company's stock began trading on Aug., 23, 1967. It started trading at $38 per share, compared to the Initial Public Offering price of $12.50. The Wang firm had a net worth of about $1 million, just before the IPO. But at the end of the first day's trading, the company's market value was about $70 million.[191] The stock closed the first day at $40.50, giving the stock a price/earnings ratio of 80, which is four to five times the value a growth stock would normally have. In its first year of trading, the stock went as high as $120 per share.[192]

Dr. Wang described the reaction at his firm: "Wang shareholders, including myself, watched our personal fortunes increase in lockstep with the stock. There was jubilation in the offices. I remember hearing my secretary, who had exercised an option to buy a hundred shares, shout 'I'm rich, I'm rich!' A number of employees did make a good deal of money, even if they did not become rich."[193] The shares held by Dr. Wang and his family, at that time, had a value of about $50 million.

Even after the successful IPO, Dr. Wang heard people tell him to change the name of his firm, to avoid discrimination. But he decided to retain the name, reasoning that many U.S. companies have names with foreign origins, including Levi Strauss and du Pont.

Dr. Wang thought his firm went public at an opportune time, between late 1967 and late 1969, when there was a lot of interest in owning high-tech stocks. The Wang firm had another public offering, in January, 1970, but that was the last favorable time until 1976, according to Dr. Wang. As he stated, "This was the last sale of stock we were to have for seven years. Shortly after this, both the stock market and the economy turned bad, and the capital markets were effectively closed until 1976. …We could have survived without going public, but it would have greatly slowed our rate of growth."[194]

He stated that the public offerings also helped them bring out their innovative calculator products, before competitors could respond. But Dr. Wang said, of the calculator market, "In fact, I made a deliberate decision to get out of it, even as the market continued to grow."[195] Wang realized that profit margins in calculators would drop sharply, as more companies entered that market.

The Wang firm decided to move on and develop computers. Their first machine was called the 4000, which was completed by spring, 1968. Dr. Wang decided that it was not as good as the more-famous DEC PDP-8 minicomputer. He decided that his firm needed better programming expertise, to write operating systems (very challenging). But they found the expertise they needed. Their company acquired Philip Hankins, Inc., located in the Boston area.

Their main business was supplying data processing services. But they also developed software for Wang's newer computers, including the 3300 Basic model and the 700 model.[196] The 3300 model included the Basic language, developed at Dartmouth college. The 700 model was later modified to change it into a calculator. It became very successful. Dr. Wang said it was easier to sell the 700 as a calculator than as a computer. Of course, managers back then knew that computers cost much more than calculators.

The 3300 model wasn't easy to use. The Basic interpreter had to be loaded into the computer's memory using paper tape, which required about 40 minutes. It also used a Teletype terminal, which Dr. Wang said was not as useful as a CRT.[197]

The Wang firm decided to get out of the calculator business, but slowly. They would slowly phase out the cheaper series, the 300, the 200 and the 100. But they would continue marketing the pricier 400, 600 and 700 models.

They then started working on another computer model, the 2200, which was much better than the 3300 machine. It came with a CRT terminal and used diskettes to read in programs and data rather than the cumbersome paper tape used with the earlier model. The Basic interpreter was kept on a ROM chip. The 2200 was completed in late 1972.

Wang's next major product line was word processors. As Dr. Wang stated in 1970, "…I decided that we should go after the word processing market in earnest."[198] The technology that they started with in that area was the 700 model calculator, which worked with IBM Selectric typewriters. Those typewriters could get information from magnetic tape cassettes. They leased, used and studied IBM's Magnetic Tape Selectric Typewriter for two years before developing their word processing system, which they called the 1200, introduced in Nov., 1971. It was based on their 700 model. The 1200 used an automatic typewriter, which could be used to edit documents. The documents could be saved or retrieved from a tape cassette. The 1200 could print letters at a speed of 175 words per minute. Dr. Wang stated that the 1200 would cut the cost of producing a business letter by 50%.

The Wang firm used the Selectric as a terminal for their 1200 model. However, the IBM typewriter often didn't work properly. IBM technicians were called in to work on the problem, and they discovered that all of the Selectrics the firm was using were missing an essential part, a spring. The technicians soon repaired all the Selectrics at the Tewksbury facility. Even so, Wang executives were irate. One of their executives placed a call to an IBM vice president. He said, "You people have been screwing us. You have been selling us a product knowingly with missing parts. We just had a loss for the first time in the company's history, and you're absolutely responsible."[199]

The 1200 had other problems. It didn't have a CRT terminal, which would have made editing much easier; the terminal was the Selectric. Wang eventually added a one-line CRT display to the 1200, to simplify editing.

Wang introduced two new products in 1976, the 2200 and the WCS, or Wang Computer System. They also introduced a new word processor about that time, called the WPS, which used a CRT terminal for editing. The WPS was introduced in June, 1976 at a trade show in New York City. Speaking of the introduction, Dr. Wang commented, "Word spread like wildfire about the machine, and within moments of the first demonstration, people were lined up ten deep at the booth. The hospitality suite became so jammed that we had to issue invitations in order to control the crowds."[200] He described the new machine as a "revolutionary piece of equipment." He said the WPS was better than any other word processors available at that time. The new WPS had a list price of $30,000. Dr. Wang had to restructure their sales department to make sure the new product would sell adequately.[201] His company also used television ads for several months to make Wang word processors more visible to potential customers. They got the idea from IBM's TV ads.[202] Wang was able to run an ad just before the Super Bowl game, in January, 1978, which helped even more. A survey showed that Wang's name recognition nearly quadrupled after their TV ad campaign. Dr. Wang said his firm's sales also soared after the ad campaign. He also said the some competitors, such as DEC and Data General, started TV advertising as a result.

The Wang firm used the foothold they got with word processing to gain market share in data processing (minicomputers) and communications. By 1985, the trade press acknowledged that Wang was the industry leader in word processing.[203]

Starting in 1975, Dr. Wang realized that his firm would need more financing, to develop a new word processing system that used CRT terminals. They were advised to issue a new class of stock. But then they would have to move from the New York Exchange to the American Stock Exchange, due to the NYSE rules. They created a new class, Class B shares. They would have a higher dividend yield, but just 10% of the voting power of the Class A shares. The new Class B shares began trading on the AMEX on April 21, 1976. The Class A shares had moved there from the NYSE. Later they renamed the Class A shares and called them Class C, to increase trading of the Class B shares.[204] Dr. Wang stated that his firm would still have grown without the new financing, but the growth rate would have been at most 20% annually. Retaining voting control for his family was an important goal for Dr. Wang.[205]

The firm's CEO predicted, in 1976, that his company would have one billion dollars in revenues in ten years. In fact, they reached that goal in six years. Their revenues were only about $100 million in 1976.[206]

Their next major product was the VS (Virtual Storage) line of computers. It was a line of minicomputers, with model 300 being the largest; it was nearly as powerful as a mainframe. That new product line was announced in Oct., 1977. Their previous minicomputer was the 2200, which Dr. Wang had some disadvantages, such as not having Fortran or Cobol available.[207] The VS series sold slowly at first, but then the firm added word processing capabilities, which helped sales.

The next year, they added networking capabilities. All of their machines were networked, which greatly helped sales.[208]

In 1979 they announced their latest innovation, IIS or Integrated Information Systems. The goal of IIS was to integrate word processing with data processing. Their intent was to provide distributed data processing, with minicomputers so that users need not wait hours or days to get their results from a mainframe computer. (Slow batch processing using mainframes was very common in the 1970s.) Each department in a large company could have their own minicomputer, which would be accessible via terminals, giving much faster response.[209]

Corporate MIS (Management Information Systems) departments didn't like the idea of distributed data processing, but they accepted it as long as the minicomputers could communicate with the company's mainframe computers.[210]

At its peak, Wang Labs was a three-billion-dollar company, with 30,000 employees. Dr. Wang said one of the keys to their success was their motto, "Find a need and fill it."[211] One of the ways they uncovered needs was the Wang Listens program. The gist of it was that they often inquired of major customers about whether Wang was meeting their needs and whether they had suggestions regarding the firm's products and services.[212]

Dr. Wang was starting to step back from his leadership post in the early 1980s and named John Cunningham as president of the firm, in 1983. But Cunningham left Wang in 1985 to become CEO of a small computer firm.

Dr. Wang stated that 1985 was a difficult year for his firm and for the industry. His response was to visit customers and Wang's field offices, despite his dislike for travel, to find out about problems and solutions. One problem that they had at that time was that the firm was missing delivery dates on some of their products. Also, customers were complaining about Wang's product support.[213]

The year 1986 was better. Wang received a contract that January for $480 million to install computer equipment at U.S. Air Force bases world wide. Dr. Wang said their bid was less than IBM's bid for the contract, but still profitable.

The CEO believed in staffing from within. Senior management positions were staffed with employees who had been with the firm for a long time. As Dr. Wang stated, "I believe in repaying loyalty with loyalty."[214] He didn't often fill higher-level positions with people from outside his company. He felt there were "fewer surprises" when executives at Wang promoted people they knew.[215] He stated that he didn't care much for MBAs. Dr. Wang felt that MBAs would often see a company as a portfolio of assets to be managed, which was not his way. But they did on occasion hire MBAs. He stated that, when they bring in someone to fill a high-level position, they would have the person serve first in a position one or two levels below the one they were trying to fill, to learn about the company's culture and how the firm works before they take on a lot of responsibility.

Dr. Wang felt that a company should serve its customers and its community; they shouldn't value profits more than ethics. Of course, some firms don't care much about their community, such as when they move a factory to a foreign country, destroying jobs in the U.S. He stated, "A study conducted by Johnson & Johnson showed that over a period of thirty years, a group of companies selected exclusively because of their reputation for social responsibility outperformed both the Dow Jones Industrial Average and the S & P stock averages by an extremely large margin."[216] That same firm, Johnson and Johnson, has its employees sign a code of ethics.

The CEO stated that his firm once owned a subsidiary in South Africa. But he was concerned that conditions in that country didn't seem to be improving, so they divested that subsidiary.

Dr. Wang stated that he only reluctantly laid off employees in 1985, when the computer industry experienced a recession. A company has to remain profitable if it is to continue serving its customers, employees and community, he stated. One way they served their employees was with a stock-purchase plan, which grew faster in value than the typical pension fund.[217]

The firm's CEO described how he happened to find out about a new building in Lowell, Mass. that eventually became Wang's headquarters. It was designed by the famous architect, Minoru Yamasaki, and included 16 acres of land. Dr. Wang liked the building, so they bought it.

That was in 1976. By 1985, they had expanded their space from 300,000 square feet to 2.3 million square feet, in the same part of Lowell. He said that by 1985, Wang was the largest employer in the Lowell area.[218]

Dr. Wang decided that he wanted to do more for the community, so he set up the Wang Institute, which began operations in Jan., 1981. It had computer science classes and granted degrees in software engineering. He planned to offer degrees in other fields later. The institute was located in Tyngsboro, Mass. It was originally a Marist seminary, which included a campus with over 200 acres. He funded it with Wang stock.[219] He and his wife also gave money to the Metropolitan Center in Boston, a facility for the performing arts. The amount was $4 million. They also gave money to Mass. General Hospital.

Dr. Wang died of cancer in 1990.

Apple Computer

Steve Wozniak and Steve Jobs, Apple's founders. grew up in the San Francisco area; Jobs was adopted. Jobs was a curious boy, who like gadgets. He watched a lot of television when he was a boy [220]—maybe too much. Jobs experimented with a carbon microphone, which a neighbor had given him. He wasn't well-liked by his classmates; one of them described Jobs as a "loner, pretty much of a crybaby."[221] As Jobs himself said, "I was pretty bored in school, and I turned into a little terror." [222] When he was attending school, he sometimes refused to do assignments. He caused so many problems that he was expelled from grade school. So he enrolled in a new school, Crittenden Middle School, in Mountain View. It was much tougher than his old grade school. He didn't spend much time at that school. His parents had to move to enroll him in another school, Cupertino Junior High. That was where he met Bill Fernandez, another electronics buff. Across the street from Fernandez lived another electronics buff, Steve Wozniak [223] Woz (a nickname) was older than Jobs and was attending the Univ. of Colorado at that time.

Woz loved electronics and spent a lot of his time designing circuit boards.

Jobs and Wozniak met in the summer of 1969, after Woz and two friends, Fernandez and Alan Baum, had built a small computer[224] Fernandez introduced them; Jobs was four years younger. Both the Steves were interested in electronics and like to build gadgets, but Woz was better at engineering, as Jobs admitted early on. Jobs said Woz was "...the first person I met who knew more about electronics than I did"[225] Jobs built a "Blue Box," which he used to make free, illegal long-distance phone calls. They built blue boxes for others, charging $150 each; Woz didn't like the idea of stealing from the phone company. Jobs was making so much money from the blue boxes that he decided not to finish high school.[226] He also started to experiment with LSD, a hallucinogenic drug, at that time and found a girl friend, Chris-Ann Brennan. He soon enrolled in college, Reed College in Portland, Ore. But he got bad grades and dropped out after one semester.[227]

By spring, 1974, Jobs had moved back to his parents' house. He tried to find work as an electronics technician at Atari Corp., known for its electronic games, and they hired him. Jobs was soon sent by Atari to Germany to fix some problems. After finishing his assignment in Germany, Jobs went on to India, seeking spiritual enlightenment. He traveled with his friend, Dan Kottke. They were shocked by the disease and poverty they found in India.[228] So, Steve returned home and got his job back at Atari.

One of Woz's early projects was a ham radio transmitter and receiver. He got them working, but soon got bored talking to adults on the radio.

In the mid-1970s, Woz joined a neighborhood club, the Homebrew Computer Club. Woz learned a lot about electronics in high school, and one of his teachers was able to get him a part-time programming job, at the Sylvania firm, writing Fortran programs. Woz later attended the Univ. of Colorado at Boulder.[229] Woz was a prankster who specialized in computer pranks. He was expelled from college at the end of his freshman year for causing too many pranks. Woz later enrolled at deAnza Community College. He spent some of his time at deAnza redesigning minicomputers, such as those from DEC and Hewlett-Packard. But the redesign work was only on paper; he never produced any redesigned machines.

Apple Computer (now Apple, Inc.) was founded on April 1, 1976; this was after Wozniak had designed and built the Apple I (See "Jobs and Wozniak" story in "Important People II" chapter). At Apple's founding, each of the Steves got 45% of the company. Ron Wayne, a Jobs friend, got 10%.

Both the Steves were inspired by an early, crude PC, called the Altair, which was a kit that needed to be assembled. It was featured in the Popular Electronics magazine of Jan., 1975. Woz decided that he could do better, and he went on to design and build the Apple I, which he finished in June, 1975.

Their first product was computer circuit boards, which they made for $25 each and planned to sell for $50. They recruited a nearby store, the Byte Shop, to buy and resell the boards. They didn't sell well, but Woz didn't care; he was already working on the Apple II computer. Woz said the Apple II was a "phenomenal improvement" over the Apple I. [230] Features of the new machine included a color display, expansion slots and a Basic language interpreter, which was developed by Bill Gates. The Basic was built into the ROM memory.[231] The new machine was nearly complete in the summer of '76, and the pair decided to show it off at an electronics show, the PC '76 show in Atlantic City. Their computer was relatively crude machine compared to the other devices on display, and their display booth was not impressive. So, they decided to finish the Apple II and put it in a fancy case with a keyboard included.

Steve Jobs, Apple's management expert, decided that he needed to start an ad campaign for the new machine. He found the Regis McKenna Agency, which also worked for the Intel firm. Jobs found it difficult to get a meeting with the founder, but his persistence paid off. The meeting didn't go well, but the firm decided to take on Apple as a client. McKenna persuaded the two Steves that they needed an investor. They found a venture capitalist, Mike Markkula. The unlikely result was that Markkula decided to invest $91,000 in the firm and wrote a business plan for the pair. He also arranged a line of credit for $250,000. Markkula's small investment bought him 30% of the firm. Markkula made a forecast about that time. He said, "We're going to be a Fortune 500 company in two years. This is the start of an industry. It happens once a decade."[232] Woz left Hewlett-Packard about that time and became an engineer at Apple.[233]

At about that time, the summer of '76, Apple relocated to its own office, in Cupertino. Apple Computer became a corporation on Jan. 3, 1977.[234] The papers were signed at Markkula's house on that date. Both the Steves became full-time employees at that time. Woz left his job at Hewlett-

Packard. They hired as president Mike Scott, formerly an executive with National Semiconductor.[235]

They learned from their mistakes at the previous computer show and spent $1500 on a new booth. Of course, their new computer looked much better at that point. They also reserved a space early, which gave them a prominent spot. They showed off their Apple II models and projected images from the Apple II machines in color on a big screen. About that time, Woz did the development work to get a cassette tape drive working with the Apple II.[236].

The Apple II didn't have a disk drive at that point, so Markkula decided that it was time to develop one, a floppy disk; that was December, 1977.[237] Woz wrote the software to work with the new drive and got it working within a month. They showed off their new diskette drive at the Las Vegas Consumer Electronics Show early the next year. The drive became "...the runaway sensation of the show."[238]

In 1978, the executives decided that they needed to produce a new machine, which they called the Apple II Plus. They also started planning for the Apple III machine.

In mid-1979, Apple was able to sell $7.3 million worth of stock, to the Xerox company and other investors. Jobs, at that time, was able to sell over $1 million of his own stock. He was now a millionaire, at age 24.[239]

Many of their Apple II's were sold to schools at that time. The schools liked the avail-able Basic language. They also liked the new spreadsheet program, called Visicalc. Initially, it was available only on the Apple II.

Also in 1979, Jobs decided to produce another model, the Lisa, which was also his presumed daughter's name.[240] The planned retail price was $2000, but it actually sold for $10,000 and was never very popular.

Apple went public in Dec., 1980, selling 4.6 million shares. Job's shares were worth $217 million at that point.[241]

Employee Jeff Raskin came up with the idea for another new PC in 1979, which he called the Macintosh[242]; the name was also a type of apple, but Apple added an "a" to the name. Raskin and a few others developed a prototype before the end of that year. That version didn't have a graphical interface, like the later Mac machines. The Mac was finally introduced on Jan., 24, 1984.

Today Apple, Inc. has annual sales over $200 billion and a capitalization of over $738 billion.

Intel Corp.

Intel isn't a computer company, but they produce a lot of hardware used by computer companies. Intel was founded on July 18, 1968, by Gordon Moore and Rovert Noyce, with the goal of producing semiconductor memories. They had previously worked at Fairchild Semiconductor. The name Intel comes from INTegrated ELectronics. They decided on that name after trying several other names, such as Moore Noyce. Moore was asked in 1968 why he and Noyce started a new company. Moore said that they "…wanted to experience once again the thrill of working in a small, fast-growing company." [243] Noyce had earlier been involved in setting up William Shockley's lab. About a year later, Noyce and seven others left Shockley to start the Fairchild Semiconductor firm. Shockley's firm was called Shockley Laboratories. [244] The employees left that firm because they didn't like Shockley.

The Fairchild firm was seriously damaged in 1967 when a Fairchild alumnus, Charles Sporck, started National Semiconductor and hired many people from Fairchild. Moore and Noyce left Fairchild one year later.

To raise some capital for Intel, Noyce called Arthur Rock, an investment banker, who agreed to invest $300,000 in Intel. [245] Noyce and Moore also invested $250K each. Grinnell College also put up $300K. Recruiting of new employees was made easier by an interview with Moore in the Palo Alto Times, which included Moore's and Noyce's home addresses.

At the time of Intel's founding, semiconductor memories were very expensive, compared to the usual magnetic core memories then in use on most computers. Their first products were static RAM memory chips, or SRAMs. Later, in the 1980s, they moved into dynamic RAMs, or DRAMs. Dynamic RAMs have to have their contents refreshed often, by special circuitry, to avoid losing data. Static RAMs do not have this problem. Intel described their first products as "memory devices." [246] At that time, many companies in California were working on semiconductor memories. [247]

Early on, Intel was working on three memory technologies. One was MOS, or Metal Oxide on Silicon. The other types were multichip memory modules and Schottky bipolar. The type they chose was called silicon gate MOS.[248]

A former Intel employee said, "Intel was <u>founded</u> to steal the silicon gate process from Fairchild."[249] But another Intel employee said about Fairchild, "We didn't bring with us recipes, mask sets, device designs, that sort of stuff...What we brought was a lot of knowledge."[250]

Fairchild often lost secrets to a competitor, National Semiconductor. As the author stated, "For a couple of years now, the best technologies developed in its research labs in Palo Alto never seemed to get put into practice at Fairchild's Mountain View manufacturing facility." [251] National Semiconductor would make use of those technologies.

Moore and Noyce used networking to find the best scientists and engineers for their new firm. They would talk to contacts in electrical engineering departments on campuses to get the names.

Early in its history, Intel had two requirements for a new employee: (1) Don't expect a raise when you are hired. (2) Expect a demotion. The latter was due to the more junior types of work they would be doing initially.[252]

Intel's first factory was an old Union Carbide plant in Mountain View, near San Francisco. That was in fall, 1968.[253] The executives planned on at least 2000 silicon wafer starts per week at that plant. The wafers had at least 100 circuits each.

Andrew Grove was the third executive to work at Intel. He was initially named Director of Operations. His responsibility was "...getting products designed on time and built to cost." [254] He was born in Hungary in 1936. His original name was Andras Grof. He arrived in the U.S in 1956 after the Soviet invasion of Hungary. He then studied chemical engineering at the City College of New York. He met his future wife at a hotel in the Catskill Mountains in New York state. She was a young Hungarian woman named Eva. Grove got his Ph.D. degree in 1963. He then went to work for Fairchild Semiconductor. Before he finished his Ph.D, he moved to U.C.-Berkeley. Grove lectured at Berkeley while he worked in R and D at Fairchild. The author stated, "Grove spoke English with an accent that was almost incomprehensible."[255]

An Intel competitor, Advanced Micro Devices (AMD), was started in 1969 by the flamboyant Jerry Sanders. He started the firm with eight guys and $1.55 million, raised from the Capital Group Companies and other investors.

Sanders was a flashy executive, who drove a Mercedes. He was also a workaholic, who sometimes kept meetings going until 9:00 p.m. on a Friday. He would sometimes start a meeting at 9:00 a.m. on a Saturday. Some of AMD's executives called him, "Monster Man."[256] AMD went public in Sep., 1972. The firm was doing well because of their second-sourcing work and because of Sanders' hard work in the sales area. But the prospectus showed that AMD was barely making money.[257]

About the time of the IPO, Sanders was only making $34,000 per year, which was more than Noyce or Grove was making at Intel.[258]

Intel's executives decided in 1970 that MOS was the best circuit type for their memory products. The bipolar circuit team wasn't pleased.[259]

Intel started building a new fab plant in Santa Clara, in early 1971. They needed it for the new 1103 memory product. The author stated that the 1103 chip "...[W]as the world's first commercially successful semiconductor memory device.[260]

But the 1103 was hard to use. So Intel developed a memory system using the 1103, making the product easier for their customers to use. Intel went after IBM's customers with its new memory systems. They designed memory systems for specific IBM mainframe models. IBM didn't want to buy the memory systems from Intel.[261]

The Inside Intel book describes the hiring and work of Sue Mcfarland, who became the secretary for Andy Grove.[262] He didn't like to have any of the words in his memos corrected, and he threw a dictionary at her when she showed him the correct word to use, "exemplified," in a dictionary.[263] That same book cites many other examples of Grove's temper and abrasive personality. Ms. Mcfarland got a "bad" performance review the first year. The reason turned out to be that she had too big a workload. After she proved that to Grove, he hired a new assistant to do the typing.[264]

Intel's engineers discovered erasable ROMs, called EPROMs. The employee responsible was Dov Frohman, who was also a physicist.[265] Intel found a way of erasing the ROM with ultraviolet light. They also discovered a way of writing new data onto the ROM chip. They produced the first working EPROM in Sep., 1970.

In 1970, Intel was asked to design some chips for a Japanese firm, Nippon Calculator Machine Corp. (sometimes called Busicom), to be used in a new calculator. The customer expected that 12 circuit chips would be needed. But an Intel employee, Ted Hoff, decided that he could eliminate most of the chips and produce a single chip that would execute the instructions from memory, a microprocessor. This would cut the total number of chips needed to four: a CPU, a memory chip, a ROM chip to hold the program and another chip to handle the input and output (I/O). Hoff got permission from his superior, Bob Noyce, to simplify the original design. Fred Faggin and Mazor, another circuit designer, got the four chips working. But then the Japanese firm asked for a discount from the original price. Intel offered to buy back the product for $60,000, and NCMC accepted. That freed Intel to sell the new microprocessor to any customer.

The microprocessor Faggin and Mazor produced was called the 4004, which became the first microprocessor. Intel still felt that their main business was memories, but they thought the new microprocessor would be a way to sell more memories. Intel didn't have high hopes for sales of the 4004 product. They expected sales of only 2000 units per year, which they based on the number of mainframes being sold.[266]

The 4004 was introduced as a product at the end of 1971. Their next microprocessor was the 8008, which processed 8 bits at a time, twice the size of the 4004's word, with an 8-bit word.

Soon Intel was producing the 8008, which was used in the first IBM PC. IBM didn't want to tell the Intel people exactly what they were developing, so they weren't allowed to see a prototype PC. At meetings with IBM, Intel people would "...ask questions, they'd tell us what was happening and we'd have to try to solve the problem literally in the dark." (from Intel web site) Initially there were no compilers available for the 8088, only assemblers (an assembler provides a simplified way to write machine language programs).

But Bill Gates and Paul Allen provided an easier way to write software for
the 8008. They wrote a BASIC language interpreter to run on that product.[267]
Intel produced another software product for the 8008, called the Intellec4, to
develop programs for the 8008.

Inside Intel describes an ethics problem that occurred at Intel. Bob Graham,
a sales and marketing executive, had disputes with Andy Grove over data sheets
for the customers, related to the 1103 memory chip. Graham didn't want to lie
on the data sheets, but Grove did. Grove said Graham had to publish the data as
Grove wanted, or he could resign.[268] So Graham resigned. The author of Inside
Intel stated, "Bob Graham and Gordon Moore had been great friends."[269]

Soon after Graham left, Intel started work on an initial public offering (IPO)
for their common stock. First they found a new market exec, Ed Gelbach, to
replace Graham. The IPO happened in Oct., 1971. Noyce and Moore were
shown in the prospectus as the largest shareholders.[270]

Intel's competitor AMD decided that second-sourcing would be a good
strategy for them. That means, for example, being a second manufacturer for
the 8008 chip. AMD's CEO, Jerry Sanders, wanted AMD to be a second source
for Intel's products. Sanders thought that would be a good growth strategy for
AMD. Of course, sometimes the primary source company didn't like the competition.[271] They would make more money being the only source.

Intel was able to get new customers for its 1103 memory chip (1K DRAM)
by telling potential buyers that they could call Intel collect to find out how much
they would save by switching to the 1103 versus the old magnetic core memories
for their products. The 1103 was smaller and faster than core but Intel said the
price was the same.[272] But customers wanted to know who Intel's second source
was for the 1103. The second source became Microsystems International Limited,
a Canadian firm.[273] But MIL made some big mistakes in the production process for
the 1103, so customers went back to Intel to get their orders filled.[274]

At the time the 8008 was introduced, Intel's executives didn't realize the
potential of the 8008 and later microprocessors. They expected sales of about

10,000 units per year. As an Intel sales engineer said, "Nobody comprehended the scale of the PC business would grow to tens of millions of units a year." (from Intel web site). Of course, the IBM PC helped to start a revolution. IBM PCs became (along with Apple's PCs) one of the two standards in the PC industry.

Intel was having a problem with its DRAM chips. They introduced a 4K DRAM product in mid-1972. But the Mostek firm introduced a 16K DRAM before Intel introduced its version.

But DRAM sales for Intel continued to rise until 1979, when they declined. The Japanese were their principal competitors in the memory area. The author of Inside Intel stated, "For the Japanese companies may have been copying chip designs and process technologies from their U.S. counterparts, but they were now making great strides in chip manufacturing itself."[275] The author also stated, "Japanese fab operators [technicians] were far more loyal to their employer," than U.S. fab operators.[276]

The Japanese also had two other advantages. The author stated, "One was that the Japanese semiconductor companies ...had much closer relationships with their suppliers and equipment manufacturers than their American counterparts did."[277] The author stated that the other advantage was due to the advice of W. E. Deming and other manufacturing experts.[278] Deming advised that "the key to cutting costs...was to increase quality."[279]

Intel bought a digital watch firm in July, 1972.[280] But it turned out to be a bad investment. They sold it in 1977. That was a decision by Intel's board. Some digital watches were selling in that year for $9.95.[281]

Intel's management believed in "constructive confrontation." This policy was due to Andy Grove, who could be "abrupt, aggressive and interrogatory," according to the Inside Intel author.[282] The author also stated that "He relished a fight," and that he liked to shout at people. Grove used two methods to control his subordinates: budgets and objectives, which were managed by "key results,"[283] related to the objectives. He had four levels of employee performance. He also used the MOMAR, or "monthly management review," where one division would give a presentation to other employees. Another Intel policy was management retreats, which would be held at a resort and would last several days.[284] Grove liked to inspect plants and offices. He would even inspect the janitor's closet on occasion.[285] Another idea from Grove was the "Late List." He wanted all first-shift employees to arrive by 8:00 a.m., even if they had worked the night before. Of course, the employees didn't like that policy.[286]

Ralph Ungermann was a talented Intel employee. But he soon grew to dislike the firm and left, along with Frederico Faggin, to start the Zilog firm, in 1974, which was partly financed by Exxon Enterprises. That organization invested $1.5 million in the new firm, which gave them a 51% stake. One of the reasons Ungermann left Intel was an assignment to work on "a chip that could recognize coins."[287]

Zilog soon produced an improved version of Intel's 8080 chip, called the Z80. It ran "any program written for Intel's 8080 chip.[288] It also would "fit inter-changeably into the same place as the 8080 on a customer's circuit board."[289] The Z80 was more advanced than the 8080, including "serial I/O" technology and "direct memory access" for faster input and output, meaning reads and writes. The Z80 was priced at only $200, just over half the cost of an 8080 chip.[290]

After the Z80 came out, Zilog started work on a new chip, the Z8000, a 16-bit microprocessor.

Intel faced a crisis in May, 1975 when its plant in Penang, Malaysia burned to the ground. That plant had more than half of Intel's production capacity. However, several competitors in the Penang area allowed Intel to use some of their factory capacity on a temporary basis. By the end of 1975, production at the Penang plant was nearly back at normal levels.[291]

Ann Bowers was the head of human resources at Intel after once having been the secretary to Bob Noyce. The author stated that she was "...slightly in awe of Bob Noyce..." since she was his secretary. But then Noyce told her about his upcoming divorce. One evening, he said, "By the way, I presume you know that I'm getting a divorce."[292] The author of Inside Intel stated that it was common for people working at Silicon Valley firms to get a divorce and marry a co-worker.

Noyce had been married for 21 years to his wife, Betty. But then they had a big fight and got a divorce. Noyce later married Ann Bowers.[293] Bowers had decided five years earlier that she wanted to marry Noyce.[294]

Jerry Sanders made good money at the CEO of Intel's competitor, Advanced Micro Devices. But the author of <u>Inside Intel</u> stated, "Despite his handsome terms at AMD, Sanders still lived beyond his income."[295] Sanders drove, for example, a Rolls Royce Corniche Model. (For comparison, this author has only seen <u>one</u> Rolls Royce being driven in his lifetime; they are pretty rare.)

A friend of Sanders, Ed Turney, asked him for a $50,000 loan. He was turned down. One reason might have been: "Sanders had complained about what he saw as slipping performance in Turney's work."[296] Turney left Intel on Dec. 4, 1974. He soon sold his 76,500 shares of AMD stock.

Despite some legal problems with Intel, AMD's Sanders signed a license agreement with Intel on their 8085 chip, the successor to the 8080A. AMD became the second source for that product. AMD wanted to become the second source for the 8086 chip, but Intel never followed up with AMD. So AMD became the second source for Zilog's Z8000 chip.[297]

Andy Grove was the organization brains at Intel. He wrote the book, <u>High-Output Management</u>, for example. One important chapter in the book was titled, "The Basics of Production: Delivering a Breakfast." He describes how to deliver all the components of a hot breakfast, a soft-boiled egg, toast and coffee hot and on time. Of course, this example was a lot simpler than describing how to produce a microprocessor, which might require over 100 steps. Grove used a lot of performance measurements. He felt it was important to recruit new college grads (NGCs). Intel used its contacts on campuses to find the best and the brightest new grads. [298] Grove would sometimes get involved in hiring of a specific, star graduate.

Intel started on a new microprocessor in 1975, called the 8800. It was intended to be an improvement over the 8080. The new processor was a 16-bit product. But that project had lots of problems. [299]

Returning to Intel's products, another microprocessor Intel produced in that era (early 1970s) was the 8086, which was a 16-bit processor, meaning the operand or word size was 16 bits. The 8086 was a more advanced version of the 8080. It was introduced in June, 1978. Intel continued with their X86 series, including the 80286. That processor was used in the IBM PC model AT. Later Intel introduced the 80386. The series ended with the 80486 processor. Later processors used the Pentium prefix. The Pentium, equivalent to an 80586 processor (a name Intel didn't use), was introduced in 1993. According to Intel, the Pentium contained 3.1 million transistors and could process 90 million instructions per second.

Another important development about that time was the Apple II personal computer, invented by Steve Wozniak, according to his book Iwoz... Wozniak stated, in the book's title, that he invented the personal computer. He invented the Apple I and the Apple II. The Apple Computer firm was started by Wozniak and Jobs. They were able to get financing from Mike Markkula, who put $91,000 of his own money into the Apple firm.[300] Apple Computer went public in a Dec., 1980 IPO. The Apple Computer story is described earlier in this chapter.

Intel started to have a problem in 1978 because its customers said the 8086 processor was inferior to the Motorola 68000, a 16- or 32-bit processor. A Motorola Programmer's Reference Manual (fourth edition) states on the cover that the product works in 16 or 32 bit mode; the manual also describes the instruction set for that processor.

Intel's response to that complaint was to produce a 100-page Futures Catalog, which described products Intel planned to deliver in the future.[301] One of the products was a co-processor chip, which allowed the 8086 to do much faster calculations. The manager responsible for the catalog was Bill Davidow, Intel's marketing whiz. They were also able to get 50 articles "published in the trade press..." But many of the products in the catalog hadn't yet been designed, so they were actually "vaporware."

To be a better competitor, Intel decided that they needed 2000 "design wins" by Dec., 1980. That meant 2000 new products designed around the 8086 processor. They called the plan "Operation Crush." The program was pretty successful. It reduced Motorola's market share significantly, to 15%.[302]

Hewlett-Packard complained about the quality of U.S.-made chips in 1980 (not just Intel's products). They said, "The parts that came from the very best American firm showed six times as many errors as those from the worst Japanese firm."[303] Another shock had earlier come from the Japanese: "Fujitsu introduced the first mass-market 64K DRAM."[304] Intel responded by stepping up work on two new technologies. One was CMOS, Complementary Metal

Oxide on Silicon. The other was chip-level redundancy, meaning extra circuitry on the chip to bypass bed cells. But it didn't work in practice.

Scott Gibson, manager of memory components at Intel, decided in 1982 that his firm couldn't compete effectively in the DRAM area. He thought they should concentrate on the CMOS technology.

Intel found that IBM had some interest in their 8088 chip, which was a slower version of the 8086. By 1981, Intel's execs realized that IBM was developing its own PC. IBM asked Intel for a second source for the 8088. Intel decided on AMD as the second source for that chip. [305] IBM's use of Intel's processor chips in their personal computers increased their market share by 1000 times. [306]

Faggin and Ungermann left Intel about that time to start their own firm, called Zilog. [307] Their first big project was the Z8000 processor. But it turned out not to be compatible with anything. The author of Inside Intel stated, "The result was that the Z8000 that emerged from three years of development was compatible with nothing." [308]

The failed Z8000 was also a big problem for AMD, which was making its own version, the AMZ8000. Jerry Sanders, the CEO, soon concluded, "I'm making the wrong part." [309]

Some Intel people started discussing how they could use an 8080 processor to produce home computers that included a keyboard and a monitor. But Gordon Moore gave his opinion: "What's it good for?...I personally don't see anything useful in it." [310] But then, in 1977, the MITS firm came out with its Altair computer kit, using the 8088 processor. Of course, AMD benefited as Intel's second source for the 8088. The new 8800 16-bit processor came out in Feb., 1981. Intel renamed it the iAPX432.

In Dec., 1980 five Intel people decided they wanted to leave Intel and start their own firm to make EPROMs, which were then in big demand. The five decided that they wanted Gordie Campbell, then a marketing manager, to head the firm. He agreed to their request in early January and the six resigned from Intel that month. [311]

Intel sued the new firm, called Seeq Technology. But Intel discovered that Seeq wasn't using Intel's process to produce EPROMs. The two firms were able to settle when Seeq agreed not to use Intel's process to make their EPROM products. Both Intel's and Seeq's executives were happy with the settlement.[312]

Intel started a new campaign, which they called Checkmate. It was a marketing campaign. Casey Powell, the east coast sales manager, was put in charge of Checkmate. In March, 1982, Intel had four new chips that they launched as part of Checkmate: the 80186, the 80286, the 82586 and the 2914. IBM used the 80286 in its new PC AT model.[313]

Powell was under a lot of pressure because of the Checkmate campaign.[314] Andy Grove was very critical, shouting at him in a meeting, several times. Powell was fed up. But he soon calmed down. After a long delay, six months, Grove apologized. Powell decided that Grove's comments were his exit cue. Powell said, "I could leave knowing that he had acknowledged I was right. That gave me permission."[315]

Powell consulted an attorney before leaving, who told him how to avoid being sued. Powell took 17 people with him from Intel's Oregon facilities.

Andy Grove wanted to sue Powell and his new firm, Sequent, but Ed Gelbach, an Intel attorney, persuaded him not to.

Powell initially use products from National Semiconductor, but he later switched to Intel. He said to Grove, "The past is behind us. I never did anything wrong. I'd like to do business with you." Grove said, "Fine."[316]

Jerry Sanders, the AMD CEO, was a flamboyant guy who became more flamboyant. He had two Rolls-Royces, three mansions and a beautiful second wife.[317]

Intel and AMD signed a "ten-year technology-sharing agreement" in 1982 which soon became less attractive to Intel. There was soon less need for a second source for Intel's products.[318]

The author describes how Andy Grove showed his temper in a meeting. He hit a table with a stick the size of a baseball bat, making a loud noise. The Grove shouted his complaint, "I don't ever, _ever_ want to be in a meeting that doesn't start and end when it's scheduled."[319]

Intel finally decided in 1985 that they had to exit the memory manufacturing business for good.[320] That actually happened in 1986. Intel again became profitable in 1987.

Fairchild Semiconductor

Fairchild Semiconductor was started in 1957 by eight people who left the Shockley Semiconductor Laboratory. Gordon Moore and Robert Noyce, who later founded Intel Corp., were among the eight. The firm still exists and is one of the oldest electronics companies in Silicon Valley.

The Microchip book[321] describes the startup: "They set up Fairchild Semiconductor, aiming to complete the work they had begun. In addition to [Jean] Hoerni, Moore and Noyce, they included Julius Blank, Victor Grinich, Eugene Kleiner, Jay Last, and Sheldon Roberts. Six held Ph.D.s. Two were mechanical engineers... Bill Shockley branded the group the traitorous eight. But in fact, the desertion by his star thinkers was just another Shockley first. Just as the Bulldog Shockley] himself set a certain high standard for the élan and esprit that would possess the best of the semicon seekers, the departures from his company established the industry's common pattern of business regeneration: The brightest researchers would run away with their best ideas to use as the basis to start their own companies... Ideas still ruled because the territory was still a wilderness, with large tracts still unexplored and important discoveries still obscured."

Fairchild was the leader in planar transistors, which had the three connections all on one surface and all of the layers were also on that surface. One of the founders, Jean Hoerni, was the inventor of that type of transistor.

But the planar transistors weren't easy to manufacture. Gordon Moore contributed his opinion: 'We could no more make planar transistors than fly."[322] But the founders knew it was an important invention. The Microchip book[323] continues: "But they could see that the planar concept was indisputably brilliant, even if its timing was awkward. Therefore Fairchild took immediate measures to patent it." Noyce and the firm's patent attorney, John Ralls, filed the patent forms.

Planar transistors led to integrated circuits at Fairchild. Discussions on integrated circuit began at Fairchild in Jan., 1959, according to the Microchip author.[324]: "According to lore, during the meeting [about the planar design], Noyce first saw with geometric clarity how the parts of transistors that had all of their features on their surface could be kind of pre-wired thin metal strips applied over the surface of the silicon. The metal pathways could approximate wires, but they'd be bonded to the surface, stuck down integrally on top of the silicon so that they became a part of the monolithic structure themselves.

The insulating oxide layer on top of the transistor—the same layer that protected it from stray dust particles—would prevent the metal pathways from touching the semiconductive zones of silicon beneath, so the metal would be insulated from the transistor at the same time it was bonded to it." The book goes on, "You could etch tiny points through that uppermost layer of oxide, aligning them precisely, so that the metal pathways flowed through the insulation to make contact only at the places you wanted them to touch the underlying transistors, thereby connecting to zones the way individual wires would connect to zones. But unlike wires, the individual pathways—the tiny metal strips—would be stuck fast to the silicon surface. They'd be part of the transistor itself, integral, built in during the same oxidizing and coating and masking and etching and bonding and all the other steps you were already using to make the device in the first place. To finish transistors, women on the production line wouldn't have to tediously solder wires to impossibly small, pinprick-size connectors anymore.

"And while you were at it, Noyce reasoned, why cut apart the transistors at all? You already made handfuls at once, all ranked and filed on a silicon wafer like the t read on a waffle. Because you were bonding tiny pathways on top of individual transistors, why not run the integral metal stripes to the next transistor, and to the next one, and the next, and the next? Why not connect a bunch of transistors on one chip of silicon? The only trick then would be to isolate them somehow, one from the other, so that the action of one transistor wouldn't bleed to the next. So that each little blinking transistor would keep its own place so that it would work singly, remain orderly and well controlled."[325]

Noyce explained the parts of an integrated circuit: "So the elements of the idea for the IC are, one, the capability of running wires over the surface. You couldn't do that with [a conventional transistor]. You had to have an insulator in there.

Secondly, the idea of being able to cut things apart with junctions rather than physically cutting them apart. And then, obviously, just the realization that other circuit elements could be built into the silicon—capacitors and resistors."[326]

Jack Kilby was also working on integrated circuits about that time. But he wasn't familiar with planar transistors, which would have made his work in that area easier.

The U.S. Patent Office had to decide who was first with the idea for integrated circuits, and they decided on Kilby. The issue also reached the courts. The U.S. Supreme Court refused to hear an appeal from Texas Instruments on the issue, in 1970. The Microchip author continues [327]: "But the [court] resolution was largely moot. Before the suit had even settled, Fairchild and TI had worked out a royalty sharing agreement in which both companies received payments from other semiconductor concerns that employed the integration concept to make silicon circuits. Neither Fairchild nor Texas Instruments held up development while the dispute crept toward a resolution. Rather than impeding the onward rush of circuit integration, the decade-long, Kilby-versus-Noyce patent wrangle caused only a distraction. Generally, informally, both Kilby and Noyce came to be regarded as coinventors of the integrated circuits, even though they came to the invention separately.

"In fact, historical circumstances encouraged the idea from both men... The competitive semiconductor business created those circumstances... Both were surrounded by the provoking, accumulating discoveries that the environment inspired."[328]

Of course, Kilby and Noyce weren't working in a vacuum. The Microchip author continues.[329]: "Both Kilby and Noyce acknowledged antecedents that suggested their innovations. Kilby had the silk screening process from Centralab. Noyce said his idea to top a chip with bonded metal pathways, replacing wires, came from a Fairchild research program called 'expanded contact.' The project sought to bond an aluminum film to Fairchild's silicon transistors, creating large contact areas so that women wielding tweezers and soldering points during final assembly steps would have an easier time attaching wires. His idea for isolating the separate transistors electrically on a chip, rather than physically—keeping all the important junctions of one transistor clearly delineated from the next—recalled a concept just proposed by Kurt Lehovec, a Czech-born physicist working for Sprague Electric Company."

Texas Instruments

Texas Instruments (TI), located in the Dallas, Texas area began in 1930 as an oil exploration company, called Geophysical Services Incorporated. It later became an electronics company when they started selling their geophysical devices to other firms. Then it became a semiconductor company when the firm decided to use transistors in its electronic devices.

TI has a number of firsts to its credit, including inventing the integrated circuit, building the first computer using integrated circuits and the first electronic calculator using ICs. The story of the latter is an interesting one. Patrick Haggerty conceived of the idea, in 1965, to make a portable electronic calculator using only integrated circuits. Haggerty was known at the time for coming up with wild ideas.

Jack Kilby described his impression of Haggerty, "He liked to explain his ideas to people, and did so, with a lot of people, at almost every opportunity. It was his style to throw out ideas. You could pick 'em up or walk away from 'em, as you choose."[330] The author continues, "Kilby dismissed a couple of his boss's airborne notions [they were on a plane flight] out of hand.... But the concept of a portable personal calculator stuck... Kilby wrapped some ganglia around the notion of a small computing machine that could drop into a pocket, run on a battery, and perform simple math. To be self-contained it would need to incorporate a key pad for punching in problems and a window of some sort to show solutions."[331]

Haggerty discussed his concept in more details in an Oct. 20, 1965 meeting. Kilby stated that the goal was to build a calculator about the size of a book on his desk, 4" X 6" X ¾" Kilby stated, "We want some kind of personal computer, and it would be nice if it was no bigger than this book. And of course, it'll have to run on batteries. And it will have to have some buttons or somethin' on it for you to tell it a problem. And it'll have some neon lights or somethin' to tell you the answer."[332] Jerry Merryman was placed in charge of the portable calculator project. This was unusual, because Merryman didn't even have a college degree. But he had learned a lot on his own and on the job. He had 18 months to produce a working calculator. At the time, that term wasn't yet in use. Kilby called it a "slide rule computer," named for the crude slide rules then in common use by engineers and scientists for doing their calculations. The project was called Cal Tech at TI. But the technology of 1965 just wasn't adequate to produce such a device.

The group had to come up with a key pad and a display mechanism, in addition to producing the appropriate integrated circuits. They chose thermal printing technology for the display. LED technology wasn't adequate yet for calculator displays.

Merryman used what were called full-slice wafers for his integrated circuits. This was because the wafers weren't sub-divided, like they are now, into tiny chips. But the technology wasn't good enough for Merryman's needs; the yields from manufacturing were only about 25%. Merryman told the technicians producing the circuits that he needed an 83% yield. They just laughed. But Merryman was serious. He said, "I'm gonna design for eighty-three percent. It's gonna use low voltage and low current and wide tolerances and big transistors and big leads and big contacts, and I'm gonna build it out of tolerant, forgiving parts, such that it's gonna work." [333] The technicians exceeded the 83% goal. Still, the components failed at random on his circuits. So, he had to route the wiring around the bad components. First, he found the bad components on each chip. Then, he used an IBM mainframe on the TI campus to come up with routing that worked. Even that wasn't adequate. They had to lay down some wiring manually.

Merryman's crew finally came up with a working calculator in Dec., 1967, which was six months later than planned. The cost was $240,000.

The Microchip author describes the resulting device.[334]: "One Cal Tech sliderule computer, a black aluminum box studded with numbered keys the size of sugar cubes, the whole assembly closer in bulk to a hardcover than a paperback, was finished in December, 1967 .... Merryman and his crew had indeed succeeded in making one working prototype that is heralded as the world's first cordless, portable calculator...But the program had failed to make a mass-consumable calculator. It succeeded in showing how far TI's ambitions outstripped its present abilities."

This author has an early-model TI calculator, called the SR-50, the SR standing for slide rule. The label on the back describes in as a "slide rule calculator." It is a scientific calculator, with a rechargeable battery and an LED display. It includes lots of scientific functions, including three trig functions, hyperbolic functions, inverse trig and hyp functions, factorial, log, exp, and power keys. The original price in 1974 was about $150. The device is similar to today's calculators, except that it doesn't do graphing, doesn't have an LCD display and is thicker than most calculators. The device went on sale in 1973, showing how far the technology had advanced in just six years at TI.

Hewlett-Packard Corp.

Bill Hewlett and Dave Packard met in the fall of 1930, at Stanford University. They didn't start their firm right after graduation. Packard wrote that he worked at the General Electric firm for a time, on vacuum tubes, at a plant in the Schenectady, NY area. GE was more involved in electrical products in that era, as opposed to electronic products. But Packard worked on manufacturing the tubes.

The Hewlett Packard company started in 1939, with a partnership agreement between Hewlett and Packard. Packard describes the agreement in his own words, "In recognition of our progress, small as it was, Bill and I began 1939 by signing a partnership agreement. I don't remember the exact terms of the agreement, but I know it was pretty informal." [335] But the pair did some earlier work together, in their now-famous Palo Alto garage, in 1938.

Packard knew he had to learn more about running a business, so he took courses at Stanford, in the fall of 1938, on business law and management accounting. [336]

One of their first products was an audio oscillator, which produces sounds of various frequencies. They sold eight of them to the Disney company for $71.50 each. [337] They were used in the Disney movie "Fantasia." They were competing with General Radio in that area, but the other firm charged much more for their oscillator product.

The HP firm made other products in those early years, including custom controls for air conditioners and a controller for the Lick Observatory. They got some early manufacturing help from Charles Litton. Litton let the pair use his shop.

Packard learned an important lesson in the 1930s. Regarding bankruptcies, he said, "Those firms that did not borrow money had a difficult time, but they ended up with their assets intact and survived during the depression years that followed." He added, "From this experience, I decided out company should not incur any long-term debt."[338] He noticed also that one of their competitors at the time, General Radio, didn't use any outside financing, so their firm could operate the same way also. Packard stated that the firm's policy is "...to reinvest most of our profits and to depend on this reinvestment, plus funds from employee stock purchases and other cash flow items, to finance out growth."[339] However, as of this writing, the HP firm has $13.9 billion in long-term debt, which is 25% of their capitalization, according to the Value Line Investment Survey.

In 1939, the firm needed more space, so they rented a building on Page Mill Road. For that year, their sales were only $5369.

About that time, the firm needed more cash, and they got a loan of $500 from Palo Alto National Bank, after talking with the bank's president.[340]

The HP company got some help from another competitor, General Radio, at that time, from its founder, Melville Eastham.

During the war, Bill Hewlett was called to active duty as an officer in the Army Signal Corps. Starting at that time, the firm made many products for the war effort and grew rapidly.[341] Their annual sales quickly reached a million dollars, according to Packard. They had two shifts going in 1943 at their factory on Page Mill Road. Bonuses for the workers increased to 85 per cent of their base pay during the war.[342] Packard's book states that HP still has a profit-sharing plan.

During the war era, the federal government didn't approve of defense contractors making too much money, as in HP's case. The limit on profits was 12% of equity. But HP's executives objected to that limit, and they were able to meet most of their profit goals, despite federal government objections.[343]

HP moved into some new lines of business during the WW II era. One of them was a microwave signal generator, which they built for the Navy. They also built a radar-jamming device for the Navy. Packard stated that they had to work around the clock on that project.

The HP firm became a corporation in 1947. Packard stated, "This allowed for some tax advantages and also provided more continuity to the business than a partnership could."[344]

The company again grew rapidly in the 1950s, due partly to the Korean War. Packard stated that his firm produced more than 100 products by 1952. Packard commented on the company's growth: "Between 1950 and 1951 our sales doubled and from 1951 to 1952 they doubled again."[345]

Packard stated that the firm built two buildings in 1956 in the new Stanford Industrial Park, which was established by Stanford University.

The Hewlett and Packard families also spent leisure time together. They started a ranching partnership in 1952, in an area south of San Francisco Bay. They called it San Felipe. Packard describes some of the family activities: "Most of the Hewlett and Packard children learned to swim in the pool at San Felipe. The children rode horses through the hills and learned about the pleasures and problems of cattle raising."[346]

Growth was still rapid at HP in the late 1950s. Packard stated that employment rose "…from 779 on January 1, 1956 to 1268 on January 1, 1957."[347]

The company went public in November, 1957. They sold 10% of the stock at $16 per share.

The advent of the European Common Market in 1957 encouraged HP to expand in that region. In 1959, they built their first factory near Stuttgart, Germany. The plant assembled electronic instruments. Previously they had exported to Europe. They established their European headquarters in Geneva in 1959. Packard stated in his book, "Hewlett-Packard now produces and sells thousands of products in more than 650 plants and offices located in 120 countries around the world."[348] At the time of his book's writing, Packard stated that the firm had several manufacturing plants in China.

In 1957, HP's managers met and agreed on seven goals in the following areas: Profit, Customers, Field of Interest, Growth, Employees, Organization and Citizenship.

Packard states in his book that one of HP's policies is to reinvest most of their profits and to use employee stock purchases to finance their growth.[349] He also lamented Wall Street's short-term focus, meaning their concentration on quarterly earnings.

HP was one of the first American companies to produce an electronic calculator. Their first product of note in that area was the HP-35, which was introduced in 1972 and cost $395 at retail. It was very popular. Packard stated, "…[T]he calculator represented such a unique value that once it hit the market, we couldn't make them fast enough."[350]

In 1964, HP developed their first minicomputer, the model 2116. In the early 1970s, they started work on a project called Omega, a 32-bit minicomputer.[351] But their management decided it was too costly, so it was cancelled. But a scaled-down project was allowed to continue, named Alpha. It was a 16-bit machine, which later became the famous HP-3000 minicomputer, which was introduced in 1972.

HP introduced their first laser printer, for use with their minicomputers, in 1982. They used technology, called electrophotographic, from Canon. The printer was the 2680 and cost about $100,000. Two years later, they introduced their first LaserJet printer, which cost only $3,495.[352]

HP started working on ink-jet printers in 1978. It was a chance discovery. David Packard explained: "An engineer working on thin-film technology for integrated-circuit applications was testing the response of thin film to electrical stimulation. The electricity superheated the medium, and droplets of fluid lying under the film were expelled. An idea was born. What if we could finely control these jets of fluid?…And it [the technology] had the advantages of requiring very little power to print and of being very inexpensive to manufacture." [353]

Their first ink-jet printer was called the ThinkJet, which was a thermal ink-jet printer. It cost $1500 and wasn't very popular. It was a low-resolution printer, with 96 DPI. They came up with a better product, called the Maverick internally, with 300 DPI resolution. But the cost would be $1500. The project was cancelled. They later came up with the DeskJet series of printers, initially at a high price of $995. But the price was soon reduced to $365, for an entry-level printer. Initially their DeskJet printers printed only with black ink. But HP soon figured out how to add color at little extra cost, which the customers liked.

Printers have come a long way from the days of the mainframe impact printers, which were big, noisy and expensive. Typically they only printed with black ink, using big, messy ribbons. They only printed text, using one font. Printing speed averaged 1000 lines of text per minute. Multiple copies and special forms were printed using specialty paper. For graphics, the alternative was plotting devices. But simple graphics, such as histograms, could be printed with the impact printers.

Twenty-One

The Control Data 6600

The Control Data 6600, the first supercomputer, was designed by Seymour Cray and his small group of engineers, working at their lab in Chippewa Falls, Wisc. The first machine was completed and shown to the media in Aug., 1963. It was about 50 times faster than Cray's previous machine, the 1604. The newer machine had two cycle times, minor cycles and major cycles. Minor cycles marked the start of each instruction, once every 100 nanoseconds. Major cycles were larger, one megahertz. If the needed functional unit was available (see below), it could start a new instruction every 100 nanoseconds. The simple instructions, such as integer adds and subtracts, took three minor cycles in all. A complex instruction, such as a floating multiply, took ten minor cycles. The average speed was about three million instructions per second. An instruction stack was built into the hardware, which could hold ten words of instructions. So, if a loop could fit into the stack, no time was needed to read up instructions from memory, and execution would be very fast.

Robert Price, the former CEO of Control Data, commented on the 6600 model: "The 6600 was the first computer to be dubbed a supercomputer."[1]

These were the functional units: Branch, Boolean, Shift, Add (floating-point), Long Add (integer), Multiply (floating-point), Divide (floating-point), and Increment. There were two Multiply and Increment units, for a total of ten. The Increment units used 18-bit operands.

The 6600's architecture was unusual, in that the machine included 11 computers. Ten of them were minicomputers, called peripheral processors. They handled the mundane tasks for the larger machine, such as input, output, memory management and console displays and commands.

They were 12-bit machines that had their own instruction set. Systems programmers working on the 6600 would often write their code in the language of the small machines, called PP code. Code for the big machine was called CP code. Commands could be issued from the big machine's CPU to a smaller machine, such as read or write commands. A typical command was CIO, to read or write a buffer of data.

The big machine had an unusual instruction set. It had a 60-bit word, which could hold two, three or four instructions. Instructions were 15-bit or 30-bit. The smaller instructions used only the registers. There were 24 operational registers, including eight 60-bit accumulators (X registers), eight 18-bit index registers (B0 was always zero), and eight address registers. The address registers A1 to A5 always did loads of the corresponding X register when changed. The address registers A6 and A7 always did stores of the corresponding X register. A0 didn't cause any loads or stores when altered, but it could hold an 18-bit value.

The CPU had a complete set of floating-point instructions, but only partial integer arithmetic. Integer multiplies and divides had to be done with the floating-point unit. The programmer had to first convert each operand to floating-point, do the multiply or divide and then convert the result to integer. Pack, normalize and unpack instructions were available for the conversions. Integer values were 60 bits, and floating-point values were 48 bits plus sign, so you could lose some accuracy when doing an integer multiply or divide. The CPU had some double precision floating-point instructions, but it wasn't a complete set of instructions. Only single precision floating-point had a complete set of instructions. Double precision values were 96 bits plus 12-bit exponent and sign in each word, for a total of 120 bits.

The CPU came with up to 262K words of memory, which is all the addressing allowed. Extended core memory was available, but programs wouldn't run in extended core. There were CPU instructions available, REC and WEC, to read or write extended core. The 6600 used a 6-bit character set, called Display Code.

The 6600 also came with fixed disks, tape drives, a card reader, for reading 80-column punch cards, and a line printer. There were also remote job entry stations available, which would read in programs to be run and print out the results. CDC developed several operating systems for the 6600, including COS, the first system (written by Seymour Cray); Kronos, for time-sharing; NOS; and Mace. COS was short for Chippewa Operating System. Mace reportedly stood for Mansfield and Cahlander Executive— named for its developers.

CDC supplied some other software for the 6600, including two Fortran compilers, assemblers and utility programs, such as UPDATE, for software development. The University of Minnesota wrote their own Fortran compiler, MNF, which became very popular. According to a U of M honors graduate in mathematics, John Norstad, "MNF was the standard compiler for teaching programming at universities all over the world in those days." A web site, http://members.iinet. net.au/~tom-hunter, describes emulators available, in 2009, for 6000-series and Cyber series machines. According to a web site, http://www.nationmaster.com/ encyclopedia/CDC-6600, a Cobol compiler was available for the 6600. The 6600 was designed for scientific and engineering work.

Other models in the 6000 series were sold, including the 6400 and the 6500, which were slower than the 6600. The 6400 had a single processor, and the 6500 had dual CPUs. Control Data later developed the Cyber series of computers, including the Cyber 70, 170 and 180 series. The 180 series were byte-oriented business computers; most of the Control Data computers were word-oriented.

7600

The 6600 became obsolete in Dec., 1968, when Control Data introduced a new model, the 7600, which was about four times faster than the 6600. The 7600 was announced about Dec. 3, 1968, as described in a Minneapolis Star article on that date: "Control Data Announces Most Powerful Computer in the World."

The 7600 model was a large, fast mainframe, the successor to the 6600 model; the 7600 was also designed by Seymour Cray and crew, working in CDC's Chippewa Falls lab. It was a fast machine, with a minor cycle time of 27.5 nanoseconds. I.e, a new instruction could start every minor cycle if the required functional unit was available. According to a CDC brochure, the 7600 central processor code was compatible with the 6000-series machines. The 7600 also had peripheral processors, like the 6000 series; they were 12-bit minicomputers. Up to 15 PPs could be connected to the central processor. It had extended memory, like the 6600, called LCM (for Large Core Memory). The main memory was called SCM, meaning Small Core Memory. The 7600 had nine functional units: Long Add, Floating Add, Floating Multiply, Floating Divide, Boolean, Shift, Normalize, Population Count and Increment. It also had an instruction stack, 12 words long, compared to 10 words on the 6600. They later developed the 8600, which didn't work well enough to sell. Robert Price, the former CDC CEO, said that the 8600 failed to achieve its performance goals. Seymour Cray had done a lot of work on the 8600, but he left to start his own firm, in 1972.

Control Data developed other supercomputers, including the Star and the Cyber 205. The ETA spinoff developed their ETA-10 supercomputer, which was sold to some customers. ETA no longer exists. It was in business from 1983 to 1989, when it was shut down by CDC.

Univac LARC

The LARC, Livermore Advanced Research Computer, was meant to be a supercomputer and was announced in Aug., 1960. But it was not successful; only two were built. The first was delivered to the Livermore lab in 1960. It came with core memory and up to 97K words of 48 bits each. The memory access time was 4 microseconds per word. Internal cycle time was 4 microseconds. Execution times were fairly fast: integer adds took 4 microseconds, multiplies took 8 microseconds, and divides took 32 microseconds, or 28 microseconds for a floating-point divide, according to the LARC General Description. The system also had hardware floating-point instructions and double precision arithmetic. Single-precision floating-point values could range from 10^{50}

to 10^{-50} in absolute value. Double precision arithmetic required at least three times longer to execute than the above figures. The circuitry in the LARC was solid-state. One LARC instruction required 12 <u>decimal</u> digits, an unusual format. To gain speed, the LARC used parallel processing. Up to four instructions could be executing at the same time, in different stages. The hardware had circuitry for detecting overflow, underflow and other calculation errors. The LARC came with up to 99 accumulators which could also be used as index registers.

Another feature to speed up execution was the Processor, which handled input and output requests and auxiliary storage (drum) operations. The CPU could issue commands for the Processor and continue with other tasks. This was similar to the way the Control Data 6600 and 7600 later operated.

The LARC came with one or two processors (CPUs). As with other models, it came with tape drives (Uniservo II or III), magnetic drums, printers, card readers. The drums had a capacity of 6 million words each, or 72 million digits. Access time for the drums was slow, at 68 milliseconds. The printer had a speed of 600 lines per minute. The console printer was slow, with a speed of ten characters per second. The tape drives could handle mylar tape, at a speed of 100 inches per second. The LARC came with an assembler, the SAL, and other software.

Other features included a punch card-to-tape facility, a tape to punch card facility, a paper tape to magnetic tape facility and a magnetic tape to paper tape facility.

The LARC used an unusual 5-bit character code. Alphabetic characters required 10 bits to represent.

IBM STRETCH

The STRETCH model was also known as the 7030 mainframe. It was announced in April, 1960 and withdrawn in 1961, according to an IBM press release. The purchase price was over $10 million. IBM stated that the first STRETCH machine was to be installed at the Los Alamos Scientific Laboratory. Execution speed was 2 million instructions per second; memory access speed was the same. These speeds were fast for that era. The STRETCH model came with card readers, card punches, magnetic tape units and printers. Disk access time was 1.25 million characters per second. A STRETCH machine required about 2000 square feet of floor space. The IBM press release describes the model's multi-programming features. IBM lost $20 million on the STRETCH machine, according to Big Blue.[2]

But the first STRETCH didn't work as promised by IBM[3], so the firm had to reduce the purchase price (originally $13.5 million). Only seven STRETCH machines were delivered to customers. Thomas Watson, Jr. admitted the failures to the press.[4].

Big Blue[5] makes an important comment about the STRETCH: "By rushing STRETCH to market prematurely, IBM again contradicted its interpretation of the antitrust laws, which stated, 'A seller may not offer to sell or offer to sell new products, until such products are actually in production and can reasonably be expected to be ready for delivery when promised, without risking charges of unfair trade practices.'"

As the author of Big Blue stated, "STRETCH proved to be a great embarrassment for IBM."

Illiac IV

The Illiac IV was manufactured by the Burroughs Corp. and was completed in 1974. Only one was completed. It had 64 processors, with two 64-bit accumulators per processor, and was an array processor, like the Star-100. I.e., each processor executed the same instruction simultaneously. Each processor had 2048 words of 64-bit memory. The instruction speed was only 15 megaflops, down from the 1000 megaflops originally estimated. The cost by 1972 was $31 million. Only one-fourth of the planned machine was ever built, meaning 64 of the planned 256 processors. There were other Illiacs; the first one began in 1961 at the Univ. of Illinois to demonstrate a new type of circuit. The Illiac IV project began in 1965. Prof. Daniel Slotnick was in charge. The machine was connected to either a Burroughs 6500, a B6700, or a DEC PDP-10 machine, according to various write-ups. The processors were connected in a linear chain. The B6500 handled the Arpa (Advanced Research Projects Agency, part of the Defense

Department) network link; that machine also had compilers and assemblers. Of course, the Arpa network later became the Internet.

The Illiac IV was installed at NASA's Ames Research Center. At that location, an operating system was used as well as the Glypnir language, which were written at the U of I.

Twenty-Two

The First Personal Computer

S teve Wozniak (Woz) designed and built the first user-friendly personal computer, which he named the Apple I. This was after the Altair, which was available to consumers, but it was a difficult-to-use PC which didn't have a keyboard or monitor, unlike Steve's machine. It was a kit, meant for hobbyists. It cost $400 unassembled.[1] To enter a program with the Altair, you had to use switches. Output was shown on lights on the front panel. An author described how to use the Altair: "One could get it to do little more than blink a pattern of lights on the front panel. And even that was not easy: one had to flick the toggle switches for each program step, then deposit that number into a memory location, then repeat that for the next step—and so on—hopefully the power did not go off while this was going on—until the whole program (less than 256 bytes long!) was in memory."[2] So, the Apple II, which came along a few years later, was a much better machine.

Imsai built a machine very similar to the Altair, called the 8080. A video monitor and diskette drives could be purchased separately to use with the 8080.[3]

Woz built his machine to use a keyboard like we now use with our PCs and a nine-inch black-and-white television as a video monitor, similar to what PCs have now. He had previously built a video terminal, with a keyboard and TV screen, for connecting to a distant computer; that was the basis for the Apple I machine. Woz was a smart guy. According to his book iWoz, he took an IQ test in sixth grade and was told his IQ was "200-plus."[4]

Woz was an amateur electrical engineer who was working at Hewlett-Packard at the time he designed and built the Apple I. He informed his managers at HP after he got the Apple I working, but they decided not to make it one of their products. This allowed Woz to sell Apple I's himself. One of the reasons for building his own PC was to show it off at the Homebrew Computer Club, a neighborhood organization of which he was a member.

Woz realized that if he could make a computer using a microprocessor (an integrated circuit), it would greatly simplify the design, since much of the logic is included in the microprocessor. He designed his computer on paper at home in a few hours. Woz initially wanted to use the Intel 8080 microprocessor, but decided it was too expensive. So he switched to the Motorola 6800, which would cost only about $40. At the WESCON show in San Francisco, in June, 1975, he was able to get 6502 microprocessors (plug-compatible with the 8080) from the MOS Tech firm for about $20 each, so he bought several of them. He also needed ROM (read-only memory) chips, to hold the operating system (he called it the "monitor" program); a complete operating system is a very complex program, but Woz wrote a bare-bones version. Woz actually wrote the 256-byte monitor program himself, in machine language. He wrote two different versions of the program, which handled the keyboard input differently. He got the ROM chips (actually PROM chips, meaning programmable) from an HP lab. Woz also needed RAM chips, for random-access memory, the computer's fastest memory. He borrowed 32 SRAM (static RAM) chips from a fellow HP employee, Myron Tuttle, giving him a total of 4096 bytes of RAM. He tried power supplies available near his desk at HP, checking the outputs with an oscilloscope.

After fixing some minor problems, such as bent pins on the microprocessor, he got the PC running! He tested it by typing something on the keyboard, but nothing happened. It turned out one of the monitor programs had a bug in it, so he replaced the two PROMs so he could use the other monitor program. It worked! He typed letters, which showed up on the screen. He also tested it with some short programs. That was June 29, 1975, a Sunday. The PC we know today was born on that day.

Woz's Apple I wasn't really a finished machine, compared to his later Apple II. His first machine was just a circuit board, which had to be connected to a keyboard and a video monitor. The Apple II was a finished machine, in a plastic case, with a keyboard included. But the video monitor and diskette drives had to be purchased separately. Hard drives for PCs weren't available until the early 1980s.

In 1975, some pieces were still missing to make PCs popular. One was a good operating system. The CP/M system, from Digital Research, was released, for the Altair. A Basic interpreter became available, from Microsoft. It allowed users and developers to create their own PC applications. Several different versions of their Basic product became available in 1975; one version needed only 4K bytes of memory to operate.[5] Diskette drives (8 inch floppies) allowed users to save their programs more easily than on paper tape or audio cassettes. [6] The floppy drive was invented by David Noble at IBM.[7] IBM used it to store the boot program and micro-programs for the System/370 series. Later floppy drives were developed for 5-1/4" and 3-1/2" diskettes. Floppy drives, of various sizes, were popular on PCs for many years, but they are now obsolete, having been replaced by flash drives having much larger capacities. Initial floppy storage capacities were low, some diskettes having a capacity of less than a megabyte. One of the Apple diskettes only held 113 kilobytes of data.[8] Later floppies from Imation and Maxell held up to 240 megabytes of data. Also, small televisions were sometimes used for PC output, such as with the Imsai 8080.[9], the Apple I (see above) and the Apple II. Keyboards began to be used, with the Apple I and the Apple II, replacing the cumbersome input procedures used with the Altair, for example.

The CP/M system was also available on the Osborne computer, in 1981. That machine was portable, but it was heavier than today's notebook machines. It also came with a small video screen, measuring about 5" diagonally. The price was under $2000.[10]

Visicalc, the first popular spreadsheet program, was announced for Apple machines. Initially it was made available for the Apple II in late 1979. It was later eclipsed by the Lotus 1-2-3 spreadsheet product, which debuted three years after Visicalc.

Also in the late 1970s, Radio Shack introduced its TRS-80 machine, which used the Z-80 microprocessor. The TRS-80 was a bargain, at $400, which included a video monitor, keyboard and cassettes for program and data storage.[11] It would run Basic programs. The Commodore PET was a competitor of the TRS-80, having been introduced in the same year, 1977. The Apple II was also introduced in that year.

Early IBM Personal Computers

The famous IBM PC was introduced in Aug., 1981. It came out five years after Apple's first PC, but IBM, according to their archives (a web site), had produced and sold other PCs before that time.

One machine that they developed was called the SCAMP, which they completed in 1973. But it was only for internal use. The name stood for "Special Computer, Apl Machine Portable." It was developed by their General Systems Division (from IBM archive web site). Two years later, IBM came out with the 5100 model, based on the SCAMP. They called it a portable, but it was pretty heavy, weighing 50 pounds. It was introduced in September, 1975. The price started at $8975, and the machine came with APL and Basic.[12] IBM had 12 models of that system available for purchase. They also offered three Problem-Solver Libraries for those machines. Of course, at that price, the 5100 wasn't meant for home users.

Another machine in that series was the 5110 model, initially shipped in 1978, which had more capabilities than the 5100, making it more attractive to small businesses. It came with general ledger and accounts payable software. Other business-oriented programs were also available. A typical system would include a printer, a diskette drive, a tape drive and the CPU or processing unit. The 5110 systems were also produced by the GSD division.

In late 1979, IBM introduced another small system, called the 5520 Administrative System, which offered text processing and electronic document distribution; that was before the Internet. They offered four different versions of the 5520. The 5520 could handle up to 12 printers and 15 display terminals. It also came with disk drives and could communicate with 370 series mainframes. The 5520 models could distribute documents over communication lines. They offered communications hardware for that purpose.

Another system from IBM was the 5110, which was a PC-size machine, which was offered for $9340 and up. It included diskette drives, dot matrix printers and 32K of RAM memory (fast computer memory). The 5110 was introduced in Feb., 1980. At that price, it still was not a machine for home users. In addition to the BASIC language, IBM offered business software for the 5110 machines, including inventory management, billing, payroll and other programs (six packages in all).

IBM also produced a small system, called the Displaywriter, introduced in June, 1980. The cheapest system sold for $7895, still too high for home use. The basic system included 160K bytes of RAM memory, a display monitor, keyboard, printer and diskette drive. It also included a word processor program. The Displaywriter could communicate with other systems over phone lines (IBM archive web site).

Another system, announced just one month before the famous IBM PC, was the System/23 Datamaster. The smallest system in that line cost $9830. It included two display terminals, a diskette drive and a printer.

But IBM's early personal computers were all too expensive for home use. So, they started developing a new PC, in Austin Texas, using a microprocessor from Motorola.[13] However, the product was running behind schedule, so IBM decided to go with an Intel microprocessor, the 8088, an 8-bit device. But first IBM wanted a second source (another company) for that product.[14] Second sourcing was common in that era. For the second source, Intel decided to use Advanced Micro Devices.[15]

Bill Lowe was one of the prime movers behind IBM's first popular personal computer (PC for short), which they called the 5150 model. Lowe was a long-term IBM employee, having spent 13 years as an engineer, working in Raleigh, N.C.[16] He was promoted several times and became the director of the Boca Raton, Florida site, in charge of the laboratory.

At IBM, the Armonk headquarters location is the center of gravity. That was one of the reasons Lowe spent a lot of time at Armonk; he wanted to be noticed. The Corporate Management Committee is one of the centers of power at Armonk. Lowe was able to get permission to address the CMC, in July 1980, about building a new PC that would be more affordable and popular than IBM's earlier PCs. One of his important points was, "…that a personal computer could not be built successfully within the current culture of IBM as it existed in mid-1980." [17] Lowe was referring to IBM's big bureau-cracy, of course. He was given permission to build a prototype pc. He had 12 engineers working on that project. One of the people Lowe recruited was Bill Sydnes, who was working at the Boca Raton facility on another project. Sydnes was "a free-spirited iconoclast," the type that Lowe wanted to work on the new PC. Sydnes was known to be a hard-working guy, sometimes sleeping on his desk or work table. He had earned five awards at IBM. [18] Lowe reached Sydnes on vacation, and he agreed to work with Lowe on that project.

Lowe was able to demonstrate a prototype PC at a meeting of the CMC in Aug., 1980. The demonstration went well, and the CMC approved the PC as a new product, to be developed. Lowe's small group became a Product Development Group. [19] The PC project was named "Project Chess" and the new model being developed was called the "Acorn," [20] which would be the first of many PCs before IBM exited that line of business.

Lowe was described by Business Week magazine as follows: "William C. Lowe is the very picture of an IBM executive: blue suit, conservative tie, square jaw and icy blue eyes. He is known as a consummate manager." [21]

IBM looked at some of its likely competitors in the 1981 PC market. They were: Apple, Tandy (Radio Shack), Commodore and Atari. Apple was the most successful at that point, but its machines weren't widely used by businesses. They decided that Apple would be a weak competitor. I.e,., "Apple's market…was ready for a company with business knowledge like IBM." [22] IBM found that only three percent of business employees were using personal computers regularly at work. [23] Another example of Apple's weakness was in the sales area: "In early 1980, for example, IBM had nearly 8400 salespeople in the field, working out of 650 sales branch offices. Apple, at the same time, had about 100 full-time sales personnel scattered among 12 branches." [24]

The Apple II was popular at that time, but it had limited capabilities. It could only accept up to 128 K bytes of RAM memory, and it only used a cassette tape drive initially, which would later be replaced with one or two diskette drives. The monitor was a small TV screen, which would only display a few lines of text.[25] In 1979 Visicalc, the first popular spreadsheet program, became available for the Apple II, helping the sales of that model.

Another manager who worked on IBM's first popular PC was Don Estridge. He was probably the best-known of the managers who worked on the first popular IBM PC. As one author stated, "...Estridge would become one of the most famous personalities in American business. Job offers would come to him from all over the world; the salaries would be in excess—often very well in excess—of what he was earning at IBM."[26] Estridge and others would meet on Saturday mornings to review progress on the new machine.

To get the new PC model out on the proposed schedule, IBM had to rely on suppliers, such as for the operating system. They originally looked at the CP/M system from Digital Research, and later looked at Microsoft and their DOS system.

One author stated that the head of Digital Research, Gary Kildall, was out flying when some IBM people came to discuss the CP/M system. The other employees present at that time refused to sign IBM's standard non-disclosure agreement. This is what happened: "What is clear, however, is that someone at Digital Research told IBM what it could do with its one-sided nondisclosure agreement. He also added that CP/M would not be changed to suit IBM's 16-bit technology, even if IBM changed the provisions of its contract with Digital Research—something which, of course, IBM was not about to do. So that was that."[27]

IBM moved on. They were impressed early on with the BASIC interpreter produced by Microsoft. As one author stated, "The [Microsoft] company's BASIC programming language [interpreter] for the Intel 8088 chip was regarded as a classic of its kind, an opinion that was substantiated by the growing acceptance of this language as the standard for many of the major desk-top computers now being produced."[28] Probably one reason for its popularity is that BASIC is a simple language, easy to learn and use.

The IBM people who visited the Microsoft firm gave their impression of Bill Gates, in 1980: "Bill Gates may look like a kid but doesn't act like one. He is, without a doubt, brilliant at developing software and programming languages [interpreters]. He's smart and knows it—but not a smart aleck. We like him. We can work with him. And his other executives are also okay. They are not running their company out of a garage or a basement. They are serious businessmen and they give us the impression that they would fall all over themselves to get a chance to work with us. We say, 'Let's go with Microsoft for the BASIC.'"[29]

Microsoft had to submit a document to the Boca Raton people explaining why they should buy their BASIC interpreter and DOS operating system for their new personal computer. It was delivered to the IBM group in September, 1980.

IBM decided to buy the BASIC product and the DOS system, which Microsoft had bought from a small company called Seattle Computer Products; SCP didn't know that IBM was interested in buying the DOS system. Microsoft was sworn to secrecy by IBM. The operating system was originally named SCP-DOS. Internally, SCP called their version QDOS, for Quick and Dirty Operating System. Bill Gates and his people were able to convince the IBM people that they should buy both BASIC and DOS. IBM's only concern was lax security at the Microsoft firm, in Seattle. They didn't want information about their Acorn product leaking to the media. The Microsoft version of DOS was called MS-DOS. IBM called their version of DOS PC-DOS.[30] It is interesting that IBM realized they didn't have the internal resources to develop a BASIC interpreter or a PC operating system internally, at least not in the allowed time frame. Of course, that was consistent with Bill Lowe's views from the start, in July 1980.

By Oct., 1980 the CMC people had approved an expansion of Project Chess, with 100 more people joining the project.[31] The Boca Raton facility became an Independent Business Unit. The CMC decided that, "The corporation and its rules and regulations, checks and balances, procedures and protocols, standards and traditions—and all that has to do with its bureaucracy—well, perhaps almost al, was tossed out. What remained were the reporting procedures."[32] Those changes, of course, allowed the Boca Raton people to get their new PC to market much faster.

The Project Chess managers were receiving many resumes from people who wanted to help design and manufacture the new PC, but none from people who wanted to help sell it. That's why Estridge recruited an IBMer named H.L. Sparks, nicknamed Sparky, to be in charge of selling the new PC. Sparks was described as a "born salesman."[33] Sparky was known for being very organized. He was able to get the computer dealers in place, by November. He also kept his office spotless, and he was detail-oriented. An associate described him as "very finicky." The associate also said, about him: "...[H]e'd be more worried about where the staples were in the documents than in what the documents had to say."[34]

Sparks hired Jim D'Arezzo as an assistant. He had experience marketing small machines, such as IBM's Displaywriter and copying machines.[35] D'Arezzo was the guy who decided to use the Charlie Chaplin look-alike in the IBM PC ads. They actually found someone to act like Chaplin's tramp character. One of the lines they used was, "The IBM Personal Computer—a Tool for Modern Times."[36] "Modern Times" was the title of a Chaplin movie.

It was decided that the new machine would be sold through Sears and Computerland stores. Selling the new PC turned out to be a long-term project for Computerland. They started working with IBM almost a year before the machine was announced to the public. Computer-land provided advice to IBM about retail sales, because IBM hadn't sold products that way before.[37] They had regular meetings with the Project Chess people. An IBM sales division decided that they wanted a part of the new PC. One of their executives said, "'This is something we must have. We've got to get this product.' By that I meant we should be promoting and selling it through the Office Products Division." But the OPD wasn't interested. They only had experience selling to businesses, not consumers.[38]

To save time, IBM had to rely on outside suppliers, besides Microsoft, to produce important parts for the new PC: Intel supplied the 8088 microprocessor, Tandon Corp. provided the diskette drives, Zenith provided the power supply, SCI made the circuit boards and Epson provided the printers.[39] It seems that IBM didn't provide many of the important parts of its new machine. They had to save time.

Using so many outside suppliers was contrary to the usual IBM policy. An author stated, "It had been IBM's custom to build its computing machines with parts made by divisions within IBM. Until the advent of Project Chess [the 1981 IBM PC], this project was all but sacrosanct—the sole exception being the acquisition of the highly sophisticated silicon chips known as microprocessors. Here, IBM lacked the expertise of such specialized corporations as Intel…"[40]

The same author commented on the need to buy parts from other firms: "If Project Chess had been forced to follow conventional IBM procedures, Sarubbi [an IBM executive] estimated that it would have taken up to another two years to complete the PC project."[41] Of course, in that case, some of the technology would have become obsolete. But older technology is typically more reliable. New technology sometimes comes with unexpected problems.

Microsoft was three months behind schedule with their operating system and BASIC for the Acorn machine, in early 1981, and IBM was getting nervous. IBM couldn't write the application programs they had planned until they had a good version of DOS. So, they were worried that the schedule for the new machine would slip if Microsoft missed their deadline. [42] IBM people said the project could be cancelled if the Acorn machine was late.

IBM and Microsoft set up an e-mail system, and Gates and his people would often visit Boca Raton. Gates had to convert his BASIC to run on the Acorn. It was originally written for the old Altair machine.[43] For its part, IBM shipped circuit boards of the Acorn to Microsoft. They didn't have complete machines at that time. By that time, Don Estridge was working 60 to 70 hour weeks on Project Chess.[44]

The machine called Acorn was introduced on Aug. 12, 1981 in New York City; Don Estridge was in charge of the ceremony. IBM also introduced eight applications programs for the new machine, including a new version of Visicalc, business applications from Peachtree Software, a game program called Adventure, and the new Microsoft BASIC. They also offered a new word-processing program called Easy Writer.[45] IBM could have just offered BASIC and Visicalc for the new machine, in addition to the DOS system, which would likely have disappointed potential buyers. The new PC used the industry-standard ASCII character set rather than IBM's standard called EBCDIC. [46] The original ASCII character set contained only 128 characters, which would fit in seven bits of memory. That made it convenient for machines using 8-bit bytes.

IBM's new PC wasn't impressive by today's standards. It came with 16 K to 64 K bytes of RAM, one diskette drive and had a price of $1600 to $2900.[47] It didn't come with a hard drive, which became available later with the XT model.

Of course, there were reactions to the introduction. The Wall Street Journal commented, "IBM has made its bold entry into the personal computer market. The computer giant could capture the lead in the youthful industry within two years."[48] Apple Computer ran a full-page ad in the Aug. 12 Wall Street Journal. It welcomed IBM to the personal computer market place.[49] Many people thought IBM was worried about Apple. But one of IBM's Project Chess executives said, "As far as we were concerned, Apple was just another competitor, a price point in the market we were going after."[50]

Demand for the IBM PC was much better than expected. The order backlogs became "intolerable."[51] The popular IBM PC created an industry. As one author stated, "By 1983, there were at least a dozen monthly or bi-monthly magazines and maybe as many as 20 weekly publications, all devoted exclusively to the IBM Personal Computer."[52]

IBM executives who worked on mainframes didn't like the new PC. According to one author, "...[M]any of the more astute mainframe marketers cursed Opel [the current CEO] for bringing the PC into IBM....It [the new PC] was like a Trojan horse within the Big Blue walls. Some of the mainframe guys were scared and, as it developed, their fears were confirmed." They knew that PCs would provide better performance per dollar than mainframes.[53]

John Opel was aware of the Trojan horse problem, but the wanted the horse inside IBM, where he could control it, rather than in some other firm, where they might take the lead in the PC industry.[54]

One result of the 1981 IBM PC was the rise of the clones, such as at Compaq Computer. That firm was started in Houston, in 1982, by three people who left Texas Instruments: Rod Canion, Jim Harris and Bill Murto. Some authors stated that Compaq began when the three drew an IBM-compatible PC on a napkin in a Houston restaurant.[55] Their plan was to reverse-engineer an IBM PC to produce a new machine that was 100% compatible, including the BIOS, or Basic Input/ Output System, which was included in the IBM PC. They created their own version of BIOS, without using any of IBM's code.[56] Their first product was the

Compaq Portable. [57] They also produced a clone of IBM's AT model. Of course, there were other clone manufacturers, such as Leading Edge, PC's Limited and PC Designs. The first of those was founded by Michael Dell. Later, Phoenix Technologies produced a BIOS chip, so customers could get a copy of IBM's BIOS when building their own PCs. [58]

Some competitors of the IBM PC weren't really clones, but they were personal computers. One example was the Osborne PC, which came with a tiny video monitor, a keyboard and two diskette drives. It sold for under $2000. Another PC was the TRS-80, which came with a small monochrome display, BASIC and a keyboard. [59] Another PC from that era was the Commodore PET.

Early in 1982 (Feb.), IBM decided to expand its PC product line, with three new product groups. The Boca Raton managers were worried about the work load if they had to produce three new machines. They eventually produced the model XT, the PC Jr. and the AT. [60] The XT model was the first one to go on sale, in March of 1983. The XT was a much better PC, which came with a ten-megabyte hard drive, in addition to more RAM memory (128 K) and a larger-capacity diskette drive. The original IBM PC didn't come with a hard drive.

At the end of 1982, Time magazine named the Personal Computer as its Man of the Year. They called it the "Machine of the Year." [61] The story wasn't just about IBM, but it said the IBM PC "...[H]as set a standard of excellence for the industry."

IBM announced the new XT model in March, 1983. XT meant eXtended Technology. It had nine times as much memory, and it had a hard disk drive (ten megabytes), which the original PC didn't have. [62] It also had a color monitor and an "integrated communications adapter" which allowed it to communicate with other IBM computers. The retail price of the XT was $4995, much more than the 1981 PC, which retailed for $2880 initially.

But the XT model was too expensive for home users, so IBM's answer was the PC Junior. It was supposed to be "a magnificent machine" meant for "the consumer markets served by mass merchandisers." [63] It would be the cheapest model in their line of PCs. The Junior model was meant to compete with the Apple II Plus and the Apple IIe. One of IBM's PC executives, Bill Sydnes, described the Junior as "...a dynamite product that could have blown the Apple II series off the map." [64] He also wasn't concerned about the new Apple Lisa model, which was introduced in early 1983. Of course, the Lisa was initially a very expensive PC, compared to IBM's models.

IBM decided to restructure its PC operations in the summer of 1983. They knew it would look bad to end the PC operations in Boca Raton. So they created a new division, called the Entry Systems Division, which ran the IBM factory in Austin, Texas and the Boca Raton facility. The Austin factory had a more traditional view of computing, being more office-oriented. The Boca Raton group had a more modern view, with PCs used for any purpose. Other factories in that division were Greenock, Scotland and Wangaratta, Australia.[65]

The Junior model was introduced on Nov. 1, 1983 in New York City. An IBM press release described the new model: "The IBM PCJr features a 16-bit 8088 microprocessor, 64 KB of permanent read-only memory (ROM), 64 KB of user memory, a cordless 62-key keyboard, a desktop transformer, two slots for ROM cartridges, an audio tone generator and a 12-month warranty."

"The enhanced model includes an additional 64 KB of user memory for a total of 128 KB, as well as a 360 KB, dual-sided slim-line diskette drive. It also has the capacity to display of to 80 columns of information."[66] The Junior initially sold for $1269, less than half the IBM PC price in Aug., 1981.

The Boca Raton IBM people weren't very optimistic about the Junior model when it was introduced, but the media seemed to like it. There was a magazine named PCJr. They had an upbeat critique of that new model: "...the design of the PCJr reveals it to be a capable machine....Junior is something much more than a scaled-down business computer. The hardware itself points in the direction that IBM believes personal computers are going (and have so far gone) [,] and it shows what IBM expects junior to do and where it expects it will do it....PCJr is designed to be a part of a home entertainment system, not just a glorified type-writer or adding machine.,"[67]

As with the original IBM PC of Aug., 1981, many business produced parts that could be added to the Junior model. But the model wasn't well-received. Sales were lukewarm. Users complained about the keyboard, which one critic likened to a bunch of Chiclets. IBM eventually came out with a redesigned key-board for that model. There was an advertising blitz for the Junior model in late

1984, and customers could get one of those machines for $799 at some stores, with a color monitor. So sales went up dramatically, for awhile.

But they phased out the Junior model after 16 months.[68] They tried to phase it out earlier, but contracts with suppliers were in effect through the spring of 1985. An IBM executive, Michael Armstrong, said they stopped making the PC Jr. model by April, 1985, but marketing, service and software development for that model would continue.[69] He said Don Estridge wasn't transferred because of any problems with the PC Jr. Estridge was "a hero in the IBM company," according to Armstrong.[70]

The AT model was introduced in Aug., 1984 in Dallas. That model was offered with up to three megabytes of RAM memory and up to 40 megabytes of hard disk space. The microprocessor was the powerful 80286 from Intel. There were also eight slots, for hardware such as extra disk drives. The AT had a much better keyboard than the Junior model. The cheapest version of the new machine sold for just under $4000.[71] The new model was popular with the dealers. Consequently, IBM had underestimated the demand, as with the 1981 PC. But some of the earliest AT machines had an electronic flaw that would cause hard disk data to be erased. The flaw was traced to a bad Texas Instruments chip.[72]

When the Boca Raton facility became part of the new ESD division, IBM's bureaucracy was taking over, and many of the original PC people didn't like it. As one author stated, "The guys on the PC team who had been around for awhile were getting the impression that bigness was settling in and many of us didn't like it. We were spending too much time communicating instead of producing. The company came in and set up multiple levels of managers, multiple disciplines, new policies and procedures, and reviews upon reviews. ...After a while, it was like a big cloud gradually engulfing us one day at a time."[73] That was a quote from Dan Wilkie, an executive at Boca Raton. The original PC team members had to get used to writing reports or creating presentations, instead of fixing new problems every day. Instead of putting in long days, they would arrive at 8:00, take lunch breaks at the usual time and leave at 5:00. They would take their weekends off for a change, and some of them looked for new jobs at some other company.[74]

The view from the Armonk headquarters was that the PC people in Boca Raton were doing well and making a lot of money for the firm. A long-term IBM executive, whose name wasn't given, stated, "There's that hard core of people down in Florida who created the PC [,] and now they want to set themselves apart from the rest of us. We can't allow that. It's disruptive to the company."[75] The headquarters executives reduced the autonomy of the executives in Boca Raton, which caused some problems in developing new products in the PC area. That was the view of the Boca Raton people. The Armonk people were concerned about the poor sales of the Junior model, for example. [76]

At that time, Don Estridge and his wife built a new house in the Boca Raton area. He would be appointed vice pres. in charge of worldwide manufacturing at that time.[77] Don was spending most of his time at the Armonk headquarters. Bill Lowe was named president of the Entry Systems Division, working at Boca Raton. The Estridges started to look for a house near Armonk. They bought a new house in New Canaan.[78]

Don Estridge and his wife were flying to Jackson Hole, Wyoming on vacation in Aug., 1985. But their plane crashed near the Dallas-Fort Worth Airport, apparently due to a downdraft from a thunderstorm. Sadly, Don Estridge and his wife were killed in the plane crash.[79] Some other IBM employees also died in the crash. The funerals started a few days later. Don and his wife were buried in a Boca Raton cemetery.

IBM produced other PC models. One of them was the model RT, an engineering workstation. It was expensive, initially selling for $11,700. It used RISC technology (Reduced Instruction Set Computing). The RT didn't sell well. One author called it "a marketing failure."[80]

IBM had to compete in the workstation market with Apollo, Sun Microsystems and Digital Equipment Corp. It wasn't an open machine, which made it difficult for other firms to develop software for the RT.

Another PC they produced was the Convertible, which was a notebook machine which could also be used as a desktop PC. The price was only $1995, but it was a failure. Toshiba produced a better notebook PC about that time.

IBM also introduced their XT-286, in Aug., 1986. The microprocessor was the 80286, like the AT model had, and it was much cheaper than the AT. But it sold poorly.

The next year IBM introduced their PS/2 series. They were well-designed machines. They used the OS/2 system, originally from Microsoft, and they had a mouse-and-icon graphics like the Macintosh. IBM initially had four models in that series: the 30, 50, 60 and 80.

Model 50 cost $3600 and had an 80286 processor. It also had a 20 megabyte hard drive and one megabyte of RAM. Model 60 could be ordered with 15 megabytes of RAM and a 185 megabyte hard drive. The model 80 PC was the fastest machine, with an 80386 processor.[81]

Twenty-Three

Univac Computer Models

Typically, the chief developer of each system described here isn't known. The LARC model is discussed in the Supercomputers chapter.

1103

The 1103 model was developed by the Engineering Research Associates, in St. Paul; it was a commercial machine, unlike the 1101 and 1102. The 1103 was announced in Feb., 1953; it was sometimes called the Atlas II by ERA people. The memory was 36-bit words, like the later 1100-series models. It had only 1024 words of RAM memory, made of Williams tubes; this was a type of cathode ray tube memory. It also had 16K words of magnetic drum memory, similar to today's disk drives.

Software for the machine included the RECO and RAWOOP assemblers and several packages to perform floating-point calculations. One of them, the SNAP floating-point system was from Ramo-Wooldridge Corp. According to William Norris[1], the first 1103 was delivered to Georgia Tech. It was described in the interview as "The first commercial 1101." Norris stated that Howard

Engstrom led the push for a commercial version of the 1101; he had made a sales call at Georgia Tech, according to Norris.

Univac soon announced a new version of the 1103, called the 1103A; it was also known as the Univac Scientific. Improvements included hardware floating-point arithmetic and magnetic core memory, making it a much better machine. There was a model called the 1102, but it was developed only for the Air Force and wasn't meant for commercial use. It had a 24-bit word and 8K of RAM memory. Again according to Norris, three 1102s were built, all for the Air Force. Norris wouldn't say how the 1102 differed from the 1101. When asked why the Air Force didn't buy 1101s, he said, "I can't answer that."[2] Norris said the 1103 machines were meant for scientific and engineering use, and the Eckert-Mauchly Univac series was for business use ("human applications," according to Norris).

Norris stated that the agreement for Remington Rand to acquire ERA was reached in 1952, with the actual closing in December of that year. Robert Price stated that ERA was purchased for $1.7 million, in 1951.[3]

1105

The 1105 model was the successor to the 1103A and was introduced in 1958.

1107

The 1107 model was the first of the modern 1100 series machines, introduced in 1962, with a 36-bit word size and one instruction per word. It came with up to 65K words of magnetic core memory. It had a sophisticated instruction set, with 16 accumulators (main arithmetic registers) or A registers and 16 index (X) registers, four of which overlapped the A registers. It also had 16 R registers, used as counters and to hold temporary values. The memory cycle time was 4 microseconds.

1108

The 1108 model was introduced in 1964 and had almost the same instruction set as the previous 1107; programs were upward-compatible. Multiple CPUs were available on this model, which came with an operating system called Exec 8, later renamed OS 1100, written in assembly language. It came with up to 262K of main memory. By this time, the Univac division had an extensive set of software for their 1100 series, including a Fortran compiler, a Cobol compiler, a Fortran interpreter, Basic, Plus and an assembler; Plus was their development language, similar to Pascal. They wrote new software in the 1970s for the 1100 series.

1110

The 1110 model was basically a faster version of the 1108, with the same word size and instruction set. It was announced in 1971. The 1100 series models initially used a six-bit character set, Fieldata, but later the new standard ASCII character set was added, making use of the 9-bit bytes available in the 36-bit words. The initial ASCII set had 128 characters, making use of 7 bits per character.

At Univac, there was a flurry of software development activity in the 1970s, including their Plus compiler (Programming Language for Univac Systems), a new Fortran, a PL/I, Conversational Time-Sharing, the Query Language Processor and MASM, the meta-assembler.

418

The 418 was an 18-bit minicomputer with a magnetic core memory and discrete-component solid state (transistor) circuitry. The memory cycle time was 4 microseconds. It had 4K to 16K words of memory. The first 418 was delivered in June, 1963. Three models were made. Model II had up to 65K of memory and a 2 microsecond cycle time. Model III had from 32K to 131K of memory and hardware floating-point instructions. The cycle time for that model was 750 nanoseconds.

494

The 494 was part of the 490 series. A brochure describes the model as the 494 Real-Time System. The machine had a 30-bit word, with 16K to 131K words of RAM memory. Memory access time was 750 nanoseconds. Double precision floating-point arithmetic was included. It had 14 index registers. It also had Drum and Fastrand mass storage, card readers and punches, magnetic tape drives, printers and remote communications devices.

The brochure describes the model: "The Univac 494 is capable of handling vast quantities of converging data in real-time, batch processing and scientific applications—concurrently. Instand response and the ability to interrupt routine for priority data makes the Univac 494 processor the center of extensive nation-wide data processing operations in real-time." Airline reservations was one of the uses for the 490 series machines.

The available printer could print up to 922 lines per minute, with 132 characters per line. A card reader could process up to 900 cards per minute. An available card punch could process 300 cards per minute. A paper tape reader could read 400 characters per second. The system also worked with VI-C and VIII-C Uniservo tape drives.

1004

The 1004 model, introduced in 1962, also worked with the 494 model, for remote batch job entry, for running jobs on larger computers. The 1004 was a small computer system. It came with a card reader, a card punch, a tape drive and a line printer. The card reader could handle the standard 80-column cards or the 90-column variety. A paper tape reader and punch was also available. It had less than 1000 characters of memory and was programmed with plug boards, like the IBM accounting machines (e.g, the 407 model). It would print up to 600 lines per minute and could read 615 cards per minute. It only allowed up to 62 program steps, with the plugboard programming.

The 1005 was an improved version of the 1004, introduced in 1966. The main improvement was the change from plugboard programs to stored-programs, running in memory.

9400

The 9400 was part of the 9000 series; that model was introduced in 1969. A brochure from Univac describes its features: disk and tape drives,

multiprogramming (up to five programs at one time) and real-time communications processing, and software packages: Cobol, Fortran, RPG and
the BAL assembler. The machine was described as a Medium-Scale System.
It came with a high-speed printer (1100 lpm maximum) and a card reader
(600 cards/minute maximum) and punch. The 9400 was built with integrated circuits (small-scale integration by today's standards), with about 50
components, such as transistors, per chip. The 9400 used a 6-bit character
set. The operating system is described as The Supervisor, but is not otherwise
described.

The memory cycle time was 600 nanoseconds, and the memory sizes were
24K to 131K bytes. The RAM memory was described as Plated Wire. The 9400
accommodated four to 16 tape drives. Each of the 8411 model disk drives would
hold 7 million bytes. The system allowed one to eight disk drives. Those drives
would operate in 7- or 9-track format and transfer rates were up to 192K bytes
per second. A Data Communications System was also available.

The brochure shows, on the first page, several disk drives, the operator
console, tape drives in the background and a register-display panel next to the
operator's console.

IBM Models

IBM's first mainframe machine was the 701 model, first delivered to a customer
in March, 1953 [4]; it was originally called the Defense Calculator. The customer
was Los Alamos Scientific lab, and the machine was installed and working in April,
1953. Another 701 was installed earlier, in December, 1952 at IBM's headquarters
in New York City. According to an IBM web site, the 701 had many components
and peripherals, including a card reader, a line printer, a magnetic tape unit and
a magnetic drum and magnetic core storage, among others. IBM described it as a
"scientific computer" but it was more likely to be used for business data processing.
Later models, such as the 705 and the 709, were better-suited for scientific work.
Thomas Watson, Jr., the CEO, described the 701 model as, "the most advanced,
most flexible high-speed computer in the world."[5] The 701 was delivered two
years later than the first Univac computer, the Univac I.

After the 701, IBM introduced a new computer model almost every year in the 1950s.[6] The 702 model, for instance, was introduced in September, 1953. Calculation speeds were 4000 integer adds or subtracts per second, and 830 multiplications per second. The machine's fast memory was electrostatic. The 701 came with a card reader, a printer, a tape drive, a magnetic drum and a card punch.

The 704 was introduced in May, 1954. The biggest improvement in that model was magnetic core storage. Earlier machines used electrostatic storage, on cathode ray tubes. Memory cycle time for the 704 was 12 microseconds, such as for retrieving a word of data. Calculation speed was about 4000 operations per second. Like the earlier 702, the 704 came with a card reader, a card punch, tape drives, printers and magnetic drums.

Their 705 model was introduced in October, 1954. Its instruction speed was 4000 per second, seven times faster than the 702. It had 20,000 bytes of magnetic core storage. Like earlier models, it had the usual set of peripheral devices.

The 709 model was introduced in January, 1957 and had built-in floating-point arithmetic. The word size was 36 bits. Fixed-point instructions were executed at a speed of 40,000 per second; floating-point multiplies were executed at a speed of 5000 per second. It also had instructions for numeric conversion. That model came with the usual peripheral devices and CRT displays, such as for graphs. There were two types of core memory available, the 737 and the 738; the latter was large-capacity memory. It also came with a Fortran compiler. The 709 model was suitable for business and scientific uses.

Another machine in the line was the 305. But customers were slow to accept the new machines. According to Big Blue[7], 95% of all IBM machines in 1959 were punch card equipment.

The 1401 computer was the first in a new line of machines which was announced in Oct., 1959. An IBM document describes the machine: "The all-transistorized IBM 1401 Data Processing System places the features found in electronic data processing systems at the disposal of smaller businesses, previously limited to the use of conventional punched card equipment. These features include: high speed card punching and reading, magnetic tape input and output, high speed printing, stored program, and arithmetic and logical ability."

The system only allowed 4000 positions (bytes or words) of core memory. It performed 3200 additions per second and just over 400 multiplies per second. The printer, model 1403, had a speed of 600 lines per minute. It was a chain printer, which used hammers to print the characters. Printers of that era used continuous-form paper (which came in big boxes), with sprocket holes at the left and right sides and perforations between each page, so the pages could be ripped apart, a process called bursting. The press release also stated that on the 1401, "…manual control panel wiring is eliminated." Their older tab equipment, such as the 407 (a type of printer), used user-alterable wiring panels for their programming. The 1401 was designed for business-oriented data processing, such as payrolls.

A newer model, the 1410, was announced in Sept., 1960. It came with the usual card reader and punch, a console, a printer and magnetic tape drives. Disk drives were also available. IBM used the word "mammoth" in their press release to describe the capacity of their disk drives. They also offered a paper tape reading device and a magnetic character reader. The press release didn't describe processor speeds or disk capacity.

In 1964, IBM introduced the System/360 series of computers, which were designed for business data processing. IBM had lots of problems with that line, but the 360s generated $16 billion in revenues by 1970 and $6 billion in profits.[8] The 360s used the OS/360 operating system, which was initially missing important features. Initially, the 360 models only allowed batch processing, which, of course, used punch cards.

But customers started to demand interactive processing on their 360s. IBM initially responded with the 360/67 model, a modified 360/65, which included time-sharing.[9] IBM also introduced the TSO product with the 360 series to provide time-sharing; it was typically used with the ISPF product, which provided a menu for users. TSO was used on MVS and OS/390, among other systems. TSO is still in use and is usually referred to as TSO/ISPF. General Electric had earlier produced a computer for time-sharing use.

Other IBM products that were or are widely used on mainframes include VSAM, for direct-access use of records residing on disk drives, CICS (Customer

Information Control System) for terminal users and IMS, a hierarchical database management system. CICS is a software product typically used by terminal users, such as bank tellers, who interact with customized screens which are retrieved and updated with short alphabetic or numeric commands, such as IQML, which are typed in by a terminal user. An IBM web site shows that CICS is an old product, from 1968, originally called CICS/OS and could only support 50 terminals.

To counter Control Data in the scientific machine market, IBM developed the 360/90 model. IBM spent over $100 million on the 360/90 series machines.[10] An IBM executive, Harwood Kolsky, described IBM's problems in the scientific computer marketplace. He lamented that the federal AEC preferred the CDC 6600 machines, which are "more modern and are more nearly [fitting] the standard problems of the AEC than does the IBM product line, which they feel is now becoming too expensive and obsolete technologically."[11] He felt that IBM had a psychological advantage in the computing industry. But, he said, "This had largely been taken over by the CDC 6600…which gives CDC the prestige of being the pacesetter in the computer industry."[12] IBM announced more 360/90 series models, to damage CDC.[13]

The author of Big Blue commented on the 360/90s: "The 360/90s swept the field…thus did its 'mediocre' 360s triumph—not by virtue of their excellence, but through a continuing exercise of power, something IBM had done since before the computer business ever existed."[14] Of course, the author meant the tabulating equipment industry, which IBM dominated for decades before selling their first computer. Another IBM product developed for the scientific market was the STRETCH, or 7030 model. IBM lost $20 million on the STRETCH machine, according to Big Blue[15]. The STRETCH model is discussed further in the Super-computers chapter of this book.

By the late 1960s, IBM had some new competitors in the peripherals area. This included card readers and punches, disk drives, tape drives and printers. IBM's tape drives, for example, were inferior. So, IBM lost 4000 tape drive installs in 1969 (estimated) and 16,000 installs total by 1970.[16] The lost installs were similar for disk drives.

Disk drives became popular in the 1960s. But IBM's drives were not the best, as described in Big Blue [17]: "...in this case the company [IBM] did not lead the industry in bringing the latest technology to market." IBM tried to manipulate the market, as much as possible, such as by packaging a new drive, the 2314, only as a package of nine spindles.

IBM's profits, according to the Big Blue book[18], were at least 50% greater than other manufacturers' (net earnings / shareholders' equity). Also, IBM's profits were much greater than those of its competitors.[19]

IBM lost a lot of sales due to the computer leasing industry, whose firms would buy 360 models and lease them to customers at attractive rates. IBM responded by altering prices and lease terms so that leasing firms would likely lose money.[20]

The federal government filed their antitrust suit against IBM in January, 1969.[21] This was after Control Data had filed their antitrust suit against IBM; the latter suit was successful.

An IBM executive, Hillary Faw, said at that time that IBM would have to destroy damaging evidence. So, he stated that IBM employees who worked on the 2319 [disk drive] would have to "clean out your files." IBM also resorted to "fixing the books to cover its tracks."[22] The federal suit was eventually dropped.

IBM announced its new 370 series line in June, 1970, partly to make the 360s owned by leasing firms obsolete. The 370s were better suited to interactive use.[23] Two of the 370 models came with virtual memory, the 370/158 and 168. Virtual memory is a feature that makes it easier to run big programs.

This is the text of the System/370 announcement, from June, 1970:

A new computer system - - the IBM System/370 - - was announced worldwide today by International Business Machines Corporation. Its two models use advanced design techniques previously available only in IBM's ultra-high-performance computers.

Introducing the new system at a press conference here, Thomas J. Watson, Jr., IBM chairman of the board, said:

"We are confident that the performance of System/370, its compatibility, its engineering and its programming will make it stand out as the landmark for the 1970s that System/360 was for the Sixties."

System/370 Models 155 and 165 can provide computer users with dramatically higher performance and information storage capacity for their data processing dollars than ever before available from IBM in medium- and large-scale systems.

Business and scientific computers users will be able to move up to the higher performance System/370 to handle their remote computing and large data base needs of the Seventies. They can do so without having to reprogram the vast majority of their existing System/360 applications.

System/370 carries forward the concept of compatibility first introduced by IBM in 1964 for the widely used System/360. Models 155 and 165 can share input and output equipment and proven programming systems that transcend specific models. They can use nearly all existing IBM peripheral devices, as well as a new 2,000-line-per-minute printer and an 800 million character-capacity disk storage. The printer and disk storage units included in today's announcement are designed to step up input and output capabilities to System/370's high internal operating speed.

Both models of System/370 are now in production - - Model 155 at Poughkeepsie, N.Y., and Montpelier, France; Model 165 at Kingston, N.Y. Model 155 is being demonstrated today in Poughkeepsie.

"We have met two very important objectives with System/370 - - price/performance and compatibility," said F. G. Rodgers, president of IBM's Data Processing Division. "First, we have achieved greatly improved performance by putting much of the advanced technology of IBM's ultra-high-performance computers within the reach of medium- and large-scale computer users."

"And we have achieved compatibility since System/360 users will be able to run most of their existing programs on the new system without change," Mr. Rodgers said.

To illustrate System/370 performance and economy, Mr. Rodgers noted that the new Model 165 operates up to five times faster internally than System/360 Model 65. Yet the user's equipment cost to achieve the increased performance level is relatively modest in comparison with the gain in processing capability. The Model 155 has up to four times the internal operating speed of System/360 Model 50.

The basic machine cycle times of the Model 165 and 155 central processors are 80 and 115 nanoseconds (billionths of a second), respectively. A cycle - - the time it takes to execute an instruction - - is a major factor in how much work the computer can do in a given period.

Each model uses a buffer memory, an advanced technique previously offered by IBM only with ultra-high-performance systems. The buffer, which operates at the same speed as the central processor, holds large blocks of data and instructions ready for immediate use, thus speeding the processing of information.

Toward expanded applications

"The applications of the Seventies will involve increased multiprogramming, remote computing, management information and tele-processing networks that make a centralized computer data base available to people in many places," Mr. Rodgers said. "The management of virtually every business wants and needs immediate access to current information organized so it can be used effectively," Mr. Rodgers said. "To do the job, banks, manufacturing firms and insurance companies - - as well as government agencies and many scientific users - - need faster, more efficient computers and larger capacity data storage. System/370 meets those requirements."

Although internal operating speed is one way to measure computer performance, users generally are more concerned with how rapidly the system can finish its assigned tasks. This capability - - called throughput - -depends on a number of factors such as memory size, input and output equipment and the efficiency of the operating systems and the user's programs.

To help customers exploit the full throughput potential of System/370, IBM has built in many advances keyed to reliable performance, including:

Monolithic integrated circuits, microscopic in size, that perform logical and arithmetic operations at speeds measured in nanoseconds.

Main core memories having capacities up to 2-million bytes for the Model 155 and 3-million for the Model 165.

Monolithic buffer storage that holds data and instructions ready before they are actually needed, streaming them into the central processing unit on demand at nanosecond speeds. The buffer effectively matches the data from the larger but slower main memory to the very high internal speed of the processor.

Expanded channels to carry more data faster between memory and other system units. These new channels are analogous to pipelines whose width and flow pressure have been increased.

The ability to handle up to 15 different program tasks simultaneously, including programs written for the IBM 1400 and 7000 series, as well as System/360.
New mass storage, printer

Users also can increase system throughput by attaching to System/370 the new IBM 3330 disk storage and the IBM 3211 printer.

Designed for large data base applications that require ready and rapid access to vast amounts of information, the 3330 combines high operating speed with the flexibility of virtually unlimited storage on removable, direct access magnetic disks. It has three-and-a-half times more on-line storage capacity - - up to 800-million bytes (more than 1.5-billion decimal digits) - - than other IBM disk storage facilities and has an average access time of only 30-thousandths of a second.

In addition to the 3330, System/370 users can take advantage of the very fast storage available with the recently announced IBM 2305 fixed head storage facility. This device previously was offered only with IBM's most powerful computers, System/360 Models 85 and 195. It is designed to provide direct access to data the central processor uses repeatedly, such as control programs and working files. The average access time of the faster of two models is only 2.5 thousandths of a second.

The new IBM 3211 printer will help speed processed information to the various users within an organization. It can turn out reports and other documents at 2,000 lines a minute, almost twice as fast as any previous IBM printer. With a smaller character set, 2,500 lines a minute can be achieved.

Control devices built into the new printer provide highly accurate spacing and clear copies. A powered stacker automatically adjusts for the height of the paper stack. Through an innovative forms control buffer in the printer, the computer can automatically specify the job-to-job formatting instructions. This eliminates the need for operating personnel to switch carriage control tapes when printing formats need to be changed. The 3211 can be used with System/370 and with most System/360 models.

Prices, programming and delivery

Monthly rental for a typical System/370 Model 155 having 768,000 bytes of main memory is $47,985, with a purchase price of $2,248,550.

Monthly rental for a typical Model 165 with 1-million bytes of main memory is $98,715, with a purchase price of $4,674,160.

Purchase customers may use IBM maintenance service for the new system. The minimum monthly maintenance charges covering the purchase systems priced above are $6,050 for the Model 155 and $12,450 for the Model 165.

Operating systems support for System/370 will be available at initial delivery of each model. System/370 education courses for customers will begin this fall at all IBM Education Centers. And a variety of new and improved program products that operate with System/370, as well as with certain models of System/360, are being announced today.

First customer shipments of System/370 Models 155 and 165 are scheduled to begin next February and April, respectively.

(Courtesy of IBM)

IBM introduced its Winchester disk drive, the 3340, in March, 1973. This was an improvement over old drives because it had an airtight container holding the disk platters. IBM used various tactics to harm disk drive competitors, such as improving disk drive technology, changing the interface between disk drives and the central processor and switching to fixed-length leases. These changes harmed Control Data, Storage Technology, and Memorex. CDC got out of the IBM-compatible disk drive business in 1985.[24]

Control Data Computers

160 and 160A

One of the earliest CDC computers was the 160 minicomputer and the newer version, the 160A. It had a 12-bit word size and 8K words of memory, which was expandable to 32K words. It was slower than the larger 1604 model, with an integer add time of 12.8 microseconds, according to a CDC brochure. It was all solid-state. It was often used with peripherals, including a card reader and several printers at the same time. It was about the size of a desk; the desk included displays of the operational registers. As the brochure stated, "The 160-A will operate up to four 1000 line-per-minute line printers at a maximum of 4000 lines per minute while simultaneously performing card-to-tape operations at the maximum rate of the card reader." Despite its small size, the 160A had its own Fortran compiler, which processed the Fortran II language. Again the brochure states, "Using the field-proven 160-A Fortran (a complete Fortran II compiler), scientific applications are quickly programmed, checked out and in production." The Fortran system included a math library and "comprehensive diagnostics." It also had an assembler, called OSAS (for One-Sixty ASsembler), and some software packages, such as one for civil engineers, called CEPS. The brochure included pictures of peripherals that worked with the 160A, including a card reader, a card punch, a line printer, and tape drives.

1604

Another early machine was the 1604, basically a scientific mainframe computer. It was a word-oriented (as opposed to byte-oriented) machine, with a 48-bit word and 200K hertz cycle time. It had an excellent instruction set, with full floating-point arithmetic built in, plus search instructions and a 24-bit instruction format. It had up to 32K words of memory. A typical installation included a card reader, a fast line printer and tape drives. It was a batch-oriented system, with the operating system processing one user job or program at a time. The 1604 was pretty advanced for its time, since it was about 50 times faster than the IBM 705 computer. The 1604's console displayed the operational registers, which wasn't unusual at that time. Communication with the operator was with an electric typewriter, used for input and output.

3000 Series

The 3000 series was a set of medium and large-scale computers. The smaller machines were the 3100, 3200 and 3300, with up to 131K 24-bit words. The large-scale machines were the 3400, 3600 and 3800, with up to 262 K 48-bit words. Memory access time was as fast as 0.8 microseconds, for all models. The series had different types of processors, designed for business or scientific use. The Fortran and Cobol languages were available for the series.

Hardware floating-point arithmetic was available, and the models had drum storage with up to 4 gigabytes of capacity. Disk storage was also an option, and peripherals included tape drives, card readers, card punches and line printers (1000 lines per minute). The card reader could read 1200 80-column cards per minute. Plotters were also available, for plotting graphs.

The 6600 and 7600 models are discussed in the Supercomputers chapter.

Cyber 70 Series

The Cyber 70 series models were successors to the 6600 and 7600 models. They had the same architecture, with the 24 operational registers and peripheral processors. The PPs had the usual 12-bit words and the CP for the Cyber 70s had ten functional units, like the 6600. Extended Core Storage was also available.

The Cyber 70s used the Scope or Kronos operating systems and had two Fortran compilers, Cobol and Algol compilers, plus Basic and the Compass assembler. A Sort/Merge package was also available and APT, for machine tools. The speed wasn't remarkable. A brochure from CDC shows that the Cyber 70/74 had a speed of 3 million instructions per second.

Cyber 170 Series

The 170 series models had an architecture very similar to the Cyber 70 models and had the usual 24 operational registers, including eight index registers, eight address registers and eight accumulators. The series was a new generation, using integrated circuits and semiconductor memory; magnetic core memory became obsolete in the early 1970s.

Addresses were 18 bits, for a maximum memory size of 262K words. The 170 series had ten to 20 12-bit peripheral processors, like the older models, with 4K of memory each. The faster 170 models had an instruction stack, like the 6600 and 7600. By this time, CDC had added another language, at least for internal use. It was originally called Pascal-X (an extended Pascal) and later renamed Cybil, meaning Cyber Implementation Language.

Cyber 180 Series

The 180 series of mainframes had a business-oriented architecture, due to customer demand, with a 64-bit word, character-oriented instructions and byte-oriented memory. Customers wanted computers that used the new, 8-bit character set (ASCII). They would also run in 60-bit mode, like the older models described above. The series had new peripheral processors, running in 16-bit or in 12-bit mode. The machines were originally called 170/8xx models and later renamed as 180/xxx models. The 180 series had a new operating system, which was called NOS/VE. Running in 170 mode, in a different address space, the machines used the older NOS or NOS/BE system. Some of the 180 models were designed in Canada.

Cyber 205

The Cyber 205 was another supercomputer from Control Data, which was newer and faster than the 7600 model. According to a document from Florida State University, their 205 had a 20 nanosecond clock cycle, 32 megabytes of main memory and 7.2 gigabytes of disk space. The maximum theoretical speed was 200 million floating-point operations per second (FLOPS). The operating system was VSOS. The languages used were:

Fortran, C and the Cyber 205 assembly language. The FSU also had a file server called the Cyber 835, which included an additional 20 gigabytes of disk space.

FSU had several supercomputers at their facility. The most reliable was the Cray Y-MP, with a mean time between failures of 2064 hours. The 205 was second-best with a MTBF of 127 hours.

Star-100

The Star-100 was a vector-oriented supercomputer, with a speed of 100 million FLOPS. The real-world speed was much less than expected, because it was difficult to use the vector feature effectively. It had a 64-bit word, to use 8-bit characters, compared to the 60-bit word in the 7600. The machine had special instructions for vector processing, such as adding a 400-word array to another 400-word array. These types of operations are built into the APL language.

The Star-100 was sometimes <u>slower</u> than the older 7600, due to its 50 nanosecond cycle time (versus 27.5 ns for the 7600). Of course, a typical program wouldn't use vector processing, which led to the disappointing speed.

There were different versions of the Star-100. The Cyber 203 was a newer version of that machine, as was the Cyber 205 (see above), an improvement over the 203 model.

Twenty-Four

M icroprocessors make possible today's portable computers, cell phones and other small electronic devices. The era of solid-state electronics began in 1947, with the invention of the transistor, by Shockley, et al., working at Bell Labs. In the 1950s, it replaced vacuum tubes in digital computers.

Initially germanium was the most-common type of material used in transistors for digital computers. After 1957, silicon became the most-used. Starting about 1960, planar transistors became common. In that type, the NPN (negative positive negative) layers are all in one plane.[1]

In 1958, another important event was the invention of the integrated circuit by Jack Kilby, in Sep., 1958.[2] He was working at Texas Instruments at that time. Robert Noyce described a similar invention, using silicon, in his notebook a few months after Kilby produced his integrated circuit.[3] Harvey Cragon and Joe Watson built the first computer entirely of integrated circuits, working at TI in 1961. It was built for the Air Force on contract and was about the size of a paperback book (or transistor radio).[4] It accepted input from mechanical keys; results appeared in a small window. TI started selling pocket-size electronic calculators, such as the SR-50, commercially in the early 1970s.

One of the drivers of the demand for integrated circuits was the Air Force, which needed them for the computers needed in the Minuteman missiles. An advanced version of that missile, the Minuteman II, included a computer using around 2000 integrated circuits.[5] Another driver of demand was the Apollo Guidance Computer, used in the Apollo Moon missions. Each of those computers required approximately 5000 integrated circuits, and about 75 of the computers were actually built. The computer was designed by the MIT Instrumentation Laboratory.[6]

Intel Corp. was founded in July, 1968 by Robert Noyce and Gordon Moore (known for Moore's Law). Intel found early on that specialty logic chips, such as for calculators, weren't very profitable. So they decided to make memory circuits, which they could produce in large quantities. Later, the memory circuits became unprofitable, so they switched to commercial microprocessors, which became a very profitable business.

Intel Corp. produced the first commercial microprocessor, the 4004, in 1971; the chip was invented by Ted Hoff.[7] It was developed for a firm called Busicom, in Japan. Busicom wanted the chip for a calculator they were developing.[8] Intel later was able to buy back the rights to the 4004 for $60,000, allowing them to sell it to any of their customers. Some people at Intel were wary of the programming required for the 4004, but Intel announced the new chip to the public anyway, in late 1971. Also in 1971, Intel was selling memory chips to hundreds of customers.[9] The 4004 is the ancestor of today's very complex Intel Pentium microprocessors. Processors that followed the 4004 included the 8008, the 8080, the 80286, etc. The Pentium 4 contains 42 million transistors.[10]

IBM had its own integrated circuits, which they developed, called "solid logic technology," which they used in their 360 series computers. One author describes them as follows: "...[C]ircuits were deposited on a ceramic substrate about half an inch thick, with metallic conducting channels printed on it."[11] For the newer 370 line, IBM used conventional integrated circuits, starting about 1970.[12]

Manufacturing microprocessors is a very complex process, which may include hundreds of steps. The process typically starts with the creation of a silicon ingot, which is cut up into thin circular wafers, on which the circuits are eventually printed. The wafers are polished to a mirror-like finish. The components in each microprocessor are connected with very thin wires of copper or aluminum. Very thin layers of various materials are deposited on the wafer. Photolithography is used to print the actual circuits on the chip.

Summary of "Making Of a Chip"[13] from Intel Corp.

The process starts with sand, meaning silicon dioxide. The material is purified in several steps, until the desired purity is reached: 99.9999%. Only one "alien" atom per billion is allowed.

The next step is to produce 100-kilogram ingots from the purified silicon dioxide.

Then the ingots are sliced to produce 12-inch wafers. Intel stated that the first wafers they used were just 2 inches in diameter.

The next step is to apply "photo resist," using a liquid.

Then the photo resist is exposed to ultraviolet light to make it soluble.

Another exposure is performed to produce transistors at this point.

The photo resist is removed with a solvent. The pattern made earlier remains.

An etching step removes the material revealed in previous step.

Then the photo resist is removed.

More photo resist is applied.

The next step is "ion implantation," where exposed parts of the wafer are bombarded with ions (doping) to change the electrical behavior of the wafer.

Then the photo resist is removed, leaving the doped parts of the wafer with the "alien atoms" included.

For each transistor, three holes are etched for copper connections to other transistors on the chip.

The next step is called electroplating, which uses copper ions to provide the connections to the transistors. The result is a "thin layer of copper" on the surface.

Now the surface is polished to remove unneeded material.

Next metal layers are added to provide wiring.

Now the wafer, with its many microprocessors, is ready for testing. Intel calls it the "functionality test." They feed "test patterns" into each chip and check the results.

The next step is to cut the wafer into pieces, which they call "dies."

The dies that failed the test are discarded.

Then the dies are packaged. Intel says they combine the substrate, the die and the radiator or "heatspreader" to make a complete packaged microprocessor. The substrate provides the "electrical and mechanical interface" for the microprocessor to interact with the PC or server system. The heatspreader radiates heat from the microprocessor.

The above steps are just a summary. Intel states that hundreds of steps are required to produce a finished microprocessor. In their words, "A microprocessor is the most complex manufactured product on earth."

Twenty-Five

Digital Equipment Corp.

Digital Equipment Corp. was founded in 1957 by Kenneth Olson and Harlan Anderson, who were electronics engineers; they graduated from MIT. They started the firm with only $70,000 which they raised from American Research and Development, a venture capital firm. The two founders had previously worked for the Digital Computer Laboratory at MIT.[1] The company had its headquarters in Maynard, Mass., in the Boston area. DEC became a large company, with 120,000 employees at one time. In its early years, DEC had a matrix-style management structure, with a manager for each product line competing with other groups for manufacturing and sales resources.

DEC's first computer was the PDP-1, introduced in 1960. It cost $120,000. It was about the size of a refrigerator. A later model was the PDP-6, a 36-bit machine, designed by Gordon Bell. The PDP-9 was introduced in 1965. The PDP-15 model was made with integrated circuits. Only a prototype was built for the PDP-3 model.[2]

DEC's first products were specialized digital devices, including the Digital Laboratory Module and the Digital Systems Module, which were introduced in 1958. DEC produced the industry's first minicomputer, the PDP-8, which was designed by Gordon Bell[3] and introduced in 1965. That model sold for only $18,000, and 50,000 of them were sold.[4]

Original Equipment Manufacturers (OEMs) bought many of DEC's machines and integrated them with their own software and hardware devices, which they resold to customers. This was a good arrangement for DEC, which didn't produce much of their own software in the firm's early years.

DEC helped to spawn some competitors, such as Data General, founded in 1968 by a DEC alumnus, Edson de Castro, who worked on the PDP-8 model.

DEC PDP-10

The PDP-10 series was a set of mainframe computers from Digital Equipment Corp. (DEC). The model numbers included PDP-10/10, /20, /30, /40 and /50. The maximum amount of memory available was 32K 36-bit words, on the 50 model. The minimum amount of memory was 8,192 words, on the /10 model. Additional memory could be purchased, up to 262K words.[5] The memory was magnetic cores. The PDP-10 series came out in the 60s. Of course, DEC was known mainly for their minicomputers, but the PDP-10 models are in the mainframe category because of their word size and capabilities. In some ways, the PDP-10 series models were similar to the Univac 1100 series models; both had 36-bit words, 18-bit addressing and 16 general-purpose registers. The PDP-10 series was instruction-compatible with the old PDP-6 series.

The PDP-10 Summary Reference Manual describes that series: "The PDP-10 system concept provides the optimum design in a solid-state, program-compatible general-purpose computer system. Its rich instruction set, speed, precision, proven software, high reliability, extreme flexibility, and ease of interface continue to find wide acceptance in physics, medical research, aerospace and simulation studies, process control, artificial intelligence, computer aided education and departmental computation studies."[6]

The PDP-10 models had 16 general-purpose registers, as mentioned. They could be used as accumulators (arithmetic registers), index registers (for modifying addresses in memory), as general-purpose registers or as the first 16 locations in core memory.

According to the Summary Reference, numerous peripheral devices were available for that series, including printers, tape drives, disk drives, punch card readers and plotters. An operator's console was also included with each machine. The machine processed commands from the operator, which had to be typed in on the "console teleprinter."

The series had 512 operation codes. 365 of them were hard-wired and 64 were trapped as programmable operators. The instructions could reference up to 262,144 words of memory with 18-bit addresses. The series allowed ASCII characters, using seven bits per character. Five byte-manipulation instructions were included. A push-down stack was also included. The instruction set also included a block-transfer instruction. Today we would call this CISC, complex instruction set computing. The opposite strategy is called RISC, reduced instruction set computing, as on the Control Data 6600 supercomputer. The RISC design provides faster execution.

The instruction set included fixed-point and floating-point arithmetic, plus all 16 boolean operations. The series also had half-word operations, such as HRL, half word right to left accumulator.

Time-sharing was also included with the PDP-10 series. As the Summary Reference Manual states, "PDP-10 monitor systems 10/40 and 10/50 offer complete general-purpose time-sharing. The terms multiprogramming, multi-usage, space sharing, and time slicing are all implied, and their respective features included. Further, individual time-shared jobs operate independently, and are protected from one another."[7] DEC supplied a time-sharing monitor with the 40 and 50 models.[8]

DEC supplied a system for the PDP-10 called TOPS-10, which allowed access as if the machine were used only by one person. The system included a text editor, for entering programs. A program debugging tool was also included.[9]

Software supplied by DEC included the Fortran-IV compiler, the Macro-10 assembler, and the editor TECO. The DEC Fortran library contained 110 functions, such as DSQRT, CONJG, CSQRT, ACOS and ALOG. Utility programs, such as DUMP and PDUMP were also included. DEC also supplied a Linking Relocating Loader, which was used with the Fortran IV compiler or the Macro 10 assembler. DEC also supplied DDT, the Dynamic Debugging Technique, which allowed dynamic interaction with Fortran IV, Cobol,, or Macro 10 programs. The user could use his own symbols during runtime with the DDT product. He could examine or modify his symbols[10] and hardware registers. Breakpoints could also be specified at execution time.

The DEC Macro 10 assembler included macros, for replicating a set of instructions. Macro definitions began with the DEFINE statement. Macro code started with the "<" operator and ended with the ">" operator. DEC calls them "angle brackets." In their words, "The character sequence, which constitutes the body of the macro, is delimited by angle brackets. The body of the macro normally consists of a group of complete statements [meaning assembly language op codes]". [11] The assembler also allowed floating-point and fixed-point constants and pseudo operations, such as RELOC or LOC, for specifying a relocatable or absolute assembly.[12] The EXTERN statement specified externally-defined symbols, and the ENTRY statement allowed defining an entry point in the current program.[13]

One of DEC's most popular machines was the PDP-11, introduced in 1970, of which 600,000 were sold during its lifetime.[14]

DEC's best-known products were the PDP (Programmed Data Processor) minicomputers, including the PDP-1, the PDP-8 and the PDP-11. There were many models in the PDP line. Some customers used the PDP-8 as a substitute for a mainframe computer. They also produced the DEC series of machines and the popular VAX series of minicomputers, in the late 1970s, using DEC's VMS operating system. Gordon Bell was in charge of developing the VAX series. But the Unix system became more popular than the VMS system. Another product from DEC was the Alpha microprocessor, introduced in 1994, which was very innovative for its time; it was a 64-bit processor. The third generation of the Alpha executed 2 to 2.4 billion instructions per second and had a clock speed of 500 to 600 megahertz, according to the IEEE Computer Society; it used RISC (Reduced Instruction Set Computing, pioneered by Seymour Cray) architecture. A paper about the Alpha is available at http://www.compaq.com/alphaserver/download/

ev6chip.pdf.[15]DEC developed other operating systems, including RSTS and OS-8. For the PDP-10 series, they developed the Monitor operating system.[16]

DEC eventually entered the personal computer market, in 1982, when they introduced the Rainbow 100 model, the DECmate II and the Professional 350. But those models were not popular, even though they came out soon after IBM's first PC model.

In 1992, DEC started to lose money, so some of their divisions were sold off, under the leadership of CEO Robert Palmer. Some of the pieces sold were their RDB data base product, sold to Oracle Corp., and the text terminals division, sold to Boundless Technologies.

The remaining parts of DEC were purchased by the Compaq Computer Corp. in Jan.,1998, for $9.6 billion; by then, DEC's headcount had fallen by more than 50% from the peak mentioned above. Compaq was later acquired by the Hewlett-Packard Corp., in 2002.

Twenty-Six

Punch cards and tabulating equipment were used in the earliest days of the computer industry, in the 1950s, because it was proven technology and the machines and punch cards were readily available. The tab equipment industry dates from the late 19th century and the inventions of Herman Hollerith. His inventions were used in the U.S. census of 1890. They included "...a gang punch, a keyboard punch, and a tabulating machine with an attached scoring box."[1] His Tabulating Machine Company began in 1896. Surprisingly, Hollerith didn't have an engineering degree. He was a graduate of the School of Mines at Columbia College. But he taught mechanical engineering, starting in 1882.[2]

Hollerith sold his TMC company to the CTR firm in 1911. CTR later became IBM. Also in 1911, a TMC competitor, the Powers Accounting Machine Company, was incorporated. It was named for the inventor James Powers. An important innovation from that firm was a printing tabulator, introduced about 1914.[3]

The medium used in tabulating equipment was the punch card, which had either 80 or 90 columns. The 80-column card was the most popular and was used in IBM's machines. The card had 12 rows, corresponding to the 10 digits, the − sign and the + sign. Letters and punctuation were coded by combinations of two or more punches in a column.

Punch cards were adapted for use with mainframe computers with the invention of card readers and card punches, for reading programs and data and for generating output, such as modified data. (The Fortran language had a PUNCH statement, for producing punch card output). Large programs and large amounts of data were read in and saved on magnetic tapes. The most important machines used with mainframe computers were the card reader and punch (connected to the computer), the keypunch, the tabulating machine, the card sorter and the gang punch. The keypunch was used to type in programs and data. The tabulating machine, besides its use for simple calculations, was used to print out programs and data. The card sorter was used to sort data on specific columns, one column at a time, into the desired order. The gang punch was used to make copies of program and data decks. Another type of machine was the interpreter, which would read duplicated decks of cards and print the coded contents at the top of the card. Binary-coded cards were sometimes used for data. The format of 80 columns by 12 rows could hold 960 bits of data, a type of compressed format. The downside of the binary format was that it was very difficult to read. Punch cards became obsolete by 1990, when nearly everyone who wanted a personal computer had one.

Paper tape was also used with early computer systems, which often had paper tape readers and punches. Data on paper tapes was represented by the presence or absence of holes in a roll or length of paper. (See "Programming in the 1960s.")

These paper media had some major disadvantages. One was that they were very low density, compared to magnetic tapes and disk storage. Another was that they were easily damaged, such as by tearing. And punch cards were occasionally dropped, by the programmer or computer operator. So prudent programmers would keep a backup copy of their program and/or data. An alternative was to use sequence numbers, as in Fortran, so a dropped deck could be sorted back into the proper order. The last eight columns of each card could contain sequence numbers.

At colleges and universities, card decks were often stored in the open, on shelves or in unlocked drawers, at computer centers, so they could easily be copied or altered, without the knowledge of the programmers or researchers.

An extensive discussion of tabulating equipment can be found in <u>IBM's Early Computers</u>, in the chapter titled, "Punch Cards and Plugwires."[4]

Arpanet/Internet

The Internet began as the Arpanet, in 1969. The Arpanet was named for the Defense Advance Research Projects Agency, which was founded in 1958. Arpanet began operations in Oct., 1969 as a host-to-host network. It used packet switching. Packet switching breaks up a message and sends it to the specified destination in pieces, by whatever paths are available. The message is then reassembled at the final destination. One of the purposes of Arpanet was to allow researchers easy access to supercomputers.

One author stated that Arpanet was first demonstrated at a hotel in Washington, DC, in Oct., 1972.[5] The same author commented that the Arpanet was dismantled in 1988. That network used DDP-516 computers, from Computer Controls Corp., to route messages in that system

By 1980, the TCP/IP standard for sending and receiving data packets, usable by any computer, was adopted. There were other networks in the 1980s, such as the NSFNET, operated by the National Science Foundation. The NSF eventually shut it down, since it was no longer needed. That occurred in 1995.

The Internet today is used for vastly more purposes than Arpanet was used for, including voice phone calls, downloading and watching movies and video, downloading and listening to music, publishing, e-mail and for other purposes.

Many tools are used on the Internet, including SMTP (simple mail transfer protocol) for e-mail, FTP (file transfer protocol) for transferring large files, HTTP (hyper text transfer protocol) for publishing text and graphics, and VOIP (voice over internet protocol) for phone calls.

The first browser for the Internet was Mosaic, developed at the University of Illinois. Mosaic was created to allow retrieval and display of files that came from the Internet. It allowed the point-and-click access method, as in today's browsers. Browsers eventually became available free, available for downloading, on the Internet. Of course, today they (one or more) come pre-installed with the operating system on new PCs. Browsers in use today include Firefox and the Internet Explorer. The standards used by browsers were developed by CERN in Europe by Tim Berners-Lee for the new World Wide Web (WWW). [6]

Individuals access the Internet using a portal, such as MSN or Netzero, provided by Internet Service Providers (ISPs). Access is available via dialup or broadband connections. With dialup access, the computer first dials a number provided by the ISP. After the connection is made and the password is verified, the user then sees his home page on the screen. He can then type in other addresses (URLs) or search for specific content using a search engine, such as Google or Bing.

Glossary

absolute
> A type of program that is ready to execute. Also a type of addressing (as opposed to relative).

accumulator
> The main arithmetic register in a computer; some computers had several accumulators

address
> A location in a computer's memory. Also part of an instruction

address register
> A register that holds an address in RAM memory

ASCII
> American Standard Code for Information Interchange, a standard character set used in the U.S.

assembler
> A language processor that translates symbolic op codes and addresses to relocatable binary or absolute machine code

batch processing
> A method for processing user programs, usually on a mainframe computer, typically using a card deck containing a program and/or data. Modern batch processing doesn't use card decks

binary
> A number system using the base 2.

binary point
> In floating-point arithmetic, the binary point marks the boundary between the integer and fractional parts of a number; the fractional part starts to the right of the binary point

bit
> The smallest unit of information in a digital computer, with a value of zero or one

byte
> Usually the smallest addressable unit of information in a computer—8 bits on most computers

card punch
> A machine, connected to a computer, which produces punch card output (obsolete)

card reader
> A machine, used mainly with mainframe computers, that reads punch cards (obsolete)

cathode ray tube
> A type of vacuum tube used to display text and graphics, or to record data (obsolete use)

CODASYL
> Conference on data systems languages, which invented Cobol and the first successful database system (hierarchical database) in the late 1960s

compiler
> A language translator that translates a specific higher-level language into relocatable binary or assembly language; the translation process is completed before the program is executed

computer science
> A field of knowledge involving digital computers, their architecture and software programs; known for its tools and techniques.

core
> A type of fast computer memory, or a unit of same (obsolete); sometimes called magnetic core memory

counter
> A circuit (sometimes a wheel) used to represent decimal or binary digits.

CPU
> Central processing unit, the part of a digital computer that executes the instructions

CRT
> See cathode ray tube

database
> A collection of records which can be retrieved and updated by specialized software

debug
> In programming, the process of finding and fixing an error in the source code.

decimal
> A number system using the base 10

delay line
> A type of fast memory used in 1940s digital computers; used a pool of mercury

disk drive
> A type of mass storage where data is directly addressable, consisting of plat-
> ters coated with iron oxide, read/write heads and related electronics

diskette
> A removable storage medium consisting of a flexible plastic disk coated with
> magnetic oxide in a plastic housing

diskette drive
> A drive that reads and writes diskettes

drum
> A type of mass storage where data is directly addressable

EAM
> Electric accounting machine

EBCDIC
> An IBM character set, Extended Binary Coded Decimal Interchange Code

editor
> A text editor; may also refer to a link-editor

electric accounting machine
> An electromechanical machine that reads punch cards, performs calcula-
> tions and prints results (obsolete)

executive
> An operating system

fixed-point
> A type of machine arithmetic, usually integer arithmetic with no frac-
> tional part

flip flop
An electronic circuit with two stable states, representing the values zero and one

floating-point
A type of machine arithmetic where the hardware keeps track of the binary point and the exponents

floppy disk
See diskette

gate
An electronic circuit whose output depends on various combinations of two inputs; a NOT gate has just one input

hardware
A digital computer or related machines or devices

hexadecimal
The base 16 arithmetic system used in some computers

higher-level language
A third-generation or higher computer language

index register
A user-addressable register in a computer used to modify the memory address

instruction
A command executed by a computer, which typically includes an op code and an address.

instruction set
A list of all the instructions executed by a digital computer

integrated circuit
>A solid-state circuit that contains usually many transistors

interactive debugger
>A feature in some compilers which allows setting breakpoints in an executing program, displaying variable values and changing values in the program

interpreter
>A language translator that translates and executes statements one at a time before processing the next statement; see compiler. Also, a machine which prints the contents of a punched card at the top edge (obsolete)

interrupt
>A transfer of control in a digital computer, typically due to an external event

JCL
>See job control language

job control language
>A language used to issue commands to an operating system

keypunch
>A machine that records characters on cards using punched holes (obsolete).

language
>A computer language such as Fortran

library
>A collection of programs, subroutines, procedures or functions (usually in relocatable binary format)

link-editor
> A program that converts relocatable binary to absolute executable binary; it may also process external references

loader
> A program that loads a program into memory and usually executes it

LSI
> Large scale integration; refers to integrated circuits

machine language
> The lowest level of computer languages, which is executable if translated into binary

macro
> A feature in some language processors which replicates source code

mainframe
> A large, powerful digital computer

memory
> The fast random access memory in a computer

mercury delay line
> An obsolete memory technology formerly used in digital computers

merge
> The process of combining two or more sorted arrays or files.

microprocessor
> An integrated circuit that executes the computer's instructions

minicomputer
A small computer, similar to a mainframe, with more limited capabilities

modem
Modulator/Demodulator, a device used to transmit data over phone lines

monitor
An operating system; also a CRT or other display device

multiprocessing
Execution of two or more programs simultaneously on one computer, typically with two or more central processors, or with one central processor and one satellite processor

multiprogramming
Running two or more programs concurrently on one computer

numerical analysis
A branch of mathematics involving the numeric solutions to equations (rather than algebraic solutions)

octal
A number system using the base 8

op code
Short for operation code, one of the instructions executed by a digital computer

operating system
The main control program in a digital computer, which runs other programs

paper tape
A data storage medium, where data is recorded with a series of punched holes, similar to punch cards (obsolete)

paper tape punch
A device that writes a segment or roll of paper tape (obsolete)

paper tape reader
A device that reads a segment or roll of paper tape (obsolete)

peripheral
A device connected to or used by a digital computer, such as a printer

personal computer
A small computer used by one person, which typically includes a keyboard and a video monitor

PROM
Programmable Read-Only Memory, ROM which is easily changed

punch card
A paper storage medium, where data is recorded with a series of punched holes; used to record programs or data (obsolete)

RAM
Random access memory, a computer's fast memory

Relay
An electrical device which can switch current flow on and off; used in the earliest digital computers

relocatable
A type of binary program which can be processed into an absolute executable program; also the format for same

ROM
Read-only memory, a type of computer memory that may contain one or more programs

software
>One or more programs written for a digital computer

sorter
>An electromechanical machine which sorted punch cards on one or more columns (obsolete)

supercomputer
>A very fast, powerful mainframe computer

tape drive
>A machine that reads and writes magnetic tapes, for use with a digital computer

teletype
>An enhanced electric typewriter than can be used to send and receive information; can be used as a computer terminal (obsolete)

text editor
>A program used to enter or modify text; an example is Notepad.exe in Windows systems

throughput
>The rate at which batch jobs are processed by a digital computer

time sharing
>A method for using a mainframe or minicomputer that uses a remote terminal connected by phone line or cable

transistor
>A small electronic device made from a semiconductor that is used for switching and other purposes; replaced the vacuum tube

translator
> A computer program that translates one language to another language, such as Fortran to relocatable binary

TTY
> Short for teletype

Turing machine
> A hypothetical machine that gets its instructions and data from a moving tape and places its output on the tape (from Alan Turing)

Unicode
> A large character set that includes Asian and Western characters

Vacuum tube
> An electronic device that is used for switching, detection and other purposes (mostly obsolete)

verifier
> A machine, similar to a keypunch, used to verify data on punch cards (obsolete)

VLSI
> Very large scale integration; refers to integrated circuits

wafer
> A thin disk of silicon or other material used to make integrated circuits

Williams tube
> A type of computer memory which used cathode ray tubes (obsolete)

word

A unit of memory in some computers, now typically 32 bits or 64 bits (size varies); a word is the normal size operand used for calculations, especially floating-point. Compare to byte.

Word processor

An enhanced text editor used to create or modify documents

Bibliography

Bashe, Charles, et al., 1996. *IBM's Early Computers* (Cambridge, Mass.: MIT Press)

Bell, Gordon, 1978. *Computer Engineering* (Daytona Beach, Florida: Digital Press)

Ceruzzi, Paul, 2003. *A History of Modern Computing* (Cambridge, Mass.: MIT Press)

Chposky and Teonsis, 1988. *Blue Magic: The People, Power and Politics Behind the IBM Personal Computer* (New York, N.Y.: Facts on File)

Control Data Corp., 1960. *Control Data 160: Programming Manual* (Minneapolis: Control Data Corp.

Control Data Corp., 1963. *Control Data 1604 Reference Manual* (St. Paul: Control Data Corp.)

Cuttle and Robinson, 1970. *Executive Programs and Operating Systems* (New York, N.Y.: American Elsevier)

DeLamarter, Thomas, 1986. *The Truth About IBM's Success and the Ominous Implications* (New York, N.Y.: Dodd, Mead)

Desmonde, William, 1964. *Computers and Their Uses* (Englewood Cliffs, NJ: Prentice-Hall)

Digital Equipment Corp., 1967, *Macro 10 Assembler Manual, PDP-10* (Maynard, Mass.: Digital Equipment Corp.)

Digital Equipment Corp., 1967, *Monitor Manual, PDP-10/20 and /30* (Maynard, Mass.: Digital Equipment Corp.)

Digital Equipment Corp., 1967, *Summary Reference Manual, PDP-10* (Maynard, Mass.: Digital Equipment Corp.)

Earls, Alan, 2004. *Digital Equipment Corporation* (Mount Pleasant, S.C.: Arcadia Publishing)

Encyclopedia Britannica, 2010. *John Atanasoff* (Chicago: Encyclopedia Britannica)

Frenzel, Louis, 1980. *Crash Course in Microcomputers* (Indianapolis: Howard Sams)

Fritz, Sandy, 2002. *Understanding Supercomputing* (New York, N.Y.: Warner Books)

Grove, Andrew, 1983. *High Output Management* (New York, N.Y.: Random House)

Hill and Peterson, 1973. *Digital Systems: Hardware Organization and Design* (New York, N.Y.: John Wiley)

Hodges, Andrew, 1983. *Alan Turing: The Enigma* (Princeton, N.J.: Princeton University Press)

Jackson, George, 1982. *Cobol: Complete, Up to the Minute Reference* (Blue Ridge Summit, PA: Tab Books)

Jackson, Tim, 1997. *Andy Grove and the Rise of theWorld's Most Powerful Chip Company* (New York, N.Y.: Penguin Group)

Kahney, Leander, 2009. *Inside Steve's Brain* (New York, N.Y.: Penguin Group)

Kaplan, Jerry, 1994. *Startup: A Silicon Valley Adventure* (New York, N.Y.: Houghton Mifflin)

Kemeny & Kurtz, 1964. *Dartmouth Basic Manual* (Hanover, N.H.: Dartmouth College)

Kessler, R. E. et al, 1996. *The Alpha 21264: Microprocessor Architecture* (Shrewsbury, Mass.: Digital Equipment Corp.)

Knuth & Pardo, 1976. *Early Programming Languages* (Palo Alto, Calif.: Stanford Univ.)

Knuth, Donald, 1968. *Fundamental Algorithms: The Art of Computer Programming* (Reading, Mass.: Addison-Wesley)

Knuth, Donald, 1969. *Seminumerical Algorithms: The Art of Computer Programming* (Reading, Mass.: Addison-Wesley)

Knuth, Donald, 1973. *Sorting and Searching: The Art of Computer Programming* (Reading, Mass.: Addison-Wesley)

Lee, John A. N., 1967. *The Anatomy of a Compiler* (New York, N.Y.: Reinhold Publishing)

Lundstrom, David E., 1987, *A Few Good Men from Univac* (Cambridge, Mass.: MIT Press)

Malik, Rex, 1976. *And Tomorrow, the World: Inside IBM* (London, U.K.: Millington)

Maney, Kevin, 2003. *The Maverick and His Machine* (Hoboken, N.J.: John Wiley)

McCartney, Scott, 1999. *Eniac: Triumphs and Tragedies of the World's First Computer* (New York, N.Y.: Walker)

Moreau, R., 1984. *The Computer Comes of Age* (Cambridge, Mass.: MIT Press)

Murray, Charles, 1997. *The Supermen: The Story of Seymour Cray and the Technical Wizards Behind the Supercomputer* (New York, N.Y.: John Wiley)

Norris, William, 1983. *New Frontiers for Business Leadership* (Minneapolis, Minn. : Dorn Books)

O'Neill, Judy, 1997. *Evolution of Interactive Computing* (Minneapolis, Minn.: University of Minnesota)

Olsen, Kenneth, 1983. *Digital Equipment Corporation: The First twenty-Five Years* (New York, NY: Newcomen Society)

Packard, David, 1995. *The HP Way: How Bill Hewlett and I Built Our Company* (New York, NY: Harper Collins)

Price, Robert M., 2005. *The Eye for Innovation* (New Haven, Conn.: Yale Univ. Press)

Pugh, Emerson, 1984. *Memories That Shaped an Industry: Decisions Leading to IBM System/360* (Cambridge, Mass.: MIT Press)

Redmond & Smith, 1975. *Project Whirlwind: History of a Pioneer Computer* (Daytona Beach, Fla.: Digital Press)

Rifkin & Harrar, 1988. *The Ultimate Entrerpreneur: The Story of Ken Olsen and Digital Equipment Corporation* (Chicago, Ill.: Contemporary Books)

Rosen, Saul, 1967. *Programming Systems and Languages* (New York, N.Y.: McGraw-Hill)

Sargent & Shoemaker, 1986. *IBM PC from the Inside Out* (Reading, Mass.: Addison-Wesley)

Shumate, Ken, 1989. *Understanding ADA, 2nd Edition* (New York, N.Y.: John Wiley)

Sippl, Charles, 1977. *Microcomputer Handbook* (New York, N.Y.: Petrocelli/Charter)

Smithsonian Inst. *Interview with Bill Gates* (Washington, DC: Smithsonian)

Smithsonian Inst. *Interview with Seymour Cray* (Washington, DC: Smithsonian)

Stein & Munro, 1964. *Computer Programming: A Mixed Language Approach* (New York, N.Y.: Academic Press)

Thornton, James, 1970. *Design of a Computer: The Control Data 6600* (Chicago: Scott Foresman)

Wang, An, 1986. *Lessons: An Autobiography* (Reading, Mass.: Addision-Wesley)

Welsh & Elder, 1982. *Introduction to Pascal* (Englewood Cliffs, N.J.: Prentice-Hall)

Wexelblat, Richard, 1981. *History of Programming Languages* (New York, N.Y.: Academic Press)

Wikipedia. *James Rand, Junior*

Wozniak & Smith, 2006. *iWoz: Computer Geek to Cult Icon: How I Invented the Personal Computer...* (New York, N.Y.: Norton)

Young & Simon, 2005. *Icon: Steve Jobs—The Greatest Second Act in the History of Business* 2005. (Hoboken, N.J.: John Wiley)

Zaks, Rodney, 1980. *The CP/M Handbook with MP/M* (Hoboken, N.J.: Sybex)

Zygmont, Jeffrey, 2003. *Microchip* (Cambridge, Mass.: Perseus)

References

1. Early Computers

1. From http://www-03.ibm.com/ibm/history/exhibits.
2. Bashe, et al., IBM's Early Computers, [Cambridge, Mass.: MIT Press, 1986], p. 31.
3. Ibid., p. 32
4. Pugh, Emerson, Memories That Shaped an Industry, [Cambridge, Mass.: MIT Press, 1984], p. 78.
5. Ibid., P. 81.
6. Ibid., p. 78.
7. Ibid., p. 91.
8. Ibid., pp. 87-88.
9. Ibid., p. 86.
10. Ibid., p. 87.

2. Electronic Computers

1. Moreau, R., The Computer Comes of Age, [Cambridge, Mass.: MIT Press, 1984], p. 44.
2. Ibid., p. 46.
3. Ibid, p. 51.
4. Ibid., p. 56.
5. Ibid., p. 59.
6. DeLamarter, Thomas, Big Blue: The Truth about IBM's Success and the Omminous Implications..., [New York, NY: Dodd, Mead, 1986], p. 35
7. Op. Cit., p. 78.
8. Ibid., p. 91.
9. Ibid., p. 91.
10. Ibid., p. 92.
11. Ibid., p. 92.
12. Ibid., p. 220.
13. Ibid., p. 70.

14. Ibid., p. 72.
15. Ibid., p. 78.
16. Ibid., p. 78.

3. Early Univac Computers

1. Sperry Corp., "Engineering Research Associates—The wellspring of Minnesota's computer industry," p. 2.
2. Ibid., p. 7.
3. Ibid., p. 7.
4. Ibid., p. 9.
5. Ibid., p. 9.
6. Ibid., p. 9.
7. Ibid., p. 14
8. Ibid., p. 17.
9. Ibid., p. 19.
10. Ibid., p. 16.
11. Ibid., p. 19.
12. Ibid., p. 19.
13. Moreau, R., <u>The Computer Comes of Age</u>, [Cambridge, Mass.: MIT Press, 1984], p. 55.
14. Ibid., p. 55.

4. IBM's Calculators

1. Bashe, et al., <u>IBM's Early Computers</u>, [Cambridge, Mass.: MIT Press, 1986], pp. 36-37
2. Ibid., p. 703.
3. Ibid., p. 44.
4. Ibid., p. 55.
5. Ibid., p. 57.
6. Ibid., pp. 132-133.
7. Ibid., pp. 182-183.

8. Ibid., p. 86.
9. Ibid., p. 86.
10. Ibid., p. 90.
11. Ibid., pp. 90-91.
12. Ibid., p. 185.
13. Ibid., pp. 386-387.
14. Ibid., p. 70.
15. Ibid., p. 71.
16. Ibid., p. 79.
17. Ibid., p. 76.
18. Ibid., p. 82.
19. Ibid., p. 77.
20. Ibid., p. 89.
21. Ibid., p. 99.
22. Ibid., p. 94.
23. Ibid., p. 98.
24. Ibid., p. 138.
25. Ibid., p. 138.
26. Ibid., pp. 136-144.
27. Ibid., p. 144.
28. Ibid., p. 146.
29. Ibid., p. 105.
30. Ibid., p. 109.
31. Ibid., p. 110.
32. Ibid., p. 110.
33. Ibid., p. 111.
34. Ibid., p. 112.
35. Ibid., p. 111.
36. Ibid., p. 126.
37. Ibid., p. 114.
38. Ibid., p. 117.
39. Ibid., p. 590.
40. Ibid., p. 593

41. Ibid., p. 596.
42. Ibid., p. 129.
43. Ibid., p. 128.
44. Ibid., p. 128.
45. Ibid., p. 127.
46. Ibid., p. 119.
47. Ibid., p. 120.

5. Early IBM Mainframes

1. Bashe, et al., <u>IBM's Early Computers</u>, [Cambridge, Mass.: MIT Press, 1986], p. 158.
2. Ibid., p. 136.
3. Ibid., p. 159.
4. http://www-03.ibm.com/ibm/ history/exhibits/mainframe
5. Op. Cit., p. 605.
6. Ibid., p. 52.
7. Ibid., p. 44.
8. Ibid., p. 62.
9. Ibid., p. 703.
10. Ibid., p. 177.
11. Ibid., p. 177.
12. Ibid., p. 176.
13. Ibid., p. 176
14. Ibid., p. 177.
15. Ibid., p. 177.
16. Ibid., p. 178.
17. Ibid., p. 178,
18. Ibid., p. 180.
19. Hill and Peterson, <u>Digital Systems: Hardware Organization and Design</u>, [New York: John Wiley & Sons], pp. 370 ff.
20. Op. Cit., p. 180.

21. Ibid., p. 180
22. Ibid., p. 180.
23. Ibid., p. 181.
24. Ibid., p. 184.
25. Ibid., pp. 299-300.
26. Ibid., p. 300.
27. Moreau, R., The Computer Comes of Age, [Cambridge, Mass.: MIT Press, 1984], p. 81.
28. Op. Cit., p. 507.
29. Ibid., p. 507.
30. Ibid., p. 507.
31. Ibid., p. 170.
32. Ibid., pp. 424-425.
33. Ibid., p. 426.
34. Ibid., p. 429.
35. Ibid., p. 427.
36. Ibid., p. 425.
37. Ibid., p. 429.
38. Ibid., p. 429.
39. Pugh, Emerson, Memories That Shaped an Industry, [Cambridge, Mass.: MIT Press, 1984], p. 164
40. Op. Cit., p. 431.
41. Ibid., p. 431.
42. Ibid., p. 451.
43. Ibid., p. 450.
44. Ibid., p. 451.
45. Ibid., p. 451.
46. Ibid., p. 452.
47. Ibid., p. 437.
48. Ibid., p. 456.
49. Ibid., pp. 437-459.
50. Ibid., pp. 457-458.

51. Pugh, Emerson, <u>Memories That Shaped an Industry</u>, [Cambridge, Mass.: MIT Press, 1984], p. 186.
52. Op. Cit., p. 366.
53. Ibid.,, p. 367.
54. Ibid., p. 367.
55. Lee, John, <u>The Anatomy of a Compiler</u>, [New York, NY: Reinhold, 1967], pp. 237-245.
56. Op. Cit., p. 367.
57. Ibid., p. 387.
58. Ibid., pp. 509-510.
59. Ibid., p. 366.
60. Ibid., p. 510..
61. Ibid., p. 512.
62. Ibid., pp. 510-511.
63. Ibid., p. 477.
64. http://www-03.ibm.com/ibm/history/exhibits
65. Ibid., p. 479.
66. Ibid., p. 479.
67. Ibid., p. 479.
68. Ibid., p. 480.
69. Ibid., p. 492.
70. Ibid., p. 491.
71. Ibid., p. 578.
72. Pugh, Emerson, <u>Memories That Shaped an Industry</u>, [Cambridge, Mass.: MIT Press, 1984], p. 194.
73. Ibid., pp. 195-196.
74. Ibid., p. 207.
75. Ibid., p. 205.
76. Ibid., p. 205.
77. Ibid., p. 206.
78. Ibid., p. 207.
79. Ibid., p. 246.
80. Ibid., p. 245.

81. Ibid., p. 216.
82. Ibid., p. 226.
83. Ibid., p. 199.
84. Ibid., p. 253.
85. Ibid.,, pp. 254-255.
86. Ibid., p. 254.
87. Ibid., pp. 258-261.

6. IBM and the Europeans

1. Malik, Rex, And Tomorrow..the World?—Inside IBM [London, England: Millington, 1975], p. 430.
2. Ibid., p. 431.
3. http://www.hagley.lib.de.us/library/collections/manuscripts/findin-gaids/ibmantitrustpart2.ACC1980.htm
4. Op. Cit., pp. 418-421.
5. Ibid., p. 66.
6. Ibid., pp. 68-69.
7. Ibid., p. 69.
8. Ibid., p. 433.
9. Ibid., p. 433.
10. Ibid., p. 448.
11. Ibid., p. 457 ff.
12. Ibid., p. 457.
13. Ibid., p. 141.
14. Ibid., p. 142.
15. Ibid., p. 140.
16. Ibid., p. 101.
17. Ibid., pp. 102-103.
18. Ibid., pp. 103-104.
19. Ceruzzi, Paul, A History of Modern Computing, [Cambridge, Mass.: MIT Press, 2003], p. 200.
20. Ibid., p. 201.

7. Speeding Up Computers

1. Hill and Peterson, Digital Systems: Hardware Organization and Design, [New York: John Wiley & Sons, 1973], pp. 376-379.
2. Ibid., pp. 380-383.
3. Bashe, et al., IBM's Early Computers, [Cambridge, Mass.: MIT Press, 1986], p. 230
4. Ibid., p. 258.
5. Ibid., p. 260.
6. Ibid., p. 253..
7. Moreau, R., The Computer Comes of Age, [Cambridge, Mass.: MIT Press, 1984], p. 118.
8. Ibid., p. 118.

8. Document Reading Devices

1. Bashe, et al., IBM's Early Computers, [Cambridge, Mass.: MIT Press, 1986], pp. 498-499.
2. Ibid., p. 500.
3. Ibid., p. 502.

9. Magnetic Tape.

1. Bashe, et al., IBM's Early Computers, [Cambridge, Mass.: MIT Press, 1986], p. 187.
2. Ibid., p. 189.
3. Ibid., pp. 194-195.
4. Ibid., p. 198.
5. Ibid., p. 195.
6. Ibid., p. 202.
7. Ibid., p. 204.
8. Ibid., p. 207.
9. Ibid., pp. 199-200.
10. Ibid., p. 210.

10. Magnetic Disks.

1. http://www-03.ibm.com/ibm/history/exhibits
2. Bashe, et al., IBM's Early Computers, [Cambridge, Mass.: MIT Press, 1986], p. 279.
3. Ibid., p. 279.
4. Ibid., p. 280.
5. Ibid., P. 280.
6. Hill and Peterson, Digital Systems: Hardware Organization and Design, [New York: John Wiley & Sons, 1973], pp. 60-63.
7. Op. Cit., p. 281.
8. Ibid., p. 281.
9. Ibid., p. 283.
10. Ibid., p. 287.
11. Ibid., p. 287-288.
12. Ibid., p. 288.
13. Ibid., p. 288
14. Ibid., p. 301.
15. Ibid., p. 291.
16. Ibid., p. 298.
17. Ibid., p. 294.
18. Ibid., p. 304.
19. Ibid., p. 310.
20. Hill and Peterson, Digital Systems: Hardware Organization and Design, [New York: John Wiley & Sons, 1973], pp. 64-65.

11. Magnetic Core Memories

1. Bashe, et al., IBM's Early Computers, [Cambridge, Mass.: MIT Press, 1986], p. 212.
2. Ibid., p. 267.
3. Ibid., pp. 234-235.
4. Pugh, Emerson, Memories That Shaped an Industry, [Cambridge, Mass.: MIT Press, 1984], p. 43.

5. Ibid., p. 40.
6. Ibid., p. 54.
7. Ibid., p. 56.
8. Bashe, et al., <u>IBM's Early Computers</u>, [Cambridge, Mass.: MIT Press, 1986], pp. 236-238.
9. Pugh, Emerson, <u>Memories That Shaped an Industry</u>, [Cambridge, Mass.: MIT Press, 1984], p. 59.
10. Op. Cit., p. 255-256.
11. Ibid., p. 257.
12. Ibid., p. 258.
13. Ibid., p. 259.
14. Pugh, Emerson, <u>Memories That Shaped an Industry</u>, [Cambridge, Mass.: MIT Press, 1984], p. 179.
15. Op. Cit., p. 260
16. Op. Cit., p. 178.
17. Bashe, et al., <u>IBM's Early Computers</u>, [Cambridge, Mass.: MIT Press, 1986], pp. 266-267.
18. Ibid., p. 270.
19. Ibid., pp. 269-272.
20. Hill and Peterson, <u>Digital Systems: Hardware Organization and Design</u>, [New York: John Wiley & Sons, 1973], p. 53.
21. Ibid., p. 55.

12. Early IBM Software

1. Bashe, et al., <u>IBM's Early Computers</u>, [Cambridge, Mass.: MIT Press, 1986], p. 296.
2. Ibid., p. 316
3. Ibid., p. 353.
4. Ibid., pp. 345-346.
5. Ibid., p. 340.
6. Ibid., p. 357.
7. Rosen, Saul, <u>Programming Systems and Languages</u>, [New York, NY, McGraw-Hill, 1967], pp. 29-47.

8. Op. Cit., p. 356.
9. Ibid., p. 357.
10. Ibid., p. 357.
11. Ibid., p. 358.
12. Ibid., p. 360.
13. Ibid., p. 360.
14. Ibid., p. 361.
15. http://www-01.ibm.com/ software/htp/cics/35/
16. Op. Cit., p. 521.
17. Ibid., p. 521.

13. Computer Languages

1. "Computer," Encyclopedia Britannica, Encyclopedia Britannica Ultimate Reference Suite, Chicago, Encyclopedia Britannica, 2010.
2. Ceruzzi, Paul, A History of Modern Computing, [Cambridge, Mass.: MIT Press, 2003], p. 202.
3. Ibid., p. 86.
4. Moreau, R., The Computer Comes of Age, [Cambridge, Mass.: MIT Press, 1984], pp. 161-162.
5. Rosen, Saul, Programming Systems and Languages, [New York, NY, McGraw-Hill, 1967], pp. 29-47.
6. Bashe, et al., IBM's Early Computers, [Cambridge, Mass.: MIT Press, 1986], p. 367.
7. Moreau, R., The Computer Comes of Age, [Cambridge, Mass.: MIT Press, 1984], p. 173.
8. Jackson, George, Cobol: Complete, Up to the Minute Reference, [Blue Ridge Summit, PA, 1982], pp. 3-4.
9. Op. Cit., pp. 173-174.
10. Ibid., p. 175.
11. Rosen, Saul, Programming Systems and Languages, [New York, NY, McGraw-Hill, 1967], pp. 119-169.
12. Moreau, R., The Computer Comes of Age, [Cambridge, Mass.: MIT Press, 1984], p. 175.

13. Op. Cit., pp. 48-78.
14. Moreau, R., The Computer Comes of Age, [Cambridge, Mass.: MIT Press, 1984], p. 168.
15. Ibid., p. 168.
16. Ibid., p. 164.
17. Ibid., pp. 164-165.
18. Ibid., p. 168.
19. Ibid., p. 172.
20. Ibid., p. 172.
21. Ibid., pp. 172-173.
22. Ceruzzi, Paul, A History of Modern Computing, [Cambridge, Mass.: MIT Press, 2003], pp. 97-98.
23. Moreau, R., The Computer Comes of Age, [Cambridge, Mass.: MIT Press, 1984], pp. 171-172.
24. Rosen, Saul, Programming Systems and Languages, [New York, NY, McGraw-Hill, 1967], pp. 160-179.
25. Op. Cit., p.181.
26. Ibid., p. 181.
27. Shumate, Ken, Understanding Ada, [New York, NY, John Wiley, 1989], p. 13.
28. Ibid., p. 12.
29. Ibid., p. 18.
30. Ibid., p. 14.
31. Ibid., p. 15.
32. Ibid., p. 16.
33. Ibid., p. 17
34. Ibid., p. 17.
35. Ibid., pp. 17-18.
36. Ibid., pp. 61-62.
37. Ibid., p. 63.
38. Ibid., p. 35.
39. Ibid., p. 225.

40. Ibid., p. 165.
41. Ibid., p. 433.
42. Ibid., p. 24.
43. Ibid., p. 461 ff.
44. Ibid., p. 477 ff.
45. Ibid., p. 515.
46. Ibid., pp. 515-516.
47. Rosen, Saul, Programming Systems and Languages, [New York, NY, McGraw-Hill, 1967], p. 160.
48. Ibid., pp. 161-162.
49. Ibid., p. 168.
50. Ibid., pp. 176-178.
51. Ceruzzi, Paul, A History of Modern Computing, [Cambridge, Mass.: MIT Press, 2003], p. 204.
52. Ibid., p. 205.
53. Ibid., p. 205.
54. Rosen, Saul, Programming Systems and Languages, [New York, NY, McGraw-Hill, 1967], pp. 79-117.

14. Computer Science—The Early Days

1. Moreau, R., The Computer Comes of Age, [Cambridge, Mass.: MIT Press, 1984], p. 193
2. Ibid., p.194
3. Stein and Munro, Computer Programming: A Mixed Language Approach, [New York, NY: Academic Press, 1964].

15. Programming in the 1960s.

No footnotes

16. Important People I

1. DeLamarter, Thomas, <u>Big Blue: The Truth about IBM's Success and the Omminous Implications…</u>, [New York, NY: Dodd, Mead, 1986], p. 10.
2. Maney, Kevin, <u>The Maverick and His Machine</u>, [Hoboken, NJ: John Wiley, 2003], pp. 77-78.
3. Op. Cit., p. 12.
4. Op. Cit., pp. 47-48.
5. Ibid., pp.57.
6. Ibid., p. 56.
7. Ibid., p. 63.
8. Ibid., p. 465.
9. Ibid., p. 67.
10. Ibid., pp 84-85.
11. Ibid., p. 87.
12. Ibid., pp. 72-73.
13. Ibid., p. 75.
14. Ibid., p. 87.
15. Ibid., p. 94
16. Ibid., pp. 99-101.
17. Ibid., pp. 155-156.
18. Ibid., p. 160
19. Ibid., pp. 179-181.
20. Ibid., p. 189.
21. Ibid., pp. 190-191.
22. Ibid., pp. 205-207.
23. Ibid., p. 209.
24. Ibid., pp. 205-207.
25. Ibid., p. 208.
26. Ibid., p. 211.
27. Ibid., p. 215.
28. Ibid., p. 220.
29. Ibid., pp. 205-207.
30. Ibid., pp. 239.

31. Ibid., p. 245.
32. Ibid., p. 250.
33. Ibid., p. 197.
34. Ibid., pp. 103-104.
35. Ibid., p. 109.
36. Ibid., p. 111.
37. Ibid., p. 111.
38. Ibid., p. 112.
39. Ibid., pp. 116-117.
40. Ibid., pp. 118-120.
41. Ibid., p. 125.
42. Ibid., pp. 132-133.
43. Ibid., p. 134.
44. Ibid., pp. 135-136.
45. DeLamarter, Thomas, <u>Big Blue: The Truth about IBM's Success and the Omminous Implications...</u>, [New York, NY: Dodd, Mead, 1986], p. 21
46. Op. Cit., pp. 138-139.
47. Ibid. p. 141.
48. Ibid., pp. 143-144.
49. Ibid., p. 299.
50. Ibid., pp. 305-306.
51. Ibid., pp. 312-314.
52. Ibid., p. 320.
53. Ibid., pp. 324-325.
54. Ibid., pp. 332-333.
55. Ibid., p. 336.
56. Ibid., p. 343.
57. Ibid., p. 345.
58. Ibid., p. 355.
59. Ibid., p. 346.
60. Ibid., p. 398.
61. Ibid., p. 399.
62. Ibid., p. 362.

63. Ibid., p. 401.
64. Ibid., pp. 372-375.
65. Ibid., p. 386.
66. Ibid., p. 423.
67. Ibid., p. 384.
68. Ibid., p. 361.
69. DeLamarter, Thomas, Big Blue: The Truth about IBM's Success and the Omminous Implications..., [New York, NY: Dodd, Mead, 1986], p. 26.
70. Ibid., p. 35.
71. Maney, Kevin, The Maverick and His Machine, [Hoboken, NJ, John Wiley: 2003], pp. 411-412.
72. Ibid., pp. 423-424.
73. Ibid., pp. 436-437.
74. Ibid., pp. 352-353.
75. Ibid., pp. 352-353.
76. Ibid., p. 264.
77. Ibid., p. 261.
78. Ibid., p. 270.
79. Ibid., p. 377.
80. Ibid., p. 437.
81. Ibid., p. 442.
82. Ibid., p. 442.
83. Ibid., p. 442.
84. McCartney, Scott, Eniac: Triumphs and Tragedies of the World's First Computer, [New York, NY: Walker, 1999], p. 30.
85. Ibid., p. 31.
86. Ibid., p. 33.
87. Ibid., p. 37.
88. Ibid., p. 40.
89. Ibid., p. 47.
90. Ibid., p. 61.
91. Ibid., p. 72.

92. Ibid., p. 82.
93. Ibid., p. 94.
94. Ibid., p. 94.
95. Ibid., p. 101
96. Ibid., p. 102
97. Ibid., p. 107.
98. Ibid., pp. 119-120.
99. Ibid., p. 125.
100. Ibid., p. 132.
101. Ibid., p. 142.
102. Ibid., p. 148.
103. Ibid., p. 152.
104. Moreau, R., The Computer Comes of Age, [Cambridge, Mass.: MIT Press, 1984], p. 51.
105. McCartney, Op. Cit., p. 171.
106. Bashe, et al., IBM's Early Computers, [Cambridge, Mass.: MIT Press, 1986], p. 240.
107. Moreau, R., The Computer Comes of Age, [Cambridge, Mass.: MIT Press, 1984], pp. 52-53.
108. Murray, Charles, Supermen: The Story of Seymour Cray and the technical Wizards Behind the Supercomputer, [New York, NY: John Wiley, 1997], p 47
109. Ibid., p. 47.
110. Ibid., p. 48.
111. Ibid., p. 48.
112. Ibid., p. 45.
113. Ibid., p. 43.
114. Ibid., pp. 52-53.
115. http://www.cbi.umn.edu/resources/norris/oral-history.html
116. Ibid.
117. Op. Cit., p. 66.
118. Moreau, R., The Computer Comes of Age, [Cambridge, Mass.: MIT Press, 1984], pp. 91.

119. Op. Cit., p. 67.
120. Ibid., p. 68.
121. Ibid., p. 70.
122. Ibid., p. 76.
123. Ibid., p. 83.
124. Ibid., pp. 84-85.
125. Ibid., p. 91.
126. Ibid., p. 91.
127. Ibid., p. 92.
128. Ibid., p. 93.
129. Ibid., pp. 113-116.
130. Ibid., p. 135.
131. Ibid., p. 123.
132. Ibid., p. 124.
133. Ibid., p. 133.
134. Ibid., p. 130.
135. Ibid., p. 146.
136. Ibid., p. 149.
137. Ibid., p. 151.
138. Ibid., p. 152.
139. Ibid., pp. 158-159.
140. Ibid., p. 155.
141. Ibid., p. 156.
142. Ibid., p. 211.
143. Ibid., p. 215
144. Ibid., pp. 216-217.
145. Ibid., pp. 219-220.
146. Ibid., pp. 137-142.
147. Ibid., p. 119.
148. Ibid., p. 114.
149. Ibid., p. 120.
150. Ibid., pp. 120-122.
151. Ibid., p. 136.

152. Ibid., p. 136.

153. Ibid., p. 217.

154. "Turing, Alan M.," Encyclopedia Britannica Ultimate Reference Suite. Chicago: Encyclopedia Britannica, 2013.

17. Important People II

1. Murray, Charles, Supermen: The Story of Seymour Cray and the technical Wizards Behind the Supercomputer, [New York, NY: John Wiley, 1997], p 11.

2. Ibid., p. 12.

3. Ibid., p. 8.

4. Ibid., p. 18.

5. Ibid., p. 21.

6. Ibid., p. 25.

7. Ibid., p. 27.

8. Ibid., p. 31.

9. Ibid., p. 37.

10. Ibid., p. 37

11. Ibid., p. 39.

12. Ibid., p. 40.

13. Ibid., p. 66.

14. Ibid., p. 70.

15. Stein and Munro, Computer Programming: A Mixed Language Approach, [New York, NY: Academic Press, 1964].

16. Op. Cit., p. 76.

17. Ibid., p. 109.

18. Ibid., p. 131.

19. Ibid., p. 110.

20. Ibid., p. 110.

21. Ibid., p. 106.

22. Ibid., p. 175.

23. Ibid., p. 176.

24. Zygmont, Jeffrey, <u>Microchip</u>, [Cambridge, Mass.: Perseus, 2003], pp. 11-12.
25. Ibid., p. 6.
26. Ibid., p. 19.
27. Ibid., p. 19.
28. Ibid., p. 19.
29. Ibid., p. 19
30. Ibid., p. 21.
31. Ibid., p. 21.
32. Ibid., p. 67.
33. Ibid., p. 68.
34. Ibid., p. 70.
35. Kilby, Jack, (autobiography)
36. Rosen, Saul, <u>Programming Systems and Languages</u>, [New York, NY, McGraw-Hill, 1967], pp. 29-47.
37. www-03.ibm.com/ibm/history/exhibits/builders
38. Ibid.
39. Ibid.
40. Ibid.
41. Smithsonian interview with Bill Gates, Washington, DC.
42. Ceruzzi, Paul, <u>A History of Modern Computing</u>, [Cambridge, Mass.: MIT Press, 2003], p. 226.
43. Ibid., p. 228.
44. Ibid., p. 229.
45. Ibid., p. 231.
46. Wozniak and Smith, <u>iWoz: Computer Geek to Cult Icon—How I Invented the Personal Computer...</u>, [New York, NY: Norton, 2006], p. 22.
47. Young and Simon, <u>Icon: Steve Jobs—The Greatest Second Act...</u>, [Hoboken, NJ: John Wiley, 2005], p. 15
48. Ibid., p. 10.
49. Ibid., p. 12.

50. Wozniak and Smith, iWoz: Computer Geek to Cult Icon—How I Invented the Personal Computer..., [New York, NY: Norton, 2006], p. 31
51. Ibid., p. 38.
52. Ibid., p. 55.
53. Ibid., p. 61.
54. Kahney, Leander, Inside Steve's Brain, [New York, NY: Penguin group], p. 2.
55. Ibid., p.190.
56. Ibid., pp. 206-207.
57. Ibid., p. 166.
58. Ibid., p. 163.
59. Ibid., p. 164.
60. Ibid., p. 112.
61. Ibid., p. 114.
62. Ibid., p. 59.
63. Ibid., p. 49.
64. Ibid., p. 68.
65. Ibid., p. 71.
66. Ibid., p. 75.
67. Ibid., p. 11.
68. Ibid., p. 35.
69. Ibid., p. 170.
70. Ibid., p. 174.
71. Ibid., p. 4.
72. Ibid., p. 174.
73. Ibid., p. 147.
74. Ibid., p. 7.
75. Ibid., p. 15.
76. Ibid., p. 25.
77. Ibid., p. 35.
78. Ibid.,, p. 7.
79. Ibid., p. 109.

80. Ibid., p. 107.
81. Ibid., p. 19.
82. Ibid.,, pp. 261-265.
83. Ibid., p. 268.
84. Ibid., p. 271.
85. Ibid., pp. 271-272.
86. Ibid., pp. 177-178.
87. Ibid., pp. 204-205.
88. Ibid., , pp. 198-205.
89. Ibid., pp. 210-212.
90. Ibid., pp. 209-210.
91. Packard, David, <u>The HP Way</u>, [New York, NY: Harper Collins:1995], p. 32.
92. Ibid., p. 41.
93. Ibid., p. 103.
94. Ibid., p. 104.
95. Ibid., p. 117.
96. Zygmont, Jeffrey, <u>Microchip</u>, [Cambridge, Mass.: Perseus, 2003], p. 172.
97. Ibid., p. 178.
98. Ibid., p. 175.
99. Ibid., pp. 190-196.
100. Ibid., p. 199.
101. Ibid., p. 199.
102. Wang, An, <u>Lessons, an Autobiography</u>, [Reading, Mass.: Addison-Wesley, 1986].
103. htttp://www-03.ibm.com/ibm/history/exhibits/builders.
104. Zygmont, Jeffrey, <u>Microchip</u>, [Cambridge, Mass.: Perseus, 2003], p. 28.
105. Ibid., pp. 30-31.
106. Ibid., p. 30.
107. Ibid., p. 32.

18. Operating Systems.

No footnotes.

19. Storage Media
No footnotes.

20. Computer Companies
1. Babbage Institute, Willis Drake Interview
2. Babbage Institute, William Norris interview
3. Ibid.
4. Lundstrom, David, <u>A Few good men from Univac</u>, [Cambridge, Mass.: MIT Press, 1987], p. 33.
5. Ibid., p. 24.
6. Ibid., p. 16.
7. Ibid., p. 22.
8. Ibid., p. 26.
9. Ibid., p. 26.
10. Ibid., p. 29.
11. Ibid., p. 30.
12. Ibid., p. 32.
13. Ibid., p. 32.
14. Ibid., p. 36.
15. Ibid., pp. 36-37.
16. Ibid., p. 37.
17. Ibid., p. 38.
18. Ibid.,, p. 41.
19. Ibid., pp. 44-45.
20. Ibid., p. 57.
21. Ibid., p. 63.
22. Ibid., p. 65.
23. Ibid., p. 71.
24. http://www.FundingUniverse.com/company-histories
25. Babbage Institute, William Norris interview
26. Babbage Institute, Willis Drake Interview
27. Op. Cit.

28. Ibid.

29. Babbage Institute, Willis Drake interview.

30. Ibid.

31. Norris, Op. Cit.

32. Ibid.

33. Babbage Institute, Willis Drake Interview

34. Ibid.

35. Ibid.

36. Ibid.

37. Ibid.

38. Lundstrom, David, <u>A Few Good Men from Univac</u>, [Cambridge, Mass.: MIT Press, 1987], p. 99

39. Ibid., p. 79.

40. Ibid., p. 99.

41. Price, Robert, <u>The Eye for Innovation</u>, [New Haven, Conn.: Yale Univ. Press, 2005, p. 255.

42. Lundstrom, Op. Cit., p. 72.

43. Ibid., pp. 75-76.

44. Ibid., p. 79.

45. Ibid., p. 83.

46. Ibid., p. 90.

47. Ibid., p. 89.

48. Ibid., p. 89.

49. Ibid., pp. 90-91.

50. Ibid., p. 93.

51. Ibid., p. 94.

52. Ibid., p. 95.

53. Ibid., p. 97.

54. Ibid., p. 117.

55. Ibid., p. 127.

56. Ibid., p. 123.

57. Ibid., pp. 124-125

58. Ibid., pp. 129-130.

59. Ibid., pp. 134-135.
60. Ibid., p. 137.
61. Ibid., p. 138.
62. Ibid., p. 140.
63. Ibid., p. 141.
64. Ibid., p. 151.
65. Ibid., p. 152.
66. Ibid., p. 163.
67. Ibid., p. 174.
68. Ibid., p. 222.
69. Ibid., p. 201.
70. Ibid., p. 207.
71. Ibid., pp. 206-207.
72. Ibid., p. 198.
73. Ibid., p. 199.
74. Ibid., p. 222.
75. Ibid., p. 224.
76. Ibid., p. 226.
77. Moreau, R., <u>The Computer Comes of Age</u>, [Cambridge, Mass.: MIT Press, 1984], p. 70.
78. DeLamarter, Thomas, <u>Big Blue: The Truth about IBM's Success and the Omminous Implications...</u>, [New York, NY: Dodd, Mead, 1986], p. 55
79. http://www.FundingUniverse.com/company-histories
80. Ibid.
81. Moreau, R., <u>The Computer Comes of Age</u>, [Cambridge, Mass.: MIT Press, 1984], p. 25.
82. Ibid., p. 63.
83. Maney, Kevin, <u>The Maverick and His Machine</u>, [Hoboken, NJ, 2003], pp. 42-43.
84. Ibid., pp. 89-90.
85. Ibid., p. 361.
86. Ibid., p. 385.
87. Ibid., p. 384.

88. DeLamarter, Thomas, <u>Big Blue: The Truth about IBM's Success and the Omminous Implications...</u>, [New York, NY: Dodd, Mead, 1986], p. 95.

89. Harrar and Rifkin, <u>Ultimate Entrepreneur, The</u>, [Chicago, Ill., Contemporary Books, 1988], p. 21.

90. Ibid., p. 23

91. Ibid., pp. 14-15.

92. Ibid., p. 26.

93. Ibid., p. 29.

94. Ibid., p. 29.

95. Ibid., p. 32.

96. Ibid., p. 32.

97. Ibid., p. 40.

98. Ibid., p. 40.

99. Ibid., p. 40

100. Ibid., p. 40.

101. Ibid., p. 41.

102. Ibid., p. 46.

103. Ibid., p. 59.

104. Ibid., p. 58.

105. Ibid., p. 62.

106. Ibid., p. 68.

107. Ibid., p. 68.

108. Ibid., p. 68.

109. Ibid., p. 116.

110. Ibid., p. 96.

111. Ibid., p. 118.

112. Ibid., p. 118.

113. Ibid., p. 118.

114. Ibid., p. 120.

115. Ibid., p. 119.

116. Ibid., p. 120.

117. Ibid., p. 116.

118. Ibid., p. 120.

119. Ibid., p. 122.
120. Ibid., p. 123.
121. Ibid., p. 125.
122. Ibid., p. 125.
123. Ibid., p. 127.
124. Ibid., p. 101.
125. Ibid., p. 127.
126. Ibid., p. 131.
127. Ibid., p. 133.
128. Ibid., p. 133.
129. Ibid., p. 135.
130. Ibid., p. 136.
131. Ibid., p. 137.
132. Ibid., pp. 140-141.
133. Ibid., p. 148.
134. Ibid., p. 163.
135. Ibid., p. 148.
136. Ibid., p. 169.
137. Ibid., p. 171.
138. Ibid., p 169.
139. Ibid., p. 172.
140. Ibid., p. 172.
141. Ibid., p. 175.
142. Ibid., p. 153.
143. Ibid., p. 153.
144. Ibid., p. 177.
145. Ibid., p. 177.
146. Ibid., p. 176.
147. Ibid., p. 178.
148. Ibid., p. 179.
149. Ibid., p. 179.
150. Ceruzzi, Paul, A History of Modern Computing, [Cambridge, Mass.: MIT Press, 2003], p. 247.

151. Op. Cit., p. 181.
152. Ibid., p. 184.
153. Ibid., p. 190.
154. Ibid., p. 190.
155. Ibid., pp. 194-195.
156. Ibid., p. 197.
157. Ibid., p. 197.
158. Ibid., p. 199.
159. Ibid., p. 200.
160. Ibid., p. 212.
161. Ibid., p. 214.
162. Ibid., p. 219.
163. Ibid., p. 229.
164. Ibid., p. 235.
165. Ibid., p. 239.
166. Ibid., p. 239.
167. Wang, An, <u>Lessons, an Autobiography</u>, [Reading, Mass., Addison-Wesley, 1986], p. 30.
168. Ibid., p. 31.
169. Ibid., p. 35.
170. Ibid., p. 43
171. Ibid., p. 52.
172. Ibid., p. 56.
173. Ibid., pp. 56-57.
174. Ibid., p. 58.
175. Ibid., p. 75.
176. Ibid., p. 75.
177. Ibid., p. 82.
178. Ibid., p. 80.
179. Ibid., p. 83.
180. Ibid., p. 86.
181. Ibid., p. 104.
182. Ibid., p. 107.

183. Ibid., p. 121.
184. Ibid., p. 116.
185. Ibid., p. 125.
186. Ibid., p. 127.
187. Ibid., p. 131.
188. Ibid., p. 133.
189. Ibid., p. 133.
190. Ibid., p. 136.
191. Ibid., pp. 148-149.
192. Ibid., p. 151.
193. Ibid., p. 150.
194. Ibid., p. 152.
195. Ibid., p. 153.
196. Ibid., p. 159.
197. Ibid., pp. 164-165.
198. Ibid., p. 173.
199. Ibid., p. 176.
200. Ibid., pp. 182-183
201. Ibid., p. 183.
202. Ibid., p. 185.
203. Ibid., p. 187.
204. Ibid., pp. 192-196.
205. Ibid., pp. 189-190.
206. Ibid., p. 199.
207. Ibid., p. 206.
208. Ibid., p. 207.
209. Ibid., pp. 209-210.
210. Ibid., p. 210.
211. Ibid., p. 214.
212. Ibid., p. 215.
213. Ibid., pp. 216-217.
214. Ibid., p. 221.
215. Ibid., p. 222.

216. Ibid., p. 226.
217. Ibid., p. 229.
218. Ibid., p. 232.
219. Ibid., p. 235.
220. Young and Simon, <u>Icon: Steve Jobs—The Greatest Second Act...</u>, [Hoboken, NJ: John Wiley, 2005], p. 9.
221. Ibid., p. 10.
222. Ibid., p. 10.
223. Ibid., p. 13.
224. Ibid., p. 15.
225. Ibid., p. 15.
226. Ibid., p. 20.
227. Ibid., p. 21.
228. Ibid., p. 27.
229. Wozniak and Smith, <u>iWoz: Computer Geek to Cult Icon—How I Invented the Personal Computer...</u>, [New York, NY: Norton, 2006], p. 58.
230. Ibid., p. 187.
231. Ibid., p. 188.
232. Ibid., pp. 196-197.
233. Ibid., p. 197.
234. Young and Simon, <u>Icon: Steve Jobs—The Greatest Second Act...</u>, [Hoboken, NJ: John Wiley, 2005], pp. 45-46.
235. Ibid., p. 46.
236. Wozniak and Smith, <u>iWoz: Computer Geek to Cult Icon—How I Invented the Personal Computer...</u>, [New York, NY: Norton, 2006], p. 211.
237. Op. Cit., p. 51.
238. Ibid., p. 52.
239. Ibid., p. 55.
240. Ibid., p. 59.
241. Ibid., p. 64.
242. Ibid., p. 67.
243. Jackson, Tim, <u>Inside Intel: Andy Grove and the Rise of the World's Most Powerful Chip Company</u>, [New York, NY: Penguin Group, 1997], p. 20.

244. Ibid., p. 20.
245. Ibid., p. 23.
246. Ibid., p. 25.
247. Ibid., pp. 25-26.
248. Ibid., p. 26.
249. Ibid., pp. 26-27.
250. Ibid., p. 27.
251. Ibid., p. 27.
252. Ibid., p. 28.
253. Ibid., p. 29.
254. Ibid., p. 30.
255. Ibid., p. 33.
256. Ibid., p. 94.
257. Ibid., p. 95.
258. Ibid., p. 96.
259. Ibid., p. 59.
260. Ibid., p. 97.
261. Ibid., pp. 99-100.
262. Ibid., pp. 61-68.
263. Ibid., p. 65.
264. Ibid., pp. 67-68.
265. Ibid., pp. 101-102.
266. Ibid., p. 74.
267. Ibid., p. 76.
268. Ibid., p. 81.
269. Ibid., p. 82.
270. Ibid., pp. 83-84.
271. Ibid., p. 88.
272. Ibid., p. 91.
273. Ibid., p. 91.
274. Ibid., p. 92.
275. Ibid., p. 243.
276. Ibid., p. 243.
277. Ibid., p. 244.

278. Ibid., p. 244.
279. Ibid., p. 244.
280. Ibid., p. 106.
281. Ibid., p. 187.
282. Ibid., p. 110.
283. Ibid., p. 111.
284. Ibid., p. 113.
285. Ibid., p. 113.
286. Ibid., p. 114.
287. Ibid., p. 117.
288. Ibid., p. 132.
289. Ibid., p. 132.
290. Ibid., p. 132.
291. Ibid., p. 140.
292. Ibid., p. 164.
293. Ibid., p. 165.
294. Ibid., p. 164.
295. Ibid., p. 166.
296. Ibid., p. 166.
297. Ibid., p. 174.
298. Ibid., p. 177.
299. Ibid., p. 161.
300. Ibid., p. 202.
301. Ibid., p. 195.
302. Ibid., p. 198.
303. Ibid., p. 247.
304. Ibid., p. 248.
305. Ibid., p. 204.
306. Ibid., p. 207.
307. Ibid., p. 198.
308. Ibid., p. 198.
309. Ibid., p. 199.
310. Ibid., p. 201.

311. Ibid., pp. 211-212.
312. Ibid., p. 217.
313. Ibid., p. 221.
314. Ibid., p. 222.
315. Ibid., p. 222.
316. Ibid., p. 226.
317. Ibid., p. 227.
318. Ibid., p. 230.
319. Ibid., p. 240.
320. Ibid., p. 253-254.
321. Zygmont, Jeffrey, Microchip, [Cambridge, Mass.: Perseus, 2003], p. 31.
322. Ibid., p. 41.
323. Ibid., p. 41.
324. Ibid., p. 44.
325. Ibid., pp. 44-45.
326. Ibid., p. 45.
327. Ibid., p. 47.
328. Ibid., p. 47.
329. Ibid., pp. 47-48.
330. Ibid., p. 83.
331. Ibid., pp. 83-84.
332. Ibid., p. 86.
333. Ibid., pp. 90-91.
334. Ibid., p. 92.
335. Packard, David, The HP Way, [New York, NY: Harper Collins, 1995], p. 40.
336. Ibid., p. 42.
337. Ibid., p. 45.
338. Ibid., p. 84.
339. Ibid., p. 85.
340. Ibid., p. 51.
341. Ibid., p. 54.
342. Ibid., p. 57.
343. Ibid., p. 58.

344. Ibid., p. 64.
345. Ibid., p. 65.
346. Ibid., p. 68.
347. Ibid., p. 70.
348. Ibid., p. 72.
349. Ibid., p. 85.
350. Ibid., p. 91.
351. Ibid., p. 103.
352. Ibid., p. 114.
353. Ibid., p. 117.

21. Supercomputers

1. Price, Robert, The Eye for Innovation, [New Haven, Conn.: Yale Univ. Press, 2005], p. 19.
2. DeLamarter, Thomas, Big Blue: The Truth about IBM's Success and the Omminous Implications…, [New York, NY: Dodd, Mead, 1986], p. 53.
3. Ibid., p. 53.
4. Ibid., p. 53.
5. Ibid., p. 53.

22. Personal Computers

1. Ceruzzi, Paul, A History of Modern Computing, [Cambridge, Mass.: MIT Press, 2003], p. 229.
2. Ibid., pp. 230-231.
3. Ibid., p. 240.
4. Wozniak and Smith, iWoz: Computer Geek to Cult Icon—How I Invented the Personal Computer…, [New York, NY: Norton, 2006], p. 15.
5. Ceruzzi, Paul, A History of Modern Computing, [Cambridge, Mass.: MIT Press, 2003], p. 233.
6. Ibid., pp. 239-240.
7. Ibid., p. 232.
8. Ibid., p. 266.

9. Ibid., p. 240.

10. Ibid., p. 278.

11. Ibid., p. 263.

12. Ibid., p. 248.

13. Jackson, Tim, <u>Inside Intel: Andy Grove and the Rise of the World's Most Powerful Chip Company</u> [New York, NY: Penguin Group, 1997], p. 203.

14. Ibid., p. 204.

15. Ibid., p. 206.

16. Chposky and Teonsis, <u>Blue Magic</u>, [New York, NY: Facts on File, 1988], p. 8.

17. Ibid., p. 9.

18. Ibid., p. 16.

19. Ibid., p. 27.

20. Ibid., p. 29.

21. Business Week magazine, Jan. 20, 1986.

22. Op. Cit. p. 11.

23. Ibid., p. 10.

24. Ibid., p. 12.

25. Ibid., p. 14.

26. Ibid., p. 61.

27. Ceruzzi, Paul, <u>A History of Modern Computing</u>, [Cambridge, Mass.: MIT Press, 2003], p. 44.

28. Op. Cit., p. 48.

29. Ibid., p. 49.

30. Ceruzzi, Paul, <u>A History of Modern Computing</u>, [Cambridge, Mass.: MIT Press, 2003], p. 270.

31. Chposky and Teonsis, <u>Blue Magic</u>, [New York, NY: Facts on File, 1988], p. 57

32. Ibid., pp. 57-58.

33. Ibid., p. 64.

34. Ibid., p. 69.

35. Ibid., p. 70.

36. Ibid., p. 80.

37. Ibid., p. 66.
38. Ibid., p. 71.
39. Ibid., p. 68.
40. Ibid., p. 86.
41. Ibid., p. 87.
42. Ibid., p. 68.
43. Ibid., p. 69.
44. Ibid., p. 70.
45. Ibid., p. 110.
46. Ceruzzi, Paul, <u>A History of Modern Computing</u>, [Cambridge, Mass.: MIT Press, 2003], p. 272.
47. Op. Cit., p. 105.
48. Ibid., p. 112.
49. Ibid., p. 111.
50. Ibid., p. 111.
51. Ibid., p. 118.
52. Ibid., pp. 136-137.
53. DeLamarter, Thomas, <u>Big Blue: The Truth about IBM's Success and the Omminous Implications...</u>, [New York, NY: Dodd, Mead, 1986], p. 108.
54. Chposky and Teonsis, <u>Blue Magic</u>, [New York, NY: Facts on File, 1988], p. 109.
55. Ceruzzi, Paul, <u>A History of Modern Computing</u>, [Cambridge, Mass.: MIT Press, 2003], p. 277.
56. Ibid., p. 277.
57. Ibid., p. 210.
58. Ibid., pp. 277-278.
59. Ibid., pp. 278-279.
60. Chposky and Teonsis, <u>Blue Magic</u>, [New York, NY: Facts on File, 1988], pp. 135-136.
61. Ibid., p. 134.
62. Ibid., p. 139.
63. Ibid., p. 142.
64. Ibid., p. 144.

65. Ibid., pp. 149-150.
66. Ibid., p. 160.
67. Ibid., p. 160.
68. Ibid., p. 165.
69. Ibid., p. 186.
70. Ibid., p. 187.
71. Ibid., p. 174.
72. Ibid., p. 175.
73. Ibid., p. 178.
74. Ibid., p. 185.
75. Ibid., p. 167.
76. Ibid., p. 167.
77. Ibid., p. 185.
78. Ibid., p. 191.
79. Ibid., pp. 192 ff.
80. Ibid., p. 214.
81. Ibid., p. 216.

23. Computer Models

1. http://www.cbi.umn.edu/resources/norris/oral-history.html
2. Ibid.
3. Price, Robert, <u>The Eye for Innovation</u>, [New Haven, Conn.: Yale Univ. Press, 2005, p. 14..
4. http://www-3.ibm.com/ibm/history/exhibits/mainframe/mainframe_profiles.html
5. Ibid.
6. DeLamarter, Thomas, <u>Big Blue: The Truth about IBM's Success and the Omminous Implications...</u>, [New York, NY: Dodd, Mead, 1986], p. 35.
7. Ibid., p. 35.
8. Ibid., p. 59.
9. Ibid., p. 92.

10. Ibid., p. 94.
11. Ibid., p. 94.
12. Ibid., p. 95.
13. Ibid., p. 95.
14. Ibid., p. 96.
15. Ibid., p. 53.
16. Ibid., p. 131.
17. Ibid., p. 162.
18. Ibid., p. 101.
19. Ibid., p. 102.
20. Ibid., pp. 154-155.
21. Ibid., p. 177.
22. Ibid., pp. 177-179.
23. Ibid., p. 168.
24. Ibid., p. 191.

24. Microprocessors

1. Moreau, R., The Computer Comes of Age, [Cambridge, Mass.: MIT Press, 1984], p. 90.
2. Zygmont, Jeffrey, Microchip, [Cambridge, Mass.: Perseus, 2003], p. 21.
3. Ceruzzi, Paul, A History of Modern Computing, [Cambridge, Mass.: MIT Press, 2003], p. 186.
4. Op. Cit., pp. 68-69.
5. OP. Cit., p. 187.
6. Ibid., p. 188.
7. Zygmont, Jeffrey, Microchip, [Cambridge, Mass.: Perseus, 2003], pp. 112-113.
8. Ibid., pp. 127-128.
9. Ibid., p. 126.
10. Ibid., pp. 129-130.
11. Ceruzzi, Paul, A History of Modern Computing, [Cambridge, Mass.: MIT Press, 2003], p. 190.
12. Ibid., p. 191.

13. http://download.intel.com/pressroom/kits/chipmaking/Making_of_a_Chip.pdf

25. Mini Computers

1. http://www.answers.com/topic/digital-equipment-corporation, p. 2.
2. Ibid., p. 22.
3. Ibid., p. 3.
4. Ibid., p. 5.
5. Ibid., p. 16.
6. Ibid., p. 2.
7. Digital Equipment Corp., <u>Summary Reference Manual for PDP-10</u>, [Maynard, Mass.: DEC, 1967], p. 7
8. Ibid., pp. 22-24.
9. Ceruzzi, Paul, <u>A History of Modern Computing</u>, [Cambridge, Mass.: MIT Press, 2003], pp. 208-210.
10. Op. Cit., p. 26.
11. Digital Equipment Corp., <u>Macro 10 Assembler Manual</u>, [Maynard, Mass.: DEC, 1967], p. 3-1.
12. Ibid., p. 2-1.
13. Ibid., p. 2-16.
14. http://www.answers.com/topic/digital-equipment-corporation, p. 6.
15. http://www.Compaq.com/alphaserver/download/ev6chip.pdf
16. Digital Equipment Corp., <u>PDP-10 Monitor Manual</u>, [Maynard, Mass., DEC, 1968].

26. Tabulating Equipment

1. Bashe, et al., <u>IBM's Early Computers</u>, [Cambridge, Mass.: MIT Press, 1986], p. 3.
2. Ibid., p. 2.
3. Ibid., p. 7.
4. Ibid., pp. 1-33.

5. Ceruzzi, Paul, <u>A History of Modern Computing</u>, [Cambridge, Mass.: MIT Press, 2003], p. 194.

6. Encyclopædia Britannica. "Internet." <u>Encyclopaedia Britannica Ultimate Reference Suite</u>. Chicago: Encyclopædia Britannica, 2010.

Index

About the Author

Steve Lindfors has a Master of Science in computer science degree from the University of Minnesota and a Master of Business Administration degree from the University of St. Thomas.

He has more than 20 years of experience in software design, development and maintenance with two computer companies and several banks.

He was also editor-in-chief of a monthly magazine for one year. Related work included writing three articles for the magazine and several editorials.

www.ingramcontent.com/pod-product-compliance
Lightning Source LLC
Chambersburg PA
CBHW051221050326
40689CB00007B/758